£15.50

GW00471805

THE DEVOUT PRAYERS
OF THY CHURCH

A devotional Commentary on the
Sunday and Seasonal Collects
in The Book of Common Prayer

by

Peter Blake

I dedicate this book
with much love and gratitude
to my wife Susan

First published March 1996
Reprinted February 1997

ISBN 1 870781 08 2

Typeset by Tarragon Press
and printed by Antony Rowe Ltd, Chippenham

Published by Tarragon Press on behalf of Canon Peter Blake
Moss Park, Ravenstone, Whithorn, Scotland DG8 8DR

CONTENTS

With a comparison between the Collects of the Book of Common Prayer and those of the American Prayer Book of 1979.

A Foreword by the Lord Charteris of Amisfield
(President of the Prayer Book Society)

"O Almighty God, who alone canst order the unruly wills and affections of sinful men"; "that most excellent gift of charity, the very bond of peace and all virtues"; "create and make in us new and contrite hearts"; "mercifully grant that thy Holy Spirit may in all things direct and rule our hearts".

These are just some of the many poetic and profound phrases from the Collects that I was privileged to learn as a schoolboy. They have remained alive in my memory ever since, and have proved a constant source of inspiration and consolation.

It saddens me to think that today the Collects are so often neglected, not only in our schools but in our churches. I hope that Canon Peter Blake's commentary will go some way to ensuring their revival, and indeed survival.

Anyone who makes use of this book will be left in no doubt as to the Collects' rich gems of faith and devotion. Without them today's Church is impoverished, as it is without the beautiful language in which they are expressed.

Charteris of Amisfield

A Foreword by The Right Reverend Edward MacBurney

(Formerly Bishop of Quincy,
The Episcopal Church of America)

There are many Christians who fault the use of set prayers, believing that liturgies deny spontaneity and get between the prayer and God. The proliferation of prayer and praise groups, in which many share in voicing special needs and concerns, surely suggest that the equation should be more of a "both/and." But Canon Peter Blake puts the case for the collected prayer of the Church, as it is focused Sunday by Sunday in her Collects, when he writes:

> "One of the main benefits of using these prayers of our Prayer Book is that they recall us to the real essentials of true religion. They do not allow us to become dominated by some passing political problem or some special social concern."

Canon Blake adds that "these prayers of our Prayer Book are not just the prayers of a Church but the 'holy Catholic Church'." And that must be their primary justification.

Anglicans inhabit a wider room than one which embraces only local causes or a pastor's pet crusades. The Church's Collects, Sunday by Sunday, provide us with the essentials of Christian doctrine because they put before us our weakness and God's power, our sin and God's grace, our redemption in Christ and our hope of glory.

The Sunday Collects, as Canon Blake shows us so very well, are not only to be prayed but also to be lived out. They point us to the Christian community, which is the Catholic Church. We are directed by them to the sacramental life: baptism, Holy Communion, absolution, healing. However, they also lead us back to Scripture. Canon Blake's book is superb in so many ways, but surely its greatest strength is his constant use of the Bible in meditating upon each Collect.

I am personally very grateful to our author, for having given us the opportunity to spend some time each week with the Church's prayer, considering its implications, looking at each Collect's Biblical foundations, and then, most important of all, using the Collect mindfully.

Americans will be grateful for the helpful listing of the Collects as they appear in the 1662 Book of Common Prayer, showing which have been kept in the 1979 American Book of Common Prayer.

Edward H. MacBurney

INTRODUCTION

There has always been the temptation for the Church to become primarily concerned with earthbound problems rather than with the heavenly vision, to allow the world to write its agenda and to behave as if works matter more than faith. Screwtape made the encouragement of this attitude the chief concern of his nephew Wormwood[1]. Any such attitude is always so easily justified at the time. Was not Esau almost dead with hunger when he sold his birthright for 'a mess of pottage'?[2] And did not Martha feel ready to drop with tiredness when she grumbled about her sister's behaviour?[3] The good is so often the deadliest enemy of the best. Screwtape is no fool, for what good to us is the merely good if we are made for the best, and do not attain it? The particular value of the Prayer Book Collects is that they help us to embrace this truth. They do not let us, as Esau did, despise our birthright, or, like Martha, become over-anxious about worldly things. Rather they help us to appreciate, like Jacob, the supreme importance of the covenant that God has made with us, and to choose, as Mary did, 'the good portion that will not be taken away from (us)'.

As we think of the importance of the Prayer Book Collects there are about them three aspects of special significance. There is their language, their history and their content. The first is widely recognised. Their language has a musical flow about it that makes it marvellously memorable, and as easy to sing as to say. Dr Bright, the Victorian liturgical scholar, said, 'It exhibits. . .an exquisite skill of antithesis and a rhythmical harmony in which the ear delights'.[4] And it is not only the ear that is enchanted by the language of the Collects. It uplifts our spirits too, for it exudes 'the beauty of holiness', and the more we use the Collects the more we are able to hear the things our spirits need to hear, and so be helped to 'worship the Lord'.[5] It was said of King David that he was 'the sweet psalmist of Israel.'[6] Archbishop Cranmer, whose birthday was just over 500 years ago, can surely be reckoned the equivalent for our Church, the inspired composer of its prayers, one through whom 'the Spirit of the Lord' also has spoken, and still speaks, and one who had God's word not so much on his tongue as at

1   The Screwtape Letters by C. S. Lewis   2   Gen 25:34 (A.V.)   3   Lk 10:38-42
4   Ancient Collects, by Dr. Bright   5   Ps 96:9   6   2 Sam:1

the end of his pen. This Commentary certainly seeks to underline the inspired nature of the language used in the composition of our Prayer Book Collects.

The history of the Prayer Book Collects is also a matter of great interest and real importance. Like the Scriptures and the Sacraments they link us with the earliest years of the Church. The great majority come from the early Sacramentaries of St Leo, St Gelasius and St Gregory that date from the 5th and 6th Centuries, and are found in the Sarum Missal, which by the 15th Century was being used throughout the country. It was consequently the Sarum Missal that Cranmer particularly turned to when choosing the Propers for his first Prayer Book in 1549. Of the Collects treated in this book only a dozen are the work of the English Reformers, and, although in translation some important amendments and additions were made to most of them, they are in the main the prayers of the early Church as known and loved in medieval England, and not merely those of the post Reformation Church of England. Like the great Cathedrals and ancient Parish Churches in which we still worship, their antiquity, as well as their beauty, uplifts us. Just as Christ is 'the same yesterday, today and for ever',[7] so are our spiritual needs and aspirations. They do not change. The tense, therefore, in which the Prayer Book Collects are written is the eternal present, and this Commentary seeks to emphasise this point.

But it is above all their content that is important. They help to establish our Church's theology as well as give words to our prayers. Archbishop Michael Ramsey has said, 'Anglican theology is not confessionalist in the sense in which Lutheran and Calvinistic Churches are confessionalist, because it holds together a Confession of Faith with a Book of Common Prayer... It is the linking of the formulation of dogma with the way of prayer which is supremely characteristic of Anglicanism. So when we Anglicans explain what we stand for to other people we say to them not just, "Come and read our documents; come and argue about theology with us", but "Come and pray with us; come and worship with us." [8] So the Collects play an exceedingly important role in our Church. They both point to and establish in our hearts and minds what it considers absolutely essential. They

7   Heb 13:8   8   Through the year with Michael Ramsey, edited by Margaret Duggan.

emphasise, first, the power and the love of God, and our need to respond to that power and love with faith and repentance. They also insist on the absolute necessity of grace, and the prime virtue of love. They confirm the passing nature of life here, and the glorious hope of eternal life hereafter. Especially they make plain the centrality of the life, death and resurrection of Jesus for the accomplishing of God's will on earth as it is in heaven, and for the overthrow of all forms of evil that resist that will. As, therefore, that which helps so much to promote our worship and establish our faith, the Prayer Book Collects are real jewels in our Anglican crown. This Commentary seeks above all to show them in this light.

The name Collect does not derive from any word meaning a prayer, as one might expect. We must start our quest for its origins in the worship of the Church in New Testament times. The earliest Christian worship naturally evolved out of Jewish worship. An important element in Synagogue worship was a time of corporate prayer that would be summed up by the service's leader, and this also became a regular element in the worship of the very early Church. In the Latin-speaking West this corporate prayer came to be called 'Oratio ad collectam plebis', which means loosely 'prayer suggested to those who have come to worship', or very simply 'led corporate prayer'. And the summing up prayer was called the 'collectio'.

In due course, after Christianity had become the main religion of the Roman Empire (and in particular the religion, usually, of the Emperor), the great liturgies of the early medieval period evolved. Although Christians then worshipped in great Cathedrals rather than in the equivalent of upper rooms, memories of those earlier simpler times were preserved, and in the West this title 'Oratio ad collectam plebis', shortened to 'Ad collectam', became a recognised introductory heading to the daily Propers. And it was from this phrase from the Latin liturgies, that were discontinued by our Reformation, that Cranmer coined this particular title 'The Collect' for the first element in the Propers in his Book of Common Prayer in 1549. The point is this. Cranmer wisely sought to preserve as much of a sense of continuity between the Church of medieval England, that worshipped in Latin, and the Reformed Church of England, that worshipped in English, and this word provided a small, but perhaps not unimportant link between the two.

The ancient Collects had a certain number of fixed endings. In the early Sacramentaries and in the Sarum Missal these were not usually printed, as it was taken for granted that the appropriate one would be known and used by the officiating Priest. In the 1549 Book this custom was clearly expected to be continued. The way the Collects were ended there varied, just as they had in the earlier Sacramentaries. Sometimes no closing ascription was given at all. Sometimes it was given in an abbreviated form, such as 'through Jesus Christ our Saviour, who liveth and reigneth, etc', or even more abbreviated, 'Grant this, etc'. The most common ending, however, was 'through Jesus Christ our Lord' (or Jesu Christ, or simply Christ). In each case an appropriate longer trinitarian ascription would have been automatically added by the officiating priest.

In the 1662 revision, however, an Amen was printed at the end of all the Collects as they stood. This had the unintended effect of cutting them short, so that the customary trinitarian endings to our Collects were inadvertently lost, except where they were already printed in full. That the later Reformers did not really desire this to happen is shown by the way in which the two Sunday Collects composed in 1662, those for Advent III and Epiphany VI, both have trinitarian endings.

The word Collect has now come to be used to describe a certain type of prayer. Such a prayer is formed of three elements. It starts with an 'invocation', in which God is addressed by Name. Nearly always this is in his first Person although, strangely, the intimate name, Father, is only once used in our Sunday Collects. (See further in commentary for Easter I). Occasionally he is addressed in his second Person; in our Sunday Collects this only occurs twice, in the Collects for Advent III and Lent I (but see also commentary for Advent IV). Then there follows the mention of some doctrine of God or some special quality in God that is appropriate to lead us into the main petition that follows.

The 'petition' is the second element of a Collect, and is the main body of the prayer. Usually this is briefly stated, indeed the more briefly the better. But sometimes it is embellished, or divided into two or more strands.

Lastly the petition is followed by the 'aspiration', the Collect's third element, whose purpose is to take the prayer to God. In this element, therefore, we often find some consequential hope expressed that arises naturally out of the petition. Just as some particular understanding of God and the Gospel may be mentioned in the invocation to prepare us to pray the petition more devoutly, so some appropriate 'hearty desire' in the aspiration may be added to assist us devotionally as we take our petition to God.

The main part of the aspiration, however, is the mention of Jesus through whom the prayer is always offered, and who, as 'the one mediator between God and man'[9] must take it to the Father. A Collect always ends, therefore, 'through Jesus Christ our Lord' (or Saviour et al), to which simple ending, as just mentioned, a trinitarian element may be added, and when the invocation is addressed to Jesus, the trinitarian ending is appropriately rephrased.

I would like to thank both Lord Charteris and Bishop Edward MacBurney most sincerely for writing Forewords to this book. They will be recognised by lovers of our Prayer Book whether in the United Kingdom or the United States.

I would also like to thank most sincerely Mrs. Joan Baxter for her kindness in typing the script of this book, and Canon Dr. David Charlton for kindly reading it and making numerous helpful comments.

I must also acknowledge my great general indebtedness first and especially to Dean E. M. Goulburn, whose famous two volume exposition of all the Prayer Book Collects has been of enormous help, and also to Canon J.

9   1 Tim 2:5

H. B. Masterman, from whose much smaller but most helpful devotional commentary on the Sunday Collects I have taken the idea of dividing the commentary on each Collect into sections, hoping that the reader will want to pause awhile to digest prayerfully what he or she has just read before moving on to read the next section. I hope, too, that the reader will not omit to read first the Collects themselves, perhaps twice, before proceeding to the commentary. As the heavy type in which they are printed properly suggests, they are the most important words of this book.

I have taken notice of the rubrics and the additional Collects included in the Prayer Book revision in 1928, which, though never authorised by Parliament, is recognised and accepted by the Church. I have therefore included the two extra Collects provided for the Christmas Season and the extra Collect for Easter Day. These are not printed in the official copies of the B.C.P., but they make very worthy additions to our Prayer Book.

The biblical quotations are taken from the R.S.V., except where it is otherwise stated, and except for quotations from the Psalms. These all come from the Prayer Book Psalter which, like the Collects, has had such a spiritual influence on Anglicans and Anglicanism and, therefore, are likely to be both familiar to and loved by those who may want to read this book. Like the Scriptures these Prayer Book Collects have proved themselves to be most 'profitable for teaching, for reproof, for correction and for training in righteousness, that the man of God may be complete, equipped for every good work'.[10] 'There is no end to their treasures.'[11]

10 2 Tim 3:16   11 Is 2:7

ADVENT I

Almighty God, give us grace that we may cast away the works of darkness, and put upon us the armour of light, now in the time of this mortal life, in which thy Son Jesus Christ came to visit us in great humility; that in the last day, when he shall come again in his glorious majesty to judge both the quick and the dead, we may rise to the life immortal, through him who liveth and reigneth with thee and the Holy Ghost, now and ever. Amen.

This Collect was the work of Cranmer in 1549 and, as was characteristic of his compositions, it was framed to harmonise with the Epistle. It is to be said throughout the Advent season after the other Advent Collects.

The dramatic phrase, 'the works of darkness', comes from this Sunday's Epistle [1]. It is fine language for an ugly thing, our sinfulness, and it is worth noticing that the Prayer Book Collects, as does the Bible, do not hesitate to emphasise both the reality and the seriousness of it. Our prayer here is that we may 'cast away' this sinfulness from our lives, but, as we know well, this is far more easily prayed for than done. The truth is that our sinfulness is not just an exterior matter, but rather an interior state.

For this reason we may feel that St. Paul's other well-known description of our sinfulness is really more apt and helpful. In Romans 7 it is described as a 'body of death', in which we are forced to dwell. Consequently, he says, there is nothing that we can do of ourselves alone to escape from its sinister and hateful power over us. Surely this is how it really is, and in consequence we can relate with ready sympathy to the vivid account of St. Paul's failure to overcome his sins in that chapter. 'I do not understand my actions. For I do not do what I want, but I do the very thing that I hate. . . Wretched man that I am, who will deliver me from this body of death?'[2] Whereas we may

1   Rom 13:12   2   Rom 7:15-24

reasonably hope of our own free will to change our 'works', if we try hard enough, there is obviously no natural way in which we can change, let alone 'cast away', our bodies.

So how are we to understand this prayer? It is only by emphasising the word 'grace' with which it starts. That is the key word in this Collect, and to pray this prayer aright we must let it dominate all that follows. In this emphasis on the grace of God the Collect is being essentially true to the New Testament, where it takes so central a place. Should we fail to do this, and there is a temptation to let our minds slip past that unfamiliar theological word as we recite it, and to fasten onto the attractively personal 'we' that so quickly follows it, two false reactions are all too likely. According to our temperament, we either find ourselves focusing all our attention on our sins and sinfulness, in which case the prayer becomes an exercise in self-centred concern; or we see it as encouragement for the self-confident belief that we can of our own will put our lives to rights, if we only try hard enough, in which case it becomes a prayer whose object is merely to inspire us to make the necessary effort to do so. The Collect, on the contrary, aims to lift our hearts and minds to God, seeking above all else his saving grace. Certainly our sinfulness is very properly being acknowledged, and our necessary cooperation with his grace being encouraged, but preeminently it is to God, who alone forgives, and who saves by the working of his grace in us, that we are being urged to turn. 'Almighty God, give us grace', that is the principal petition. As we pray this prayer, therefore, we must not fail to give these words their full weight. These words 'give us grace', which are so vital for the proper understanding and praying of this first Collect, are repeatedly found in subsequent Collects. It should cause us no surprise that there is no petition more frequently made than this.

Having stressed the negative, the casting away of what is sinful, the Collect goes on to stress the positive, the putting on of righteousness, described here as 'the armour of light'. This too comes from the Sunday Epistle. Our

Lord specifically warned us of the dangers of half finishing the spiritual task. 'When the unclean spirit has gone out of a man...he says, "I will return to the house from whence I came", and when he comes he finds it empty, swept and put in order. Then he goes and brings with him seven other spirits more evil than himself, and they enter in and dwell there; and the last state of that man becomes worse than the first.'[3] Our experience confirms the danger the parable depicts. A casting away must be followed by a putting on, and for this also we need God's grace. All virtue or wisdom is to be acknowledged as the work of grace, 'the grace of our Lord Jesus Christ', 'apart from (whom we) can do nothing'.[4]

In the Epistle, taken from Romans 13, St. Paul uses this phrase 'the armour of light' without elaboration. However, in Ephesians 6 he develops it in stirring fashion. There he makes it clear that he does not only have in mind that which will protect us against evil, which the word armour might suggest, but also that which will carry the fight to the enemy, for he speaks of the sword as well as the shield and helmet. Yet that famous passage on 'the whole armour of God'[5] is not really an easy one for us to relate to today, any more than we would find a suit of armour easy to wear! Later in the Epistle, however, we find the whole matter put with sublime simplicity, in words that are, and will always be, truly inspiring, plumbing the depths of our Christian faith. 'Put ye on the Lord Jesus Christ', says St. Paul.[6] Can we find anywhere the mystery of the Gospel more succinctly expressed? This is what we always want as well as need to hear, for this command is the one that never loses its attraction to Christian ears, nor its power to help us.

What a mystery our spiritual lives are! What does this instruction mean? We know perfectly well what it means, even though it is virtually impossible to find words to describe it. This ability of ours to have an intimate relationship with someone who lived 2000 years ago, of whom we know so comparatively little, is surely the basic mystery of the Christian religion.

3   Matt 12:43-45   4   Jn 15:5   5   Eph. 6:10-20   6   Rom 13:14 (A.V.)

St. Peter said of the earliest Christians, 'without having seen him, you love him; though you do not now see him, you believe in him and rejoice with unutterable and exalted joy. As the outcome of your faith you obtain the salvation of your souls'.[7] St. Paul said of himself, 'It is no longer I who live, but Christ who lives in me, and the life I now live, I live by faith in the Son of God, who loved me and gave himself for me'.[8] So with us, if we seek to analyse or explain our spiritual lives, we have to use some such words as these. Christ's influence on our lives is so much more than that of a man, who lived long ago and left behind a memory and some teaching. It is that of a living presence, both being with us and indwelling us. It is as he himself promised it would be; 'I will not leave you desolate; I will come to you. . . you will know that I am in my Father, and you in me and I in you.' So it is for anyone 'who has his commandments and keeps them'.[9] But how this can be true for us must not be ascribed to our own virtue or spiritual maturity. It is only possible because of the grace of God. Here some words of Christ come to mind as we consider this mystery. 'I thank thee, Father. . . that thou hast hidden these things from the wise and understanding and revealed them to babes; yea, Father, for such was thy gracious will.'[10] It is by grace alone that we are able both to cast away our sinfulness, and to put on Christ as an armour of light; and this experience is only possible because such is God's gracious will for us.

The Collect continues by stressing the contrast between the first and second comings of Christ, and relating them to our spiritual lives in him. His first coming was 'in great humility'; his second will be 'in glorious majesty'. We are not to consider that there is any strangeness in this, but rather just as we should expect. The New Testament emphasises this. 'He humbled himself. . . therefore God has highly exalted him'.[11] So it is now for his Mother,[12] and so it must be for us all, 'A servant is not greater than his master. . . If you know these things, blessed are you'.[13] Humility and glory

7   1 Pet 1:8, 9   8   Gal 2:20   9   John 14:18-21   10   Luke 10:21
11   Phil 2:8-9   12   Luke 1:46-53   13   John 13:16

are related, and humility here leads inevitably to glory hereafter. 'He that humbles himself will be exalted.'[14]

His first coming was in humble service, but it was nevertheless a coming that was to set in motion the divine judgement, which will be completed when he comes again in his glorious majesty. This divine judgement is essentially a revelation of the truth. 'For judgement I came into this world', said Jesus, 'that those who do not see may see, and those who see may be blind'.[15] This judging truth both sets us free and shows us up, so it is a truth that saves as well as a truth that condemns. To us the word judgement must have an ominous ring about it because we are sinners. But that there is an encouraging side to this doctrine of the divine judgement is confirmed by Jesus, who also said, 'I did not come to judge the world, but to save it'.[16] The Holy Spirit, moreover, whom Jesus brings to us, confirms this two sided truth about God's judgement. 'When he comes', said Jesus, 'he will convict the world of sin, and convince it of righteousness and judgement . . . He will glorify me, for he will take what is mine and declare it to you. All that the Father has is mine; therefore I said that he will take what is mine and declare it to you'.[17] Is this not exactly how it is in our experience? It is the Holy Spirit that convicts and convinces us of these vital things, and then at the same time reassures us that all such matters belong to Jesus, and that both our ultimate salvation and our final judgement are in his hands. Therefore we are led on and enabled to find in him our Saviour as well as our Judge. In consequence we can sing, 'We believe that thou shalt come to be our Judge. We therefore pray thee help thy servants, whom thou hast redeemed with thy precious blood.'[18] Judgement and salvation are intimately connected. Both meet in Jesus.

This truth introduces us to the two contrasting emphases that are particularly characteristic of Advent, penitence for sin and hope of salvation. Because of grace, which is the saving power of God in our lives, we sinners,

---

14 Lk 14:11   15 Jn 9:39   16 Jn 12:47   17 Jn 16:8,14
18 Te Deum

who stand condemned by God's law, and who cannot of ourselves cast away our sinfulness, and who experience all the suffering, shame and sorrow that sin brings upon us, can nonetheless always 'abound in hope'.[19] So it is trust in the grace of God, which this Collect so particularly encourages, that gives to Advent its special paradoxical flavour of penitential hope. It is appropriate, therefore, that it should be used throughout the season.

———————

Finally, the coming of Christ to judge is said to be for 'both the quick and the dead', a phrase from the Creeds. All will be judged. 'And I saw the dead, great and small, standing before the throne, and books were opened', says the Seer.[20] What, we may wonder, is written in those 'books', not just in ours which are still being written, but also in those of others who have passed on? When we think of divine judgement it is inevitable that we should be concerned for others, as well as ourselves, especially those we love. 'Lord, what about this man?'[21] is a natural question to ask of Jesus. But the reply that Peter received, when he asked that question in a somewhat different context, will be the same that we will receive in this one, which is that the eternal fate of others is not our direct concern, and is among those things that 'the Father has fixed by his own authority'.[22] But the dual aspect of our Lord's coming to be both Judge and Saviour, which this Collect emphasises, enables us to pray for the departed always in a spirit of hope. St. Paul certainly greatly encourages us in this hope when he says, 'God desires that all men should be saved and come to the knowledge of the truth'.[23] There can be no denying the distance our sins take us from God, but if salvation for all is the will of our loving Father, (and who can doubt it?), how can we fail to hope and pray that such will indeed come true for all?

19 Rom. 15:13   20 Rev. 20:12   21 Jn 21:21   22 Acts 1:7
23 1 Tim 2:4

ADVENT II

Blessed Lord, who hast caused all holy Scriptures to be written for our learning: Grant that we may in such wise hear them, read, mark, learn and inwardly digest them, that by patience and comfort of thy holy Word, we may embrace and ever hold fast the blessed hope of everlasting life, which thou hast given us in our Saviour Jesus Christ. Amen.

This Collect is by Cranmer and was composed in 1549. As was character-istic of his method, Cranmer has used the Epistle to provide the theme of this new Collect. The outstanding feature of the Reformation was the rediscovery of the Bible and the reading of it by ordinary people in their own language. It fitted, therefore, Cranmer's sense of spiritual priorities to have a prayer about the Bible and Bible reading at the very beginning of the Church's year.

In the Collects the initial relative clause is always of great devotional importance. Here we pray, 'Blessed Lord, who hast caused all holy Scrip-tures to be written for our learning'. What a difference it makes to our attitude towards Scripture when that truth really grips us! St. Paul ex-presses the Christian attitude towards the Bible in today's Epistle,[1] and also in 2 Tim. 3 : 16-17, where he says, 'All Scripture is inspired by God and profitable for teaching, for reproof, for correction and for training in righteousness, that the man of God may be complete, equipped for every good work'.

Modern theologians have shed much light on the Scriptures, but they may also seem to have undermined their unique authority. Let us remember then that Christ himself held the view that the Scriptures are the very word of God. 'Truly I say to you, till heaven and earth pass away, not an iota, not a dot, will pass from the law till all is accomplished.'[2] In many subtle, as

1   Rom 15:4   2   Matt 5:18

well as obvious ways, the Gospels show us how Christ was soaked in the Old Testament Scriptures. He often quoted them; he knew them better than the Scribes themselves, and from a boy this was one of the things that most astonished men about him; and his message is expressed in words and images that make it unintelligible without reference to them. The New Testament is connected to the Old as leaves and fruit are connected to branches and trunk. Cut down one and you cut down the other. And just as the fruit sums up the life of a tree, so the life of Jesus fulfils the whole of the Bible. 'Think not that I have come to abolish the law and the prophets; I have come to fulfil them.'[3]

It was Luther who said, 'The holy Scriptures are the manger in which Christ is born,' and if Christ is to be born in our hearts, it is going to be necessary for us to read our Bibles. Do we not all have a Bible somewhere on our shelves, but how often do we reach out for it? How many, who would certainly call themselves Christians, are bored by the idea of Bible study, either private or corporate? Not a few. No doubt we can give reasons for not being regular Bible readers, if we are not. But we would not look for any excuses if we were really convinced that all holy Scriptures were inspired by God and 'written for our learning'. Once this grips our hearts and minds we will study the Bible gladly and willingly. We can use this prayer as an intercession to this end.

The Collect teaches us how to set about Bible reading. First, it says that we must 'hear' the holy Scriptures, only secondly does it mention that we must read them. This may surprise us, but when this prayer was first written most people could not read, and so, if they were to learn what the Scriptures said, they had to hear them read aloud. This Collect reflects that spiritu- ally exciting time when men were experiencing the thrill of hearing and reading the holy Scriptures in their own language for the first time. To men

3   Matt 5:17

then the words of Scripture glowed with a freshness that set their hearts pulsing with excitement and joy. Because our times are so different, modern English Christians find it hard to understand the power and wonder of the Bible as it broke upon the ears of our countrymen four hundred years ago. However, many others today can. I discovered this for myself during my time in Central Africa. One of my outstanding memories is of Africans reading the Bible to each other near their front doors. Many there could not read, and few possessed a Bible, so there was the twofold need to hear it read aloud. The power of the Bible in such a place is very much like it must have been in England in the sixteenth century. Have we forgotten the converting power of the holy Scriptures that rest unread upon so many shelves? Perhaps we have need to remind ourselves of how Jesus said to the Sadducees by way of rebuke, 'You know neither the Scriptures nor the power of God'.[4]

But there is much more to the word 'hear' as used in the Bible than just listening to what is said. There hearing is almost synonymous with obeying. This is because biblical theology is all about man's relationship with a God that speaks, and whose word is creative and imperative. He speaks his word to man, and man must hear and obey. Central to this idea is the description of Jesus as 'the Word made flesh'[5]. We must 'hear' this Word, which means that we must respond to Jesus with faith and obedience. Therefore faith as well as obedience is intimately connected with hearing. 'Faith comes from what is heard, and what is heard comes from the preaching of Christ'.[6] So the Bible is a book that 'preaches' Christ, and to the Scriptures we must respond in faith and obedience, that is we must 'in such wise hear them'. 'He that has ears to hear', said Jesus, 'let him hear'.[7]

There are two main ways to read the Bible. One way is broadly, as one would read any other book, seeking to get the sweep of the narrative, and to see it as a whole. This might be called the way of 'learning'. Here a modern translation can be of particular value. It can make half-remembered stories, and even familiar ones, come alive with remarkable freshness. It is this freshness which is so spiritually important, and which has such power to convert us, and which we find so hard to experience today.

The other way is the slow thoughtful way, the way of meditation. In the words of the Collect it is the way of 'inwardly digesting'. Several Saints have given us their methods of doing this, notably St. Ignatius and St. Francois de Sales. None is likely to suit us today unless adapted, although both the principles and the eager spirit that they set before us are as relevant today as they always have been. By and large they add up to this: we read a passage of Scripture slowly, and then ask ourselves three questions about it. "What does this passage mean? What does it mean to me? What must I do about it?"

Essentially Bible reading is so simple, but nonetheless in practice it is hard. What makes it hard, beyond the initial need to believe in its special importance, is the need for us to ask ourselves honestly such questions as we read, and then to listen to, and ultimately to act upon, the answers we may hear. As we ruefully acknowledge this common weakness, let us remind ourselves of the true meaning in this Collect of those two important words 'patience and comfort'. In ordinary usage they have both become far weaker words than they used to be and, consequently, this Collect can be drained of much of its ability to help and inspire us.

Patience had the meaning of being brave, loyal and determined rather than being careful, unhurried and calm, as it has today. So the Greek word (hupomone) translated in the A.V. as patience is translated in later versions by words like perseverance and resolution (i.e. in Heb. 12 : 1 'run with patience' becomes 'run with perseverance' (R.S.V.) and 'run with resolution' (N.E.B.)) So our prayer here, therefore, is for that loyal persevering spirit that will enable us to keep our resolutions to study the Bible faithfully and carefully, and not be side-tracked by any circumstance. The word comfort, too, has subtly changed its meaning since the 16th century. Today it usually means to make someone happier, whereas then it meant to make someone stronger. But in spiritual matters to be stronger is also sure to make us happier too, which is a connection of ideas well taught by the Psalmist when he said, 'In God's word will I rejoice: in the Lord's word will I comfort me.'[8] Therefore, 'by patience and comfort of thy holy word' should remind us of the determination that is required, if we are to get what we should from Bible study, and of the moral and spiritual strength that is the welcome result in our lives, if only we will persist in this vital exercise.

———————————

Finally, the ultimate purpose of Bible reading is spelt out for us in this Collect, 'that we embrace and ever hold fast the blessed hope of everlasting life'. It is a tender image. An embrace is a two-way action between those who love each other. God, however, can only embrace us wholly as we seek to embrace him wholly. Through a devout and persevering reading of the Bible we shall be wonderfully helped so to reach out in love to God as to enable him to hold us fast to himself, and so confirm in us 'the blessed hope of everlasting life'.

We may notice, consequently, how this Collect appropriately emphasises Advent's special theme of hope, for it echoes this Sunday's Epistle passage from Romans 15. As we 'hear and read' our Bibles, 'the God of hope (will) fill (us) with all joy and peace in believing, that (we) may abound in hope, through the power of the Holy Ghost'.[9] This is regular Bible reading's rich reward.

8   Ps 56:10   9   Rom 15:13 A.V.

ADVENT III

O Lord Jesu Christ, who at thy first coming didst send thy messenger to prepare thy way before thee: Grant that the ministers and stewards of thy mysteries may likewise so prepare and make ready thy way, by turning the hearts of the disobedient to the wisdom of the just, that at thy second coming to judge the world we may be found an acceptable people in thy sight, who livest and reignest with the Father and the Holy Spirit, ever one God, world without end. Amen.

This Collect is unusual in that it is addressed to Jesus. In the Collects prayer is usually addressed to the Father through the Son. The only other Prayer Book Collects to take this form are those for Lent I and St. Stephen's Day, although in its original form the Collect for Advent IV was also addressed to Jesus.

This Collect was composed by Bishop Cosin for the Book of 1662. Characteristically for those composed later it echoes both the Epistle and the Gospel. The Collect is particularly for those who are ordained, with the Advent ordinations set to take place on the following Sunday, although it retains the special Advent theme of preparing us for the second coming of our Lord.

The main petition is for 'the ministers and stewards of Christ's mysteries', and in this it echoes the Epistle. There we read, 'Let a man so account of us, as of the ministers of Christ and stewards of the mysteries of God'.[1] The word for minister means under-rower, and the word for steward means one who looks after a household. Both words refer to one who works for another. Now, 'it is required in stewards that a man be found faithful'.[2] The essence of the Christian life is that we live as men under authority, as those

1   1 Cor 4:1 A.V.   2   1 Cor 4:2 A.V.

who serve a master, and especially this is so for the clergy.

Who are the clergy? And what is special about them? The Prayer Book Ordinal and the New Testament agree; in the administration of the Word and Sacraments the clergy are 'ministers and stewards' of the divine 'mysteries'. This ministry is the result of a secret call from God heard by the individual, but one which must be tested, recognised and confirmed in ordination by the Church. The clergy are to feel themselves as those chosen by God. No one may take this work of handling 'the mysteries of God' upon himself, as of his own choice. 'You did not choose me, but I chose you and appointed you',[3] said Jesus to his Apostles.

The Epistle speaks about the faithfulness that is required in the clergy, and the way in which they are under special judgement. Do they not need in consequence special prayer? In the Church's calendar there are four groups of days, called Ember Days, in which prayer for the clergy is specifically enjoined. The first group is on the Wednesday, Friday and Saturday after this Sunday. The others come after Lent 1, after Whitsunday, and after 13th September, in the fortnight before Michaelmas. They should certainly not be forgotten.

The purpose of a priest's work is described here as that which helps 'to prepare and make ready thy way, by turning the hearts of the disobedient to the wisdom of the just'. This recalls the prophecy of the angel to Zechariah about his son, John the Baptist. 'He will turn many of the sons of Israel to the Lord their God, and he will go before him in the spirit and power of Elijah, to turn the hearts of the fathers to the children, and the disobedient to the wisdom of the just, and to make ready for the Lord a people prepared.'[4] John the Baptist is the Collect's 'messenger', and it may at first sight appear inappropriate that he is picked out to be the pattern of a Christian priest, seeing that in spirit he is much more an Old Testament figure than a New Testament one. However, could there be a finer description of the role of a priest than that given of John the Baptist by his priestly father, Zechariah, in the Benedictus? 'And thou, child, shalt be called the prophet of the highest, and thou shalt go before the face of the Lord to prepare his ways; to give knowledge of salvation unto his people for the remission of their sins,....to give light to them that sit in darkness and in the shadow of death, and to guide (their) feet into the way of peace'.[5] Moreover, in stressing the role of John the Baptist as the exemplar of a Christian priest, the Collect is only echoing the words of Jesus, which end the Gospel for this Sunday, 'This is he of whom it is written, Behold I send my messenger before thy face, which shall prepare thy way before thee.'[6]

John the Baptist was the pre-ordained messenger or forerunner of the Messiah, the one who pointed to Jesus. This is vividly illustrated in that scene 'in Bethany beyond the Jordan where John was baptising'. He was with some of his followers, and St. John's account in his Gospel continues, 'the next day he saw Jesus coming towards him and said, "Behold the Lamb of God, who takes away the sins of the world"'.[7] A priest is to be one who, in like manner, points to Jesus as our Lord and Saviour. And, as John was, he too is able to do more. He is able to help others to meet him and know him for themselves. This is what happened in the case of Andrew who, in this story, followed Jesus, met him, and then was able to say to his brother, 'We have found the Messiah'.[8] So it is with the priestly ministry of Word and Sacrament. Through it others can meet and accept Jesus as their Lord and Saviour. They too can say for themselves with conviction and joy, 'we have found the Messiah'. Down the ages and to this day this is the experience of millions, who receive and share in the Church's ministry of Word and Sacrament. And what joy for the priest when he sees this happening in the lives of those to whom he is ministering!

In this connection another famous scene comes to mind. On Easter Day, probably at the time of sunset, Cleopas and a companion met the risen

5   Lk 1:76-79 A.V.   6   Matt 11:10 A.V.   7   Jn 1:29   8   Jn 1:41

Christ. It was all so mysterious, for at first they did not realise that this is what was happening. But in due course they did realise, and were able to say, 'Did not our hearts burn within us as he talked to us', and 'he made himself known to us in the breaking of the bread'.[9] Such is the mystery of the Church's ministry of Word and Sacrament, that we can say the same things, when we hear the Word and partake of the Sacraments. We too can say 'he talked to us' and 'he made himself known to us'. This is why the Word and Sacraments, of which the clergy are the ministers, are rightly described in this Collect as Christ's 'mysteries'. Through them the risen Christ comes to us personally. As we have said, is not this experience for us the ultimate mystery of our religion?

As we have recalled, John the Baptist, pointing to Jesus, said, 'Behold the Lamb of God, who takes away the sins of the world'. Yes, that pre-eminently is why our Lord came, and still comes, to be the Saviour of the world. 'For God so loved the world that he gave his only Son, that whoever believes in him should not perish, but have eternal life. For God sent his Son into the world...that the world might be saved through him.'[10] By pointing to Jesus, within the context of their ministry of Word and Sacrament, the clergy proclaim our salvation in him and impart to sinners God's forgiveness and grace. This priestly function is specially emphasised in their ordination, when the Bishop repeats Christ's words to his Apostles after his resurrection, 'Whose sins thou dost forgive, they are forgiven, and whose sins thou dost retain, they are retained'.[11] And then he goes on to add, 'And be thou a faithful dispenser of the Word of God and his holy Sacraments, in the name of the Father and of the Son and of the Holy Ghost'. This Word of God and his holy Sacraments concern 'the redemption of the world through our Lord Jesus Christ, the means of grace and the hope of glory'.[12] Whatever else the clergy may be called upon to do, the Collect very properly places special emphasis upon their spiritual ministry of 'turning the hearts of the

9   Lk 24:32,35   10 Jn 3:16,17   11 Jn 20:23   12 The General Thanksgiving

disobedient to the wisdom of the just' by being faithful dispensers of these divine mysteries.

It is a wonderful privilege to be called to this ministry. But it is also a great responsibility. It has to do with nothing less than other people's eternal salvation, as the last clause of the Collect makes plain. How, therefore, should the clergy consider themselves? 'What we preach', said St. Paul, 'is not ourselves, but Jesus Christ as Lord, with ourselves as your servants for Jesus's sake'.[13] This is the proper vision of the priestly life. Jesus said, 'For their sakes I consecrate myself, that they also may be consecrated in truth'.[14] Just so, and the priest must continually seek to consecrate himself for his ministry, after the pattern of his Lord. The cry of St. Paul will find an echo in the heart of every priest, 'Necessity is laid upon me. Woe to me if I do not preach the Gospel!'[15] But he will find much comfort also from St. Paul's assurance, 'He who calls you is faithful, and he will do it'.[16] Let not the Church, however, forget its duty to pray for those whom God has called, and is calling, to be ministers and stewards of his mysteries. This Collect is a fine prayer to use for this purpose.

If we are to pray for the Clergy today, however, we can hardly evade the question of the ordination of women. When this Collect was composed the idea of female priests had not arisen, and our Prayer Book Ordinal speaks of a male-only priesthood, as does the New Testament.[17] However, the main truth emphasised in our Ordinal is that those being ordained are made 'Priests in the Church of God'. The Reformers certainly claimed that they were creating a self-governing Church, distinct in its government from other Churches. But that was all. They did not believe that this change in any way broke their essential unity with the Holy Catholic Church of the Creeds. So its Clergy were still 'Priests in the Church of God'. There was no such thing for them as Anglican Orders, any more than there were such

13 2 Cor 4:5   14 Jn 17:19   15 1 Cor 9:16   16 1 Thess 5:24
17 1 Tim 3:1-7, Tit 1:5-9

things as Anglican Scriptures, Anglican Sacraments or Anglican Creeds. Consequently, to be loyal to our Church's Ordinal in relation to this current question of the ordination of women, we have to answer such questions as, "Can we proceed unilaterally in this matter and remain in fellowship not only with our fellow Catholic Christians in the present, but also with our fellow Anglicans in the past? And, if we do proceed unilaterally, are we creating a second Reformation more radical than the first, which will invalidate the claim that our clergy are 'Priests in the Church of God', whatever their sex may be, since neither Scripture nor Tradition support this change?"

As this matter stands both the first women priests have been ordained, and the decision to ordain women is considered irrevocable. However a considerable minority, who still desire to stay within the Church of England, refuse to accept either this decision or the women recently ordained as Priests. It is, therefore, a time of peculiar tension in the Church and 'great searchings of heart'[18] for many of its faithful worshippers. But we have to recall that in our Church's history there have been similar times of great tension. From its new beginning in the 16th Century the Church of England has with remarkable success sought to hold together what may loosely be called the Catholic and Protestant elements in the Church, that the Reformation elsewhere had only succeeded in separating. Indeed, the willingness of these elements to live together in our Church, accepting each other in spite of their marked differences of emphasis, has created a peculiar character for it that many deem its special glory. Its desire to acknowledge unity within diversity, although once again being severely tested, is nonetheless as evident as ever at this time. The efforts of the disaffected minority to create a third Province within the Church of England, in which women priests would not be accepted, have failed, but a compromise response of creating special Bishops sympathetic to their position to minister to their needs is now actively in place. And the future is still unfolding.

18 Judg. 5:15

As we consider this Collect, which was composed at another period of great tension in our Church's history, in which the question of who were to be accepted as 'true ministers and stewards of (Christ's) mysteries' was also most prominent, we may ask, 'Can it help us now?' Surely it can. There is a particular relevance in the petition that 'we may be found an acceptable people in thy sight'. That is, after all, what all desire. And then there is the mention made of 'the wisdom of the just'. This surely is one with the all-important charity that is 'patient and kind...not arrogant or rude... that bears and hopes all things.'[19] Where this wise and generous charity exists we may entertain the hope that God will take charge and his will be done. There is no force more creative. It is able to create fellowship in spite of disagreement. Prayer is both the way into and the way of preserving such fellowship, and the desire expressed in this Collect that we may experience this 'wisdom of the just' is, therefore, profoundly relevant to the very special needs of our Church today. This Collect, therefore, can be used as an intercessory prayer at this most difficult time for our Church by all who desire, in spite of deep-seated disagreements, to continue as loyal and active members of it.

---

19 1 Cor 13 : 4-7 (AV)

ADVENT IV

O Lord, raise up (we pray thee) thy power, and come among us, and with great might succour us; that whereas, through our sins and wickedness, we are sore let and hindered in running the race that is set before us, thy bountiful grace and mercy may speedily help and deliver us; through the satisfaction of thy Son our Lord, to whom with thee and the Holy Ghost be honour and glory, world without end. Amen.

This is the first of the medieval Collects that Cranmer translated, but it is interesting to notice that in this case he went behind the version in the Sarum Missal to the earlier version in the Gelasian Sacramentary. The Sarum version was Gregorian and addressed to Christ, whereas the Gelasian version was addressed to the Father, as this Collect is. Why 'we pray thee' is put in brackets is not clear, except perhaps because it was part of the Sarum Collect, where it was not in brackets, or because it was not in the Gelasian Collect that otherwise Cranmer preferred. The brackets, which seem unnecessary, may have the effect now of spoiling the flowing start to the Collect, but nonetheless it is still a lovely prayer. Some other changes and additions made in translation are dealt with in the commentary.

This Collect is a cri de coeur. It does not wait, as we have said, to preface the main petition with an appropriate relative clause, but rushes headlong into urgent prayer. We are in deep trouble, it declares, and no attempt is made to hide the reason. 'Our sins and wickedness' are the cause of it all. A simple and straightforward honesty and humility motivates the prayer. In our trouble we are turning to God as the only power with sufficient 'great might to succour us', and we are asking him to act 'speedily'. Does such a prayer merit the description 'childlike', or is it, as it may appear today, frankly childish?

Much certainly has changed since the times from which this prayer comes. In recent years spiritual writers have been urging us to put away childish attitudes and to acknowledge that man has 'come of age.'[1] Involved in this plea is not only that we realise that we now have 'great might' of our own with which to succour ourselves, as well as all the other needy and distressed throughout the world, and that therefore our prayers today should be more in the direction of possessing grace to use these powers aright, than in asking for new acts of divine intervention on our behalf; it is also a plea that we interpret the old images of God, on which the old prayers are based, with what might be called spiritual sophistication. It is all part of the divine will, it is stressed, that we are not any longer like defenceless and ignorant infants, but rather like grown adults. This being so, our relationship with our heavenly Father must change accordingly, and consequently the content of our prayers should change also. No doubt there is reason and sense in this teaching, and it is right that we abandon childish images of God as Father and King (no beard, no crown). But there is no need for us to lose all sense of being God's children and of being his subjects. Indeed at all cost we must not do so.

The difference between the childlike and the childish in our spiritual lives is of great importance, and it is not always easy to avoid the latter in seeking after the former as the New Testament requires. We hear, for instance, our Lord saying to his disciples, 'Unless you turn, and become like children, you will never enter the kingdom of Heaven'.[2] But we also hear St. Paul saying that we are called to a 'mature manhood' in Christ, and that we are 'no longer to be children, tossed to and fro.'[3] A childlike faith that is so praiseworthy in its initial simplicity can degenerate into childishness, if it never matures. Yet the mature Christian should never lose his sense of dependence on God and his spiritual status as child of his heavenly Father. This clearly is the witness of the Saints. Growing into 'mature manhood' means growing up into a deepening relationship with Christ,

1   Honest to God, by John Robinson   2   Matt 18:3   3   Eph 4:13,14

who is the eternal Son, both of man and of God, and becoming a more active fellow-worker with Christ, and sharing more spontaneously in his creative and redemptive activity in the world. The late Archbishop Michael Ramsey, put the contrast between the childish and the childlike Christian like this, 'It is one thing to be childish, with a religion which never grows up; it is another thing to be childlike, with a religion which matures into a manly independence, and yet discovers an ever-deepening dependence on God as our origin and our goal.'[4] Although we never cease to be a person in need of divine help, we should mature into a person who, out of the help we ourselves have received from him, can become a means by which God can also help others.

Recently an entirely new, but nonetheless related, consideration to that of childishness in the interpretation of images, and one that is altogether more serious, has emerged to disturb the life of the Church. Feminists are demanding the abandonment of all wholly male images of God, if they cannot be balanced by female ones, because they claim that by implication they falsely aggrandise men and diminish the status of women. Such thinking naturally makes even the Lord's Prayer uncongenial, as well as several other famous prayers, notably the doxology, and the historic Creeds themselves. Much that has been and still is the staple diet of church-going Christians they would like to see appropriately rephrased or abandoned.

In their demands for radical change, however, the feminists are not alone. Liberal theologians, who reject the virginal conception and the bodily resurrection of Jesus, and social liberals, who no longer accept traditional attitudes towards marriage and divorce and sexual relations generally, be they heterosexual or homosexual, are also calling for radical changes in the Church's formularies and sacramental practice. Beside these there are

4   Through the year with Michael Ramsey, edited by Margaret Duggan

also the prophets of a New Age that they claim is dawning, one that should be called Charismatic rather then Christian, in which the dominant divine personality is the Holy Spirit rather than Jesus. They perceive this change to be analogous to the change that took place when God in Christ brought to birth the Catholic Church out of the Jewish Church; God in his Spirit is, they believe, now doing a new thing, bringing into being a new Church that will take his truth forward into the future, gathering as it does so into one the great religions of the world. They are not afraid, moreover, to reject both Scripture and Tradition if they appear to hinder this New Age's full acceptance.

So we are living in a time when some of the Church's main doctrines, traditions and practices are being attacked from within and radical changes demanded. These various critical voices are becoming increasingly audible and insistent, and there is no denying that they constitute a real threat to the unity of the Church.

What can be said in response to these events by and for those who do not feel part of them, whose spiritual lives remain at peace within the historic traditions of the Church? This is not the first time the Church has been faced with danger and difficulty, and prayer has always been its first response. This, therefore, must be our immediate response now. It is surely apropos to recall how this particular Collect came out of another time of great confusion, when Catholics and Arians confronted each other in western Europe. This prayer in its original form, as we have said, was addressed to Jesus. It was a cri de coeur that he should 'come among' the confused people of that time to 'succour' them by means of his 'great might', for the times were evil. All could see that the consequences of the conflict then raging between Christians of different persuasions was potentially disastrous. Does it not seem, therefore, an appropriate prayer for our time too?

The image of life being like a race comes three times in the Epistles, in Hebrews, 1 Corinthians and 2 Timothy, and we find it in this Collect as an element added in 1662. The Hebrews' passage is particularly dramatic. 'Since we are surrounded by so great a cloud of witnesses, let us also lay aside every weight, and sin which clings so closely, and let us run with perseverance the race that is set before us, looking to Jesus, the pioneer and perfecter of our faith, who for the joy that was set before him endured the cross, despising the shame, and is seated at the right hand of the throne of God'.[5] If we wish to 'run the straight race', sin is like a handicap that we carry. We may long to shed it because it clings so closely, but we cannot of ourselves cast it off. We are returning in essence to the problem prayed about and discussed in the Collect for Advent I, which we continue to use throughout the Advent season, and so with this Collect.

How can God then 'help and deliver us'? Better still, how can he do it 'speedily'? The Collect for Advent stresses the need for grace, and so the continued use of that Collect is most appropriate. But we are not automatons, but free agents. We must contribute to our own salvation. To this end the way St. Paul uses this image of life being like a race in 1 Corinthians is most apposite, for he introduces that vital element in the spiritual life called mortification. 'Do you not know that in a race all runners compete, but only one receives the prize? So run that you may obtain it. Every athlete exercises self-control in all things'. Mortification means the practice of such self-discipline and self-denial as may be necessary to preserve and strengthen our spiritual lives. Serious progress in any ordinary profession demands self-discipline and self-denial, and in this the scientist or business-man is the same as the athlete. They do it to receive rewards that are merely temporary, whereas we are to practise mortification to gain eternal blessings. 'Put to death, therefore, what is earthly in you.'[6] 'If your eye causes you to sin, pluck it out.'[7] We all really know the essential wisdom of such teaching, however hard it may be to practise properly. St. Paul is in

5   Heb 12:1,2   6   Col 3:5   7   Matt 18:9

no doubt of its necessity for him. 'I do not box as one that beats the air, but I pommel my body and subdue it, lest, after preaching to others, I myself should be disqualified'.[8] The unmortified life will not be a good instrument of God's will, and our determination to avoid sin to the point of regular self-discipline and painful self-denial both proves the reality of our faith and repentance, and also opens the way for God's needful grace. Since we live in such comparatively comfortable times, perhaps few truths concerning the spiritual life are more in need of emphasis today than this.

This is the Collect for the last Sunday in Advent. Our prayer to God 'to raise up his power and come among us' does two things. On the one hand, it points us to Christmas, which can now be only a few days away. On the other, it points us to the second coming of Jesus, which may be at any time. 'Come Lord Jesus'[9] was the characteristic prayer of the early Church, which we can tell from the New Testament lived its first years in the expectation that our Lord's second coming was imminent. This expectation is echoed here, and Advent is very much the season in which the second coming of Jesus is brought before us, as we prepare to celebrate the anniversary of his first coming.

While we continue our lives here we are going to need God's 'bountiful grace and mercy' to help us. In the end, however, we look for a time when even grace and mercy will be needed no more, for their work will be done, and God's kingdom will finally have come. How mysterious is this ultimate Christian hope! Then it will fully be known that 'from him and through him and to him are all things', and 'to him (shall) be glory for ever'.[10] Christian hope is based upon the conviction that God is 'the Alpha and the Omega, who is and who was and who is to come, the Almighty'.[11] We are to delight in this truth, and to desire and pray for this divine culmination

8   1 Cor 9:24-27   9   Rev 22:20, 1 Cor 16:22   10   Rom 11:36   11   Rev 1:8

of all things. In spite of sin, and in spite of divine judgement on sinners, Christian hope assures us that nothing could be better for us all than that this divine culmination should take place.

The ending to this Collect uses the unusual word 'satisfaction', which has taken the place of the difficult phrase 'the indulgence of his propitiation' in the original medieval Collect. Satisfaction and propitiation, however, are words which have similar theological meaning, and they refer here to our atonement won by the redeeming sacrifice of Christ upon the cross. (The only time the word 'satisfaction' is used in the A.V. to describe an act of propitiation it is translated 'ransom' in the R.S.V.[12]). This Collect, therefore, links the themes of Advent and Christmas with those of Good Friday and Easter. It could hardly be more wide-ranging in its content, and without doubt it is a prayer to ponder. God's love and power, our sin and weakness, the availability of God's grace and forgiveness through the redeeming sacrifice of his Son, whose coming was in the past, but also is now, and will be at the last day, are all emphasised. The whole Gospel seems to be included in it.

12 Num 35:31

CHRISTMAS DAY AND THE SUNDAYS AFTER CHRISTMAS

Almighty God, who has given us thy only begotten Son to take our nature upon him, and as at this time to be born of a pure Virgin; Grant that we being regenerate, and made thy children by adoption and grace, may daily be renewed by thy Holy Spirit; through the same our Lord Jesus Christ, who liveth and reigneth with thee and the same Spirit, ever one God, world without end. Amen.

Collect for Christmas Eve, added in 1928.

O God, who makest us glad with the yearly remembrance of the birth of thy only Son, Jesus Christ: Grant that as we joyfully receive him for our redeemer, so we may with sure confidence behold him, when he shall come to be our judge; who liveth and reigneth with thee and the Holy Ghost, one God, world without end. Amen.

Collect for Christmas II, added in 1928.

Almighty God, who didst wonderfully create man in thine own image, and didst yet more wonderfully restore him; Grant, we beseech thee, that as thy Son our Lord Jesus Christ was made in the likeness of men, so we may be made partakers of the divine nature; through the same thy Son, who with thee and the Holy Ghost liveth and reigneth, one God, world without end. Amen.

Since Christmas is kept with its octave, the Sunday after Christmas always falls within it. (An octave covers a span of eight days.) For this reason the Collect for both days is the same.

Within the octave are the four major Saints' days of St. Stephen, St. John, Holy Innocents and the Circumcision of our Lord which, falling on New

Year's Day, ends the octave. Each has its own proper Collect, Epistle and Gospel (its Proper) and in medieval times each had their own octave, which in the case of the Circumcision was cut short by the feast of the Epiphany on 6th January. Although with the introduction of the B.C.P. octaves for Saints' Days were discontinued, a remnant of the medieval practice remains in the B.C.P. in that no Proper is provided for a second Sunday after Christmas, and, when there is one, that for the Circumcision is expected to be used. In the 1928 revision of the B.C.P., however, a Proper was provided for this Sunday, which occurs in the Calendar whenever a Sunday falls between January 2-5. It also required the Proper Preface for Christmas to continue until the Epiphany.

The beautiful Christmas Day Collect is by Cranmer, although he clearly is indebted to the medieval Collect for the Sunday after Christmas. It is a great improvement on any of the regular medieval Collects set for the Day current at the time of the Reformation, for by then there were three for the Day and one for the Vigil. In the 1549 book two Propers were set for Christmas, one for the Day and one for the Vigil, which simplification was a direct return to the custom in the ancient Church. In 1662, however, the Vigil was dropped from the B.C.P., but in the 1928 revision the Vigil with its Proper was returned, as well as a Proper for the second Sunday after Christmas being introduced. The Collect for Christmas Eve is the old Roman Collect for that day and the Collect set for the vigil in 1549, and is well worthy of a place again in our Prayer Book. The Collect for Christmas II is from the ancient Leonine Sacramentary and is equally worthy of a place in our Prayer Book.

The keeping of Christmas Day on 25th December, with its special season of twelve days, came surprisingly late into the liturgical calendar of the universal Church. In the Church in the East the birth of Jesus was celebrated on 6th January, the feast of the Epiphany, until the middle of the sixth century. Only then did the Church there come into line with the practice of the Church in the West by keeping Christ's birthday on 25th December, and the days between it and the Epiphany as a special Christmas season. However, in the Armenian Church, which by that time lay outside the Roman Empire, the birth of Jesus is still celebrated on 6th January, and still today in the Orthodox Churches the Epiphany, as the older festival, has that same kind of popular appeal that we in the West associate with Christmas.

The main substance of the Christmas Collect is the prayer that we may be born again and that we may be made as little children. ('Regenerate' means born again.) Christmas certainly is a day for children. How often this is said, and what a lot of money changes hands in consequence! It is the day of presents and Santa Claus. St. Nicholas, who is the innocent originator of the reindeer-driving, present-laden figure in red, singled out the children of his home town for his visitation, so the legend goes. Very little, however, is known for certain about this most popular of Saints, who is the patron Saint of sailors and of Russia, as well as of children. In the nineteenth century he became Santa Claus, a pseudonym we must lay at the door of the Americans.

The commercial world may seem to have hijacked our great Christian festival, turning Christmas into Xmas, and substituting the bearded old Santa Claus for the Babe of Bethlehem as the hero of the hour. But let it be stressed that, for Christians especially, Christmas is indeed the day for receiving gifts. Nowhere, perhaps, is the true spirit of Christmas better felt than by little children looking forward eagerly to what they will receive. For Christmas is the day of 'God's inexpressible gift'.[1] It is a day to receive, more than a day to give. 'Truly I say to you, whoever does not receive the kingdom of God like a child shall not enter into it.'[2] The kingdom

1   2 Cor 9:15   2   Mk 10:15

of God is a gift, and no one can earn or purchase it. That is the reason why our Lord said that the poor and destitute are likely to find it easier to enter the kingdom of God than the rich and important.[3] The real spirit of Christmas is excitement about God's gift of his Son, and our proper activity is to hurry, as the shepherds did to the stable, or as children do to their stockings, 'to see this thing that has happened, which the Lord has made known to us.'[4]

Before we as Christians can give anything of distinctive value to others, we must ourselves 'receive Christ'. What does this often-used phrase mean? What a mysterious thing it is, this necessary spiritual act of receiving Christ as the Lord of our lives! Christ himself likened it to becoming as little children and being born again. No wonder Nicodemus was perplexed. 'How can a man be born again when he is old?' said Nicodemus. 'Can he enter a second time into his mother's womb, and be born?'[5] Christ replied that this new birth must be the work of the Holy Spirit, and in this Collect we pray that we 'may be renewed by thy Holy Spirit'. Unless he does it, it cannot be done, for this new birth is supernatural.

This truth points us to the sacrament of Baptism. 'Truly, truly, I say to you unless one is born of water and the Spirit, he cannot enter the kingdom of God.'[6] This Collect reminds us also of our Baptism when it speaks of us 'being regenerate'. There we pray that through 'holy Baptism' we may receive remission of our sins by spiritual regeneration, and so our baptism is our spiritual birthday. Christmas Day is, therefore, an excellent day for us to renew those baptismal promises, which were most likely made for us when we were babies, who now as adults worship the Babe of Bethlehem.

The Collect also refers to the Pauline doctrine of adoption, which, one must say, bristles with difficulties. By nature, he teaches, we are not any longer

3   Mk 10:23   4   Lk 2:15   5   Jn 3:4   6   Jn 3:5

children of God, but rather children of wrath, for our divine sonship has been so marred by sin as to disqualify us from claiming that title for ourselves.[7] Unless we are 'saved', therefore, we are 'lost'. The logic of this teaching took St. Paul into theological waters which even he perceived were taking him out of his depth, as we can read in Romans Chapters 9-11. However, this doctrine has been one that has stirred the hearts and minds of the greatest theologians, notably St. Augustine in the fifth century and Calvin in the sixteenth. It was held to be of particular importance at the time of the Reformation when this Collect was composed.

It is the positive side of this doctrine that should be stressed; that is, that through Christ we are 'saved' and do most certainly become the children of God. In this spiritual experience we find our true selves. We become what God meant us to be, but otherwise are not. It is likely to surprise and even shock us today to read how this doctrine in the thinking of St. Paul is related to the grim custom of slavery, that was so firmly part of the world in which he lived. His point, however, was that through slavery a human-being could become so changed in status as no longer to be treated as fully human. He could become utterly lost. This is what sin had achieved for us all in St. Paul's thinking, making us slaves rather than sons. Becoming a child of God 'by adoption and grace', however, was like being emancipated from slavery, and becoming gloriously free to be what God wants us to be. Sonship and freedom are, therefore, closely related in St. Paul's thinking. 'So with us', he says, 'when we were children we were slaves to the elemental spirits of the universe. But when the time was fully come, God sent forth his Son, born of a woman, born under the law, to redeem those who were under the law, so that we might receive adoption as sons. And because you are sons, God has sent the Spirit of his Son into your hearts, crying "Abba, Father". So you are no longer a slave but a son, and if a son then an heir.'[8] It is this teaching that lies behind this phrase in our Collect, and that it may be our experience is the heart of its petition.

7   Rom 3:9, Eph 2:3   8   Gal 4:3-7

This important theme is also particularly that of the Leonine Collect that is set for the second Sunday after Christmas in the 1928 version of the B.C.P. Jesus comes to restore to us what was lost by us, but here the wording is taken from 2 Peter.[9] The truths of our creation and our redemption by God are linked in this prayer, and declared to be 'wonderful'. We cannot just be Christmas Christians, for the Gospel is not fully present in the story of Christmas, however much it is foreshadowed there. The wonder of Christmas demands that we go on to appreciate the subsequent wonders of Good Friday, Easter, Ascension and Whitsun, to which it points us. This ancient Collect, therefore, is the perfect prayer with which to end the Christmas season, for it encourages us to progress expectantly along the liturgical road lying ahead, which will enable us to appreciate, one by one, those other wonders of our faith, that it declares are 'yet more wonderful'.

The prayer of the Christmas Collect, we should notice, is not only that we may experience 'being regenerate and made God's children by adoption and grace', but also that this experience may be renewed in us 'daily'. The word daily reminds us of the Lord's Prayer and of our Lord's injunction to take up our cross daily and follow him. 'New every morning is the love, our wakening and uprising prove.'[10] His love is new each day. Therefore, his grace is given daily, which is just as well for our problems too are renewed daily. 'Mine enemies are daily in hand to swallow me up', said the Psalmist.[11] We know what he means! Consequently how necessary it is that we train ourselves to pray first thing in the morning and before we face the demands of each new day. So many of us leave waking up to the last possible moment. How valuable an extra half-an-hour would be, or even an extra five minutes! It would give us time to renew our touch with God, that we 'may daily be renewed by his Holy Spirit'. How much we need to enjoy this strengthening experience. It is a sure sign that we are in

9   2 Pet 1:4   10 J. Keble in his 'Christian Year', now a morning hymn
11 Ps 52:2, 56:2

earnest about doing God's will in life, if we find time to pray in the morning. If we really know ourselves to be God's children, we will find it quite natural to turn to him, as if by a natural spiritual pull, the moment we wake. 'My voice shalt thou hear betimes, O Lord; early in the morning will I direct my prayer unto thee and look up.'[12]

Christmas, we have stressed, is a children's festival. So it is a festival for us all, for we are all God's 'children by adoption and grace'. The Son of God came among us at the first Christmas to bring us all into his own family. The family, therefore, that we see gathered in that dim stable in Bethlehem spreads out on all sides throughout all time, incorporating all that will be included in its circle. And let us be sure to notice that it includes not only humans but animals too, for it was among animals that Christ was born, and his first bed was a manger. In Romans this wider, or perhaps the proper word is widest, aspect of Christian hope, that redemption includes all creation, is expressed in words which echo the idea contained in St. Paul's doctrine of adoption. The truth is that it is not just mankind that is enslaved by sin; all creation has been affected by the power of evil. Man being made free is to be the beginning of an universal emancipation from the malign power that separates all things from God. What a mystery this is, but what an exciting one! 'The creation waits with eager longing for the revealing of the sons of God; for the creation was subjected to futility, not of its own will, but by the will of him who subjected it in hope; because the creation itself will be set free from its bondage to decay and obtain the glorious liberty of the children of God.'[13] This vision of cosmic redemption through Christ is one that St. Paul fills out in his Epistles to the Ephesians and Colossians and that he expresses precisely in 2 Cor 5 : 19, where he declares, 'God was in Christ reconciling the world (the Greek is 'kosmos') to himself'. It is also one which is delightfully and powerfully depicted for us in the traditional Christmas crib. There rich and poor, represented by

12 Ps 5:3   13 Rom 8:19-21

wise men and shepherds, kneel alongside sheep and ox and ass, all recognising in the infant in the manger their great redeemer. Phrases from the Benedicite come to mind, such as, 'O all ye beasts and cattle, bless ye the Lord; praise him and magnify him for ever.' In that great hymn of praise the heavenly host, all flora and fauna, and the inhabitants of heaven itself unite with 'the children of men' in praising and magnifying God. It is surely appropriate that we owe the Christmas Crib to the devotional genius of St. Francis.

Then there is one further point. The Christmas Collect clearly presumes the traditional biblical doctrine of the Virgin Birth. Mary is described as 'a pure virgin'. Although the adjective is particularly attractive to our ears as we think of Mary, the emphasis is on the noun. This is because what is being stressed is not something about Mary, but something about Jesus. He was not the natural son of Joseph. His birth was wholly miraculous and unique, 'a great and mighty wonder.'[14] The conception of Jesus in the womb of Mary was a happening 'not of the will of the flesh, nor of the will of man, but of God.'[15] It was the work of the Holy Spirit,[16] and so is called the Incarnation. This means the 'taking flesh' by God. (The Latin 'in carne' means 'in human flesh'). St. John says, 'the Word became flesh'; the Nicene Creed says that he who is 'of one substance with the Father...was incarnate by the Holy Ghost of the Virgin Mary, and was made man.' It is this doctrine that is presupposed and confirmed in this Collect.

We have mentioned the shepherds as being models of Christians, as they hurried in wonder and excitement to see this amazing event told them by the angel, and to worship the Babe that they found 'lying in a manger'.[17] Let us also consider Joseph, and recognise in him a contrasting model of a Christian. Let us see him standing there, watching, also with wonder and excitement all that is taking place in that stable in Bethlehem, filled with

---

14 St. Germanus, Christmas Hymn   15 Jn 1:13   16 Lk 1:35
17 Lk 2:12

adoration and thanksgiving and joy, since he was the first after his wife to know the full secret of the true Father of this child. We too can share his feelings, so long as we share his faith.

What a blessed time Christmas is, with its own mysterious brand of happiness! How delightfully and truthfully the Collect for Christmas Eve puts it! 'O God, who makest us glad with the yearly remembrance of the birth of thy only Son, Jesus Christ'. And surely such a melodious sentence reminds us of that special joy of Christmas, the singing of Christmas Carols. The Christmas Carol Service is now as firmly part of our Christmas celebrations as the Midnight Mass and the Nativity Play, if one can link the sublime with the hilarious (no, not the ridiculous in this case). The purpose of all our Christmas devotion is also so well expressed in this ancient Collect, when we pray that 'we may joyfully receive him for our redeemer'. The introduction to the famous Carol Service in King's College, Cambridge, that is now so widely adopted in our Parish Churches, emphasises this special spirit of glad remembrance and joyful receiving by encouraging us 'in heart and mind to go even unto Bethlehem and see again this thing which has come to pass with the babe lying in a manger', and in so doing to make our lives once more 'glad with (this) yearly remembrance'.

EPIPHANY

O God, who by the leading of a star didst manifest thy only-begotten Son to the Gentiles: Mercifully grant, that we, which know thee now by faith, may after this life have the fruition of thy glorious Godhead; through Jesus Christ our Lord. Amen.

The Collect is Gregorian. In translation, however, the second element in the petition, which had been a simply expressed hope for the beatific vision, has been heavily elaborated. (See commentary)

The Epiphany in our Prayer Book is called 'the Manifestation of Christ to the Gentiles'. This follows the general attitude of western Christianity towards this Feast, where it was given a missionary slant. Moreover in the West it was neither given an octave nor considered a major festival. In the East the attitude towards it has always been different. There the Feast is called The Theophany, or the Manifestation of Christ as God, and the Gospel tells of the Baptism of Christ, not the visit of the Magi. In the East the Epiphany for centuries took the place of Christmas, as has been mentioned in the commentary on the Collect for Christmas, and still today is the more popular festival.

In the 1662 Book the Collect is said only until the Sunday, but in the 1928 revision the Epiphany was given an octave, and so this Collect is now also said after the Collect for Epiphany I on that Sunday.

The Collect stresses that it was God who led the wise men to Christ. The biblical story emphasises the same truth. The wise men were not just curious astrologers, but godly men coming to worship, and their hopes and desires were marvellously fulfilled. 'Where is he who has been born King of the Jews. For we have seen his star in the East, and have come to worship him', they said. 'And lo, the star which they had seen in the East went before them, till it came to rest over where the young child was. When they saw the star they rejoiced exceedingly with great joy; and going into the house they saw the child with Mary his mother, and they fell down and worshipped him.'[1] The keynotes of this famous story are eagerness in the search and joy in the finding, with a spirit of reverence pervading all. This, too, is the spirit of our Collect. Faith is like the star, a means whereby we may eagerly search and joyfully find our Lord, and finally, through him, experience 'the fruition of (God's) glorious Godhead'. It implies that the life of man is a thrilling journey with a glorious objective in mind. Heaven is our goal, as Bishop Wand has put it with splendid simplicity, and our guiding star is faith.

Faith in the New Testament rests upon the virtue of steadfastness or loyalty in the Old Testament. To believe in the Old Testament had the meaning of to hold on to firmly, and the object of this steadfast loyalty, this holding on to firmly, was God and his Law. This trusting in, obeying, holding firmly to God and his Law was the very heart of Old Testament spirituality. There are innumerable passages that illustrate this, but of all perhaps Psalm 119 is the most compelling and explicit. 'Blessed are they that keep his testimonies, and seek him with their whole heart.'[2] Faith in the Old Testament is summed up in those words, 'with my whole heart', that are repeated like a refrain throughout that tremendous Psalm. 'I call with my whole heart: hear me, O Lord, I will keep thy statutes'.[3] This is Old Testament faith.

In the New Testament this faith is switched from God and his Law to God's Son and his Spirit. We want to recognise the drama involved in this. The whole-hearted trust in God, which expressed itself in whole-hearted obedience to the Law in all its details, is shown in the New Testament to have been disastrous. The spiritual life of Saul, the Pharisee, was heroic,

1 Matt 2:2, 9-11   2 Ps 119:2   3 Ps 119:145

yet tragic. St. Paul in Romans and Galatians stresses both the heroism and the tragedy. He realised to his horror that he had come to be, through his devotion to the Law, the enemy of God, the rejecter of the Messiah and the persecutor of his disciples. Saul had to be changed to Paul. He had to become a new person. The faith of the Jew in the Law had to change into the faith of the Christian in the living Christ and his indwelling Spirit. This change was nothing less than to experience spiritually a second birth.

Quite what a tremendous problem this was for the Jews of those days is shown clearly in the personal confessions, as well as the theological arguments, of St. Paul's Epistles, particularly Romans 1-11. But perhaps the most succinct and most personal statement of the problem is in Galatians. 'For I through the Law died to the Law, that I might live to God. I have been crucified with Christ: it is no longer I who live, but Christ who lives in me; and the life I now live in the flesh I live by faith in the Son of God, who loved me and gave himself for me.'[4] 'To live by faith in the Son of God' was for St. Paul to seek Jesus with his whole heart as passionately, relentlessly, obediently as he had sought to keep God's Law when he was a Pharisee. The long, arduous journey over fierce and arid deserts undertaken by night marches by the godly searchers from the East is a picture of the journey that St. Paul had to make to find his Saviour. And in its way it is a picture of the pilgrimage required of us all.

The guiding star can certainly be likened to our faith, but because the faith of Christians is in 'the Son of God, who loved (us) and gave himself for (us)', the star can also be likened to Christ himself. It is after all he whom we follow, rather than our faith in him. The light of faith is a light indeed, but it falls short of 'the light of the world', 'the light that lightens every man'.[5] Our faith is a variable light. It fades and grows, but Christ remains constant. So the stars are always there, even though by day they are

4   Gal 2:19-20   5   Jn 8:12, 1:9

invisible. It is our limited vision, made so by the circumstances of this life, that causes them to be hid from our eyes. So we read that 'the star went before them', but we must presume that they lost sight of it when daylight came. Equally, Christ goes before us and in faith we follow him. But we cannot say that we see him clearly always. Often we must wait with patience for the vision of him to become sharp and obvious again. Often we peer after him 'as through a glass darkly'.[6] It is the activity of hope, which is so close to faith, even, as it were, the other side of the same coin to faith, that enables us to do this with eager expectation, sure in our hearts that we will find Christ, if we continue in faith. 'Now hope that is seen is not hope. For who hopes for what he sees? But if we hope for what we do not see, we wait for it with patience.'[7] There is always an element of real heroism in faith. In Hebrews faith is the virtue of the heroes of the Old Testament. It is spiritual vision, so that we, like Moses, 'can endure seeing him who is invisible'.[8] Faith in the New Testament is linked with the virtues of hope, patience and endurance. The journey of faith may be a glorious one, but it is not an easy one.

The Epiphany Collect, no less than the Epiphany Gospel, stresses the arduous nature of the spiritual life based on faith. Certainly there is a sense of pathos in the acknowledgement, 'who know thee now by faith', just as there is in the uncertainties of the wise men as they looked for Jesus. But they both stress the ultimate joyful fulfilment that awaits those who will live by faith. We have to follow faithfully, but Christ is as concerned as we are that we should not lose him as we do so. As St. Paul says, Christ draws us after him, 'from faith to faith'.[9] It is the will of God, no less than our prayer, that we should 'have the fruition of his glorious Godhead'. As already mentioned this ultimate Christian hope is far more simply expressed in the original Gregorian Collect, in which the second element of our petition, rendered here as having 'the fruition of thy glorious Godhead',

6   1 Cor 13: 12 A.V.   7   Rom 8:24-25   8   Heb 11:27
9   Rom 1:17 A.V.

was that we may 'gaze upon thy majesty by sight'. The 'by sight' was clearly being contrasted with the 'by faith' earlier in the petition, and we were being reminded of St. Paul's dictum that here 'we walk by faith, not by sight'.[10] In heaven, however, the veil will be lifted, and the eyes of our spirits will be able to see God in a way that they cannot see him now. This is a major theme of the Book of Revelation in which we hear of this ultimate fulfilment in words that may owe something to the story of the wise men. To the Christian in Thyatira who continues faithful the Spirit says, 'I will give him the Morning Star'.[11] Yes, he whom we follow faithfully will be ours for ever. Faith will give way to sight and knowledge. Here both are limited. 'We see through a glass darkly, but then face to face.' At the last our knowledge of God through Christ will be so intimate and complete that it may be for us, as it was for Moses, to whom 'the Lord spoke face to face, as a man speaks to his friend.'[12]

'The fruition of thy glorious Godhead' is a phrase that suggests in a general way something becoming ripe, full grown and ready to be picked. What we may believe is that, while we grow spiritually within the family of the Church, led on by Christ along the path of faith, what is growing within us will ripen, become full grown, and in the end be gathered in as God meant it to be. Our soul may be likened to fruit of which God is the grower. Such an analogy was often used by Jesus. Is it not the message of his many harvest parables? In John 15, too, we have the analogy of Jesus being the vine and ourselves the branches and grapes, with the Father being the husbandman. Jesus is surely teaching us in these parables that it is God's intention to bring our lives to a 'fruition', in accordance with his loving purpose for us. And this, when it takes place, will be, as our Collect stresses, something 'glorious'. In his analogy of the vine, the branches and the grapes, Jesus ends with the declaration, 'these things I have spoken to you, that my joy may be in you and that your joy may be full'.[13] And when the wise men came to their journey's end, we are told that 'they rejoiced with exceeding great joy'.[14]

10 2 Cor 5 : 7   11 Rev 2:28   12 Ex 33:11   13 Jn 15:11   14 Mt 2:10

EPIPHANY I

O Lord, we beseech thee mercifully to receive the prayers of thy people which call upon thee; and grant that they may both perceive and know what things they ought to do, and also may have grace and power faithfully to fulfil the same; through Jesus Christ our Lord. Amen.

The B.C.P. does not give the Epiphany an octave, although the Church at the time of the Reformation did. The history that lies behind this change is interesting and indicative of the way in which the Reformers in compiling our Prayer Book sometimes sought to go behind the customs of their day to those of earlier times.

As mentioned last week, there had been originally a comparatively unenthusiastic attitude towards the Epiphany in the West, which was in marked contrast to the importance given to it in the East. However, in later medieval times the Epiphany also gained its octave in the West. In most liturgies this had the effect of moving the Epiphany Propers forward one week, with the Proper for the Epiphany serving for this Sunday. The Reformers, however, decided to follow the usage of the earlier Sacramentaries; they turned back the clock, as it were, replaced the Epiphany Collects to their original Sundays and took away the Epiphany octave.

In the 1928 revision of the Prayer Book, however, the Epiphany was once more given back its octave, and a Proper Preface was provided. However, no attempt was made to disrupt this Sunday, whose Proper remains, with the Epiphany Collect said as an additional Collect.

This is the Gregorian Collect. In translation some changes and additions were made, one being of particular importance. (See commentary)

This is a very practical prayer. It has a busy ring about it. It is a prayer that we may be up and doing, and that we should get our priorities right. It is the sort of prayer, therefore, that is sometimes read before committee meetings, and it is one that we may well use when we have special decisions to make in our own lives.

It is essential to our understanding of God, and for our faith in him, that his wisdom is such that he knows in every conceivable circumstance in life what ought to be done. Such wisdom is part of his omniscience. 'God knows' is still a common saying, but sadly it is usually said with a hopeless shrug of the shoulders. We, however, should be able to say it with faith and hope. The Psalmist speaks of this mystery with awe, but also with confidence. For him it is a cause for courage and thanksgiving. 'O Lord, thou hast searched me out and known me. Thou knowest my downsitting and my uprising; thou understandest my thoughts long before.' Therefore he is always able to hope for the best, even when things go badly, even when all seems lost. 'Yea, the darkness is no darkness with thee, but the night is as clear as the day: the darkness and light to thee are both alike.'[1] Because this is true of God, we are consequently able 'to go forth in the name of the Lord God',[2] confident that at all times the loving purpose of God is an ingredient in all that happens to us, and that his foreknowledge of events, as they happen, always precedes them.

However, it is not only essential for us to know that God understands, but also that he cares. But what he primarily cares about is our righteousness, not our comfort! And our righteousness consists in our doing his righteous will. This is the consistent teaching of the Bible, and this is the truth to which our Lord witnessed above all others. To do the Father's will was the motivation of all that he did, even from his youth to his death. 'Wist ye not that I must be about my Father's business', says the boy Jesus to his anxious parents, according to the reading favoured by the Authorised Version.[3] 'Thy will be done' is the heart of his special prayer. When his

1 Ps 139:1-11   2 Ps 71:14   3 Lk 2:49 A.V.

disciples returned from Sychar in Samaria with food they found Jesus, whom they had left hungry and exhausted, elated and refreshed. They asked him if he had somehow received food already. He answered them, 'I have food to eat of which you do not know. My food is to do the will of him who sent me, and to accomplish his work.'[4]

But before we can do God's will, we need to know what it is. And this will be no easy matter, as the Gospels emphasise. Even for Jesus 'the perceiving and knowing of what he ought to do' was neither easy nor straightforward. This is made particularly clear in the stories we have of Jesus at prayer. We see him at prayer in the wilderness, on several occasions throughout the night, on the mountain of Transfiguration, and in the garden of Gethsemane, and on all these occasions we see him seeking 'to perceive and know what things he ought to do'. He too, as we are, was tempted to deviate from the Father's will. And here it may be helpful to stress that, although it is not expressly mentioned in the Collect, to perceive and know what we ought not to do is often just as vital as to know what we should do. In the wilderness Jesus needed to discard false options, as he prepared himself to begin his ministry. It is quite wrong for us to imagine these were not real and painful temptations for him to do that which was mistaken and sinful. Like him we must seek to understand the Father's will before we act, and this may take time, and perhaps more time than we would wish. Jesus, however, was forty days in the wilderness. Such a waiting upon God shows a proper patience, and this Collect guides us towards this virtue.

As we take this prayer on our lips, however, it is quite easy not to appreciate the seriousness of this matter. Do we really want to perceive and know God's will? It may, after all, be hard and dangerous. Was it not so for Jesus? And did he not warn us it would be so for us also?[5] It is certain to be testing to the best in us and disagreeable to the worst in us. Thomas Gray's words

4   Jn 4: 32-34   5   Matt 10:24-25

come to mind, 'Where ignorance is bliss, 'tis folly to be wise'. Yet in the Bible the warning that men may only come to realise what was God's will for them after the time has passed when it is possible for them to do it is often repeated. This is the lament of the prophets: 'The ox knows its owner and the ass its master's crib, but Israel does not know, my people does not understand.'[6] And soon for Israel and for Judah it was too late. It was the same for the Messiah as for the prophets. Jesus wept over Jerusalem, just as Isaiah and Jeremiah had done before him. 'When he drew near and saw the city he wept over it, saying, "Would that even today you knew the things that make for peace! But they are hid from your eyes".'[7] Then he prophesied the terrible things that would happen soon to both the city and its inhabitants.

So this is an urgent, as well as an important matter, about which we are being guided to pray. Perhaps it is the urgency and importance of this matter that made the framers of this Collect start in such a seemingly strange way. Why otherwise should we first beseech God to receive our prayers? Surely we can take that much for granted before we pray. The only justification for such an opening would seem to be to lay emphasis on the vital urgency and importance of this prayer. How dreadful to hear the words 'too late' addressed to us![8]

The second part of our petition is that we may have the ability to do God's will, having first understood what it is. In the original Latin Collect the words 'grace and' are not there. They were added by Cranmer. How right that they were included. We can never do the will of God without the grace of God. The New Testament stresses this truth. Although in the perception and the doing of God's will we need certainly to use our natural faculties, without the addition of God's grace, we can, in our Lord's words, 'do nothing'.[9] Yet it has to be admitted that a paradoxical situation faces us

6   Is 1:3   7   Lk 19:41-42   8   Matt 25:10-13   9   Jn 15:5

here. Although we cannot do all our duty in our own strength, nevertheless the exertion of all our strength will be required of us to do it, even while we pray for grace to help us. It has been said that 'God helps those that help themselves', and 'act as though all depends on you; pray as though all depends on God'. If we have perceived aright, we will always be given strength to perform aright, but both the perceiving and the performing are a combination of God's grace working through his natural gifts to us, inspiring and activating them. Gary Player, the famous golfer, has said, 'The more I practise, the luckier I get!' The combination of our striving and God's grace is what brings results, and can give us that sort of experience! We can find that we have achieved the apparently impossible, or at least far more than we imagined possible. This is the way of miracles, and the reason why they happen in the lives of some and not in all. But we all could know this power. Jesus said 'If you have faith as a grain of mustard seed' extraordinary things would happen.[10] The sort of spiritual life that achieves wonderful things is not beyond any of us.

To the doing of God's will we will find many obstacles. Jesus not only shared our difficulties in perceiving and knowing the Father's will; he also shared our difficulties in doing it. Many tried to stop him, including his own family and friends. Three times in St. Mark's Gospel Jesus spelled out to his disciples what was God's will for him, and each time they sought to deflect him from doing it. 'And he began to teach them that the Son of man must suffer many things and be rejected....and be killed, and after three days rise again. And he said this plainly. And Peter took him and began to rebuke him. Turning and seeing his disciples he rebuked Peter and said, "Get behind me Satan! For you are not on the side of God but of man." ' [11] Even his mother was someone that might have lead him astray,[12] and his brothers also were often a trouble to him.[13] We may expect the same experience.

10 Matt 17:20   11 Mk 8:31-33   12 Mk 3:31-35   13 Jn 7:1-5

There was also the natural weakness of his human nature to be overcome, for he shared all our natural weakness, though not our sinfulness. In the garden of Gethsemane particularly we hear of the greatness of his struggle. When he returned from prayer, seeking the companionship of his closest disciples, he found them asleep. He said, 'The spirit is indeed willing, but the flesh is weak'.[13] Were these words more a comment on his own bitter struggle to fulfil the Father's will than on the weakness of the Apostles to assist him? They certainly sound more appropriate if taken in that way. In spite of temptations and amid extreme suffering, in the power of the Holy Spirit that filled him, Jesus in no way failed 'faithfully to fulfil' the Father's will. As he had said earlier, his meat and drink was 'to do God's will and to accomplish his work'.[14] In the end upon the Cross he fulfilled it perfectly. According to the R.S.V. his last words in St. John's Gospel were, 'It is finished'.[15] In the Greek the tense gives a sense of completeness to what has been finished, so 'it is accomplished', as in the N.E.B., is surely the better translation. We may be certain that, as it was for him, a cross awaits us as we seek to do the Father's will, but through prayer grace will be given to us too to take it up. Even so, as it was with him, straightforward effort and natural courage will also be required of us. We must not grow weary in well-doing; the real test of faithfulness is doggedly to carry on even in the face of difficulty. [16] We shall not be left to struggle alone. 'The Lord be with you', is what we truthfully and repeatedly declare in the course of our Prayer Book services. 'He who calls you is faithful, and he will do it' [17], for he is as concerned as we are that we 'faithfully fulfil' 'the things we ought to do'.

---

13 Mk 14:38   14 Jn 4:34   15 Jn 19:30   16 Mk 10:22   17 I Thess 5:24

EPIPHANY II

Almighty and everlasting God, who dost govern all things in heaven and earth; mercifully hear the supplications of thy people, and grant us thy peace all the days of our life; through Jesus Christ our Lord. Amen.

This Collect is Gregorian. It has been given a more personal ending in translation, the original merely praying for 'thy peace for our times'.

The opening clause is one that slips off the tongue easily, but can we really believe it? Does God indeed govern all things in heaven and earth? The Bible in many places speaks of the sovereign power of God. Yet perhaps it is noteworthy that such thoughts are usually expressed in the context of prayer and praise. None is more explicit than King David's prayer of thanksgiving: 'Blessed art thou, O Lord, the God of Israel our father, for ever and ever. Thine, O Lord, is the greatness, and the power, and the glory, and the victory, and the majesty; for all that is in the heavens and the earth is thine; thine is the kingdom, O Lord, and thou art exalted as head above all. Both riches and honour come of thee, and thou rulest over all. In thy hand are power and might; and in thy hand it is to make great and to give strength to all. And now we thank thee, our God, and praise thy glorious name.'[1] It is one of the high points of the Old Testament, and a passage, one feels sure, that fed the devotional life of Jesus himself. In our hearts we surely say "Amen", but in our minds we are still likely to ask, "Is it true?" Or if that should appear to be too faithless a query, we are almost certain to ask ourselves the question, "How are we to understand the sovereignty of God in the face of events that make this doctrine so profoundly difficult to believe?"

1   1 Chron 29:10-13

It would appear that such difficulties have always been apparent to religious men. The Bible, which asserts this doctrine, also highlights its difficulties. If God is sovereign, why do the innocent and the righteous so often suffer at the hands of the guilty and the wicked? The Psalmist speaks for us all when he complains, 'Why standest thou so far off, O Lord, and hidest thy face in the needful time of trouble?' It cannot be that God is frankly ignorant of what happens upon earth. 'Surely thou hast seen it, for thou beholdest ungodliness and wrong?' And the indignation of the Psalmist is not merely born out of concern for human need; after all we might, when all is weighed up, deserve even more than we receive; 'For who can tell how oft he offendeth?'[2] What above all the Psalmist cannot bear is the mockery of the unbeliever and the justification that such events and circumstances appear to give for his unbelief. 'Wherefore should the wicked blaspheme...and say in his heart, "Tush, thou God carest not for it."'[3]

The answer to this problem lies at the very heart of the Gospel and can only be found there. It was the central theme of our Lord's teaching, where the sovereignty of God is usually termed the kingdom of God. Jesus came above all else to establish this sovereignty or kingdom. But has it not always been established? Yes, it has; but herein lies the mystery, and for us the problem; it is not a sovereignty or kingdom such as the world readily understands. Its power is the power of love. Therein lies the nub of the matter, and the cause of all our perplexity. The sovereignty or kingdom of God is not something that God simply sets up, although he does; it must also be received for its reality to be experienced. Christ came both to show forth its eternal existence, and to call us into sharing that sovereignty or kingdom. The sovereignty or kingdom of God's love is an eternal reality, because it has existed for ever within the life of the eternal Trinity, within whom for ever love reigns. Through his incarnation Christ brought this eternal sovereignty of perfect love, which has always existed and governed

2   Ps 19:12   3   Ps 10:10-15

in heaven, down to earth. His life here made that kingdom come on earth as it is in heaven. Now he lives on in his new earthly body, the Church. Through that body God's kingdom will continue to come on earth as it is in heaven, and that this will be finally and fully accomplished is central to the Church's great prayer, the Lord's Prayer. Meanwhile through the Church he bids us enter that kingdom, and share in and extend that sovereignty.

This rule, this sovereignty, this kingdom of God is mysterious and not 'of this world', but nonetheless we may still comprehend the way it 'governs' from personal experience. In our lives we can see how nothing is weaker than love, and yet at the same time nothing is stronger. It is possible for all to ignore or spurn love, but it is impossible for any to destroy it. As St. Paul pointed out, 'it bears all things....endures all things....it never ends.'[4] It must have the last word as it had the first, for it is because of love that we 'live and move and have our being'.[5] It is in this sense that we must see it as the force that is sovereign and that 'governs all things in heaven and earth'.

The reality and the mystery of God's sovereignty is illustrated perfectly in the life, death, resurrection and ascension of Jesus. In him God's kingdom came, and since he ever lives it remains, on earth as it is in heaven. Love ruled in his life, and it ruled as he died. There the weakness of love is revealed in all its starkness. 'He saved others, himself he cannot save.'[6] Coming to redeem all, even those who hated, rejected and killed him, he is unable to rescue himself. Christ in his passion reveals on the one hand God's weakness, because he is love. However, on the other he revealed there God's strength, again because he is love; for nothing could destroy it, and in his Resurrection the power of love is confirmed. It must reign. It is sovereign. St. Paul in a purple passage, as he considers this mystery of God's sovereignty revealed in Christ, rejoices in 'the immeasurable great-

4   1 Cor 13:7-8   5   Acts 17:28   6   Mk 15:31

ness of his power' and the 'might which he accomplished in Christ when he raised him from the dead and made him sit at his right hand', and how that God now 'has put all things under his feet'.[7] Nevertheless, the writer of Hebrews makes the relevant comment that this total sovereignty of God's love awaits its consummation in time as well as in eternity. Certainly God has 'left nothing outside his control, (but) as it is, we do not yet see everything in subjection to him'.[8] So the kingdom of God has come, is coming and will come. Because it is a kingdom ruled by love, it must wait to be received by willing subjects. It has not yet been fully received. As we receive it, therefore, we assist its coming, and widen its domain.

This, then, is the cause of all our perplexity. But this is a mystery to be welcomed. How awful it would be if the sovereign power of all was not love! What good news it is that love, and not mere law, governs all things in heaven and earth! Consequently there is always room for hope. We may now endure believing that 'mercy will triumph over judgement'.[9] The Crucifixion shows that there are no lengths to which divine love is not prepared to go. Jesus shows us that divine love goes far beyond even the greatest of human love, in that he was prepared to lay down his life for his enemies, and not merely for his friends, 'the righteous for the unrighteous, that he might bring us all to God'.[10] It is in this spirit of faith and hope that we are able to understand the sovereignty of God, 'who dost govern all things in heaven and earth'.

The petition in this Collect is now the personal one that we may experience 'peace all the days of our life'. But let us notice that our prayer is specifically for 'thy peace'. As in divine sovereignty there is a similar mystery about God's peace. Just as Jesus came to establish God's kingdom on earth as it is in heaven, so he came to give us God's peace here too, but neither is 'of this world'. Just as he said, 'My kingdom is not of this world,' so too he said,

---

7 Eph 1:15-23   8 Heb 2:8   9 Jas 2:13   10 1 Pet 3:18

'My peace I give to you, but not as the world gives do I give to you.'[11]

The peace of God passes all understanding.[12] It is not natural to sinners; 'there is no peace for the wicked'.[13] It is a peace that has to be experienced amid struggle and suffering. Certainly these are not to be understood as opposites to God's peace, but rather as the inevitable complements to it. In John 14 Jesus speaks much of peace, as he prepares his disciples for his Crucifixion and all the hardships that will soon overtake them. In that passage the opposite to peace would appear to be fear or anxiety or faithlessness, but not suffering. He links peace there with love and joy, as St. Paul does in his famous passage in Galations 5. And in both passages peace is linked with the coming of the Holy Spirit and portrayed as his gift. In John 16 peace and joy are again linked, and this time both are described as permanent divine gifts, such as cannot be taken away from us by any man or by the world. These promises give the justification for our prayer that God will grant us his peace 'all the days of our life', which would otherwise sound at the very least unreasonable.

Above all, peace in our Lord's teaching is linked with the Resurrection. We can know the peace of God now, because we can enter into the meaning of and have an experience of the Resurrection now. This peace of God amid struggle and suffering is a foretaste of victory in heaven after our struggles are over and our sufferings are no more. This peace is a victorious peace, that enables us to rise above struggle and suffering in such a way as to make them creative of good. There is a false peace, a peace brought about by defeat, a resting in the peace of death. The peace of God, however, is a peace full of life, in which we may also rest, even if that rest is only the quiet centre of fierce storms. None of us can escape struggle and suffering 'all the days of our life' and be a disciple of Jesus Christ, but through Jesus Christ, as we pray here, we may all experience the peace of God always. The Crucifixion and the Resurrection are both to be in our lives constant spiritual experiences, for amid the struggle and suffering that goes on in

11 Jn 18:36, 14:27   12 Phil 4:7   13 Is 57:21

one way or another all the time, there is to be God's peace that makes it all bearable and also creative of good, both to ourselves and to others. It is a both-and reality, and therein lies the mystery, and, according to St. Peter, the wonder.[14] So it is that St. Paul can say to the Thessalonians, 'Now may the Lord of peace himself give you peace at all times in all ways'.[15] This peace, which may be for 'all the days of our life', and indeed for our times, is also a peace that will continue in even fuller measure when earthly days for us are over.

14 1 Pet 1:3-9   15 2 Thess 3:16

EPIPHANY III

Almighty and everlasting God, mercifully look upon our infirmities, and in all our dangers and necessities stretch forth thy right hand to help and defend us; through Jesus Christ our Lord. Amen.

This Collect is Gregorian and is very similar to that for Lent III. In translation it has been strengthened by the addition of the phrase 'in all our dangers and necessities', but perhaps weakened by the omission 'of thy majesty' after 'right hand'. Interestingly the whole phrase is kept in the Collect for Lent III.

In this Collect we are encouraged to recognise our weakness, and therefore to ask for God's help. This simple theme is often the main consideration of the Collects, and indeed it is repeated in that for next Sunday. This should hardly surprise us, for the recognition of human weakness and man's need of divine assistance is surely the stuff of all religions, including our own. Indeed, it is the height of folly, and in Christian theology the essence of sin, for us to deny either our weakness or our need for divine help. However, we are much tempted these days to do so. We are told that man has 'come of age'[1], and without doubt today much power does belong to man. So much is this the truth, at least for us who live in the developed world, that we are probably more frightened of our strength than of our weakness! Indeed this prayer would perhaps seem more realistic to many if it was that God would mercifully look upon our power to do almost anything, including destroy ourselves, and save us from that. Dangers resulting from our infirmities seem to be receding as fast as dangers from our strengths are increasing.

Moreover, because we have apparently become so much the masters of our own destiny, there is impatience in some quarters with those who plead weakness, for to plead weakness is so often to stifle action. There would

1 Honest to God, by John Robinson

seem to be biblical support for this impatience, for did not St. Paul rule that those who would not work should not eat?[2] Are we not becoming increasingly conscious that ill health is frequently related to foolish habits and wrong behaviour, and the refusal to change them? Did not Jesus say to the man who lay beside the pool waiting for someone to help him, 'Do you want to be healed?'[3] And was not St. Paul's injunction that we help each other linked with what he saw as the complementary responsibility, that we do all we can to see that we are not a burden on anyone else?[4]

However, there is a peculiar paradox about so much of 'the truth as it is in Jesus'.[5] In him to die is to live, and to be weak is to be strong. This is a lesson that St. Paul had to learn with difficulty, as he confesses in 2 Corinthians. But in the end he came to glory in his weaknesses rather than in his strengths. The reason for this was that he perceived that, whereas his weaknesses were factors that united him with Christ, his strengths were inducements to pride, and hence to behaviour that separated him from Christ. In our Collect we pray that God may 'mercifully look upon our infirmities,' and we should do the same! It was the error of the Pharisee that he looked on his strengths, and the wisdom of the tax collector that he recognised his 'infirmities'.[6] Today we may well pray for grace not to make the same mistake. But if we look upon our 'infirmities', we must do so 'in Christ,' or they will fill us only with fear and despair. To look upon them 'in him,' however, is to transform them; then they become the basis of faith and hope, and therefore of strength.

And this is what we can do, because Christ took our weaknesses upon himself and 'bore our sins in his own body on the tree'.[7] In him we may look upon our 'infirmities', both physical and spiritual, and discover in them through him a source of strength. This is surprising, even mysterious, even though experience constantly confirms its truth. This is how St. Paul speaks of this matter: 'Therefore, since we are justified by faith, we have peace with God through our Lord Jesus Christ... and we rejoice in our hope of sharing in the glory of God. More than that, we rejoice in our sufferings,

2 2 Thess 3:10   3   Jn 5:6   4   Gal 6:1-5   5   Eph 4:21
6 Lk 18:9-14   7   1 Pet 2:24

knowing that suffering produces endurance, and endurance produces character, and character produces hope, and hope does not disappoint, because God's love has been poured into our hearts through the Holy Spirit which has been given to us.'[8] As we look upon our 'infirmities' 'in Christ', the Holy Spirit leads us on from weakness to strength and from fear to confidence, not in ourselves or in our own power to cope with our 'dangers and necessities', but in God's grace and power to do so, working in and through us.

Nevertheless, in spite of our modern strengths and our increased ability to look after ourselves, 'infirmities', 'dangers and necessities' still exist to harass and distress us. This Collect lays distinct emphasis upon them - 'all our dangers and necessities'. We ask God to look mercifully upon them, because we are naturally fearful of what they may do to us. So behind this prayer lies fear.

In the Bible fear is constantly mentioned. It is after all the commonest of human experiences. No one escapes its chilly grip upon their spirits, at least from time to time, and some know it very frequently. A distinction is made, however, in the Bible between godly and ungodly fear. The one leads to an earnest seeking after God's protection, and so to faith and hope in his mercy and power. The other is merely our natural reaction to danger, leading simply to the urge to escape. Behind this Collect there is the former, leading us to faith in God, who has power to protect us 'in the needful time of trouble'. [9]

Godly fear is portrayed in the Old Testament as the crowning gift of God's Spirit[10] and a spiritual experience of the greatest value. 'The fear of the Lord is the beginning of wisdom'[11] is an often repeated saying, and to the writer of Ecclesiastes it was the only motivation for true religion. 'The end of the matter is this; then all is heard. Fear God and keep his commandments, for this is the whole duty of man.'[12] This may sound a rather gloomy

8 Rom 5:1-5   9 Pss 37:40:10:1   10 Is 11:3   11 Ps 111:10 et al
12 Eccles 12:13

summary of the spiritual life to Christian ears, but we should remember that we are specifically strengthened in this gift of godly fear at our Confirmation.

There is, moreover, much about godly fear in the New Testament, where it is often very properly translated 'awe' in the more modern versions. Several stories tell of how Jesus frequently inspired this feeling in people. In the story of the storm we see, interestingly, the two kinds of fear contrasted. The disciples, understandably, were terrified at the violence of the waves and the prospect of drowning. 'Teacher' they said, waking Jesus, 'do you not care if we perish?' He, however, 'rebuked the wind' and then rebuked them too, '"Why are you afraid? Have you no faith?" And they were filled with awe, and said to one another, "Who then is this, that even the wind and sea obey him".'[13]

It is the teaching of Jesus that godly fear should drive out other kinds of fear that are spiritually harmful, for godly fear promotes the courage we need to face ordinary fear. Equally, to be overcome by ungodly fear is to lose our needful 'fear of the Lord'. 'Do not fear those that kill the body, but cannot kill the soul', said Jesus, 'rather fear him who can destroy both body and soul.'[14] In our 'fear of what man may do unto us' we may grow to have 'no fear of God before our eyes'. And this, as the Psalmist says, is 'abominable' ![15] This Collect, however, bids us take the advice of the Psalmist in another place, 'Though I am sometimes afraid, yet put I my trust in thee.'[16]

That this is possible is central to the Gospel. Although it is true that 'the wrath of God is revealed from heaven against all ungodliness and wickedness', the Gospel proclaims the answering truth that 'the power of God is for salvation to everyone who has faith'.[17] Which brings us to the second petition in our Collect, in which we pray, 'Stretch forth thy right hand to help and defend us.' The Psalmist declares confidently 'The right hand of the Lord bringeth mighty things to pass.'[18] The right hand of a man was

13 Mk 4:35-41   14 Matt 10:28   15 Ps 36:1-2   16 Ps 56:3
17 Rom 1:16-18   18 Ps 118:16

deemed his strong hand, and so at the right hand of God was the place of divine power and authority. Christ in the Epistles is frequently described as being now at the right hand of God, enthroned in majesty and power,[19] and this phraseology is kept in the Creed. Nowhere, however, is the meaning of this phrase better described (without it being used) than in the famous hymn to Christ in Philippians. 'Therefore God has highly exalted him and bestowed upon him the name that is above every name, that at the name of Jesus every knee shall bow...and every tongue confess that Jesus Christ is Lord to the glory of God the Father.'[20]

How marvellous! How encouraging! Nevertheless, having pointed out there the glorious power and protection that those who are in Christ can rely upon, since Christ now possesses the plenitude of divine power, St. Paul immediately goes on to stress the continuing need for earnest endeavour, and to warn against over-confidence. 'Therefore' he says 'my beloved, as you have always obeyed, so now... work out your own salvation with fear and trembling.'[21] Because Christ is at the right hand of God, it does not mean there is nothing left for us to do or fear. Nevertheless we may go on in faith and hope, because through Christ 'God is at work in us, both to will and to work for his good pleasure.'[22]

In effect this 'right hand of God' is Christ himself, who is 'the man of thy right hand'.[23] Although at that mysterious but glorious place of power and authority in heaven, he is also at work in us on earth to bring mighty things to pass. And the most mighty thing that Christ can bring to pass in us is our salvation. Because of his presence at our right hand, as well as at God's, we are able to face, without ungodly fear, 'infirmities', 'dangers and necessities'. Godly fear will never leave us. Indeed, as we grow in Christ, it will only deepen, as the lives of all the Saints clearly show. Meanwhile the Psalmist sums up this Collect's theme, and the way in which we may hope it will be answered: 'Thou shalt show me the path of life; in thy presence is the fulness of joy, and at thy right hand there is pleasure for evermore.'[24]

19 Rom 8:34 et al   20 Phil 2:9-11   21 Phil 2:12   22 Phil 2:13
23 Ps 80:17   24 Ps 16:12

EPIPHANY IV

O God, who knowest us to be set in the midst of so many and great dangers, that by reason of the frailty of our nature we cannot always stand upright; Grant to us such strength and protection, as may support us in all dangers, and carry us through all temptations, through Jesus Christ our Lord. Amen.

The first half of this Collect is a translation of the Gregorian Collect for this Sunday with one small but important addition, the word 'always'. The second half, which followed the original in the translation for the 1549 Prayer Book, and prayed then specifically for 'health of body and soul', was changed considerably in 1662, giving the prayer a much more general aspect. (See commentary)

Surely this is a very important prayer, for great issues arise from it. However, the general theme is essentially the same as last week's Collect; only here we appeal to God to help us from a different spiritual premise. Last week it was from a belief in his mercy; this week it is from a realisation of his knowledge. He knows the full extent of both our need and of our weakness, and it is this knowledge that gives us the confidence to pray. The introduction to the prayer, then, reminds us of three things, God's knowledge, our dangers and our natural weakness.

This divine knowledge of all our 'many and great dangers', and also of the full extent of 'the frailty of our nature', must be just as much a cause of suffering for God, as they are for us. Just as a human parent must suffer when he sees the children he loves facing danger and temptation, so must God. And Jesus surely confirms this truth in his parable of the Prodigal Son.[1] The prodigal goes to his ruin all unconscious of the 'many and great

---

1   Lk 15:11-24

dangers' that characterise life away from his father's home, and quite unaware of the 'frailty of his nature' to cope when temptation, danger and hardship come upon him. Such foolish self confidence, of which the father is well aware, only adds greatly to the parent's anxiety and distress.

Is it not so with us? And with God, because of us? God knows our dangers and our frailties, but often we do not. We are like children who play in the road, unmindful of parental warnings and thoughtless of our own safety. So often the dangers that beset us are avoidable and our frailty is compounded by our wilfulness. So we suffer, but so does God, who, like the father in the parable, longs after us. It was out of his knowledge of our need and his compassionate longing after us, that God sent his Son that we might not perish in our 'many and great dangers' and from 'the frailty of our nature'. It was in obedience to this divine love of the Father for weak and foolish mankind, that the divine Son took the road to this earthly place of 'many and great dangers', and lived here in all 'the frailty of our nature', to provide us with all 'the strength and protection' that we may ever need. So it is in Christ, and in the contemplation of his life and death, that we shall find the answer to this prayer, and the inspiration to pray it with faith and hope.

As already stated, the first half of this Collect is a translation of the medieval Collect for this Sunday. In the English, however, there is the notable addition of the word 'always', which is not in the Latin, and which at first sight seems to change the sense considerably. The Latin says simply that we cannot stand upright, or firm, because of our weakness of nature. To say, however, 'we cannot always stand upright' suggests that our dependence on God for help is not essential to us, but contingent on circumstances. However, we may take it as certain that Cranmer did not at all mean us to give this Collect such an interpretation. The fact is that our way of saying things has changed, and the 'always' added was meant to emphasise our dependence on God rather than to limit it. Today we would probably use 'ever' rather than 'always' - 'we cannot ever stand upright'. That certainly is the meaning Cranmer meant to convey, and we should pray it in that sense.

However, we may argue, nonetheless, that there is a case for keeping 'always' and understanding it in its usual sense. An important theological point is involved. It is right to stress human dependence on God, but it is not right to consider human nature as essentially evil, only as essentially weak. If it was otherwise, Christ's humanity was not a true humanity, and there was no Incarnation. And then there is no Gospel. Christ who shared 'the frailty of our nature' could 'stand upright' amid 'the many and great dangers' that beset him, and therefore, potentially, we can too. When we sin, however, we stand apart from God. Without sin, therefore, life would be so very different. We would stand before God upright and unashamed, as Adam and Eve are depicted as doing in the days of their innocence.[2] And as Christ did, always.

It is easy to confuse weakness of nature with sinfulness of nature, but the difference between the two is important. Our weakness of nature is of God, whereas our sinfulness is not. God made us weak so that we may enjoy the more readily our dependence on him, and it is the essence of sin to reject this and seek our enjoyment in dependence on ourselves. In the Incarnation the Son did not lose his dependence on the Father, in which his joy for ever consists, and which he eternally enjoys in his equality with the Father in heaven. But there was a change in the nature of that dependence when he became, through the womb of Mary, Jesus of Nazareth. He surrendered his dependence born of divine equality for a dependence born of human weakness. This is the truth that St. Paul speaks of in Philippians 2, and is called by theologians the kenotic theory of the Incarnation. (Keno in Greek means 'I empty'). There St. Paul depicts the divine Son emptying himself

2   Gen 2:15-25

of divine equality with the Father, in order to become our Brother and our Saviour. In so doing, however, his perfect union with and dependence on the Father was in no way broken. It was lived, however, at a different level of existence, the human and temporal, where it was lived in weakness, rather than the divine and eternal, where it is lived in glory and power.

Because of what Christ has done for us, we too may hope in the end to stand upright, for such is the Father's gracious will for us. St. Paul speaks of the power of Christ to do this for his disciple. 'He will be upheld, for his Master will be able to make him stand.'[3] In the Book of the Revelation St. John sees the redeemed 'standing before the throne of God and before the Lamb' praising God with joy.[4] So for the redeemed it will be as Jesus said it would be. They shall be as the angels who, like Gabriel, 'stand in the presence of God'.[5] It is, therefore, not so much our frailty, as our sinfulness of nature, that we must blame for our inability to 'stand upright', at least in spirit if not in body, amid 'the many and great dangers' that beset us. Meanwhile we are to take to ourselves all the varied protection of God's grace, which St. Paul likens to spiritual armour. We are to put it on so that we 'may be able to stand against all the wiles of the Devil... and having done all to stand.'[6] The words of the Psalmist, therefore, have a wonderful prophetic ring about them, and to Christian ears perfectly express our ultimate hope; 'we are risen and stand upright'.[7]

We have already taken notice of the truth that so many of our trials and tribulations are the result of our own foolishness and disobedience, and therefore avoidable. But not all. Trying to live as a Christian will inevitably bring with it 'dangers and temptations', for the spirit of the world is opposed to the Spirit of God, and to follow Christ is a dangerous enterprise, in which temptation is going to be a permanent feature. The Greek word for tempt can also mean test, but there is spiritually a world of difference

3 Rom 14:4 (cf 1 Cor 15:1)   4   Rev 7:9   5   Lk 1:19   6   Eph 6:10-13
7   Ps 20:8

between the two words in English. We are tempted by evil, never by God.[8] But God does test us. Jesus was led up into the desert by the Holy Spirit to be tested by God and tempted by the Devil. So it will be for us. In practice, however, it is hard to know just how to describe what is happening to us! This prayer inevitably invites comparison with the Lord's Prayer. There we pray, 'Lead us not into temptation', which certainly seems to need the following phrase, 'but deliver us from evil', to be readily understood. St. Paul stresses that temptations are 'common to man', and there is no evading them. However, it is part of God's 'faithfulness' that he will not let us be tempted beyond our strength, but will provide for us 'the way of escape, that we may be able to endure it'.[9] We should trust him implicitly to provide us with all the inner 'strength and protection' that we may need to carry us through all temptations. The writer of Hebrews underlines this teaching by emphasising how Christ was 'tempted as we are, yet without sin'. It is this, he says, that above all else makes him a worthy High Priest, since he is able fully 'to sympathise with our weaknesses'.[10] This Collect, therefore, gives at least one sense in which the Lord's Prayer may be, and probably usually is, interpreted, for I expect many pray in their minds 'carry us through all temptation', when they say with their lips 'lead us not into temptation'.

However, if we compare this Collect closely with the Lord's Prayer, we have to notice one particular difference. In the Lord's Prayer temptation is in the singular. There Jesus may have been referring to temptation in general, in which case 'all temptations' in the Collect and 'temptation' in the Lord's Prayer mean the same thing. But modern translators of the Lord's Prayer do not support this. They believe Jesus had some special temptation or testing in mind that was so terrible that we should pray to the Father that we should never experience it. The N.E.B., for instance, renders this phrase, 'bring us not to the test'; other versions have 'the time of trial'. If Jesus had in mind a particular event, to what was he referring? Was it his

8 Jas 1:13 9 1 Cor 10:13 10 Heb 4:15

Crucifixion, which he saw approaching? In support of such a suggestion we may notice that the words in the Lord's Prayer are almost identical to those he used to his disciples in the garden of Gethsemane.[11] In his own prayer to the Father in the garden it is clear that Jesus sought escape from crucifixion, if it was not contrary to the Father's will, but also it is clear that through his prayer he became fully and finally convinced that it was the Father's will. He believed that he was indeed being led by the Father to a testing, to his time of trial, through which he would finally fulfil the purpose of his life. So in the end he went willingly to face it.[12]

In St. Luke's version of the Lord's Prayer this puzzling phrase, 'Lead us not into temptation' ends the prayer, but in the Matthean version, 'but deliver us from evil' is added. Yet here again there is doubt and disagreement as to what Jesus meant, if the longer version is favoured, as in fact it always is in the B.C.P. and in our ordinary prayers. In the Greek there is an article before the noun for evil, which indicates a personal rather than an impersonal force of evil; so the Evil One, rather than simply evil, is almost certainly what Jesus meant. This translation is now favoured by nearly all modern versions of the Bible. It seems possible, even probable, therefore, that what Jesus meant by a temptation or testing that was so awful that we must pray constantly not to experience it is a face to face encounter with the Devil and a deliverance into his power. In that case the latter phrase says positively what the former says negatively, and they have the same essential meaning. (See also commentary for Epiphany VI.)

In his Crucifixion we do believe that it was nothing less than this that Jesus experienced, and, moreover, that it was 'for us that he hung and suffered there'[13]. He was delivered into the Devil's power, that we may be saved from that power. He was delivered into the power of the Evil One, but he overcame him in that momentous encounter.[14] Since in this Collect we pray that we may be 'supported in all dangers and carried through all temptations' we must not exclude what we may call our own personal time of

11 Matt 26:41   12 Jn 18:11
13 Mrs. Alexander – Passiontide hymn, There is a green hill.   14 Col 2:14-15

trial or crucial test, such as may overwhelm us. And do we not all have in our lives, not merely passing temptations to resist, but some experience much more deep-seated to cope with, or a particular problem, or unfortunate tendency, or peculiar difficulty that must be faced up to, or overcome, lest it overwhelm us? Its origin may be obvious or mysterious; our inheritance, our environment, our acquaintances, our physical make-up or appearance may be some of any number of causes for what is for us our personal time of trial, our special temptation, our peculiar test of character that constitutes this vital feature of our lives.

In as far as this is true for us, we must not think it strange, even less that we are wicked, to have such a problem to face. Jesus himself had his time of trial, his special temptation, his peculiar test of character, the agony of which was not limited to the hours of his Passion, for he saw it approaching long before.[15] So too for us; our main problems are also seldom sudden ones, but usually long-standing and long-lasting ones, perhaps even life-long. How many forms they can take, and how deep-seated they can be! As we struggle to face up to them, or escape from them, we may be absolutely sure that God will be with us to help us. Has he not said, 'I will never fail you, nor forsake you'?[16] Most importantly we must make them constantly the subject of prayer, as Jesus himself did.

So this is indeed a very important prayer, out of which surely great issues arise, even, spiritually speaking, matters of life and death. But it is also a very helpful prayer, one that guides us and inspires us to trust in God's power to help us in the most personal, deep-seated and difficult areas of our lives.

15 Lk 9:22, 12:50, 17:25, 18:31-34, 22:39-46   16 Heb 13:5

EPIPHANY V

O Lord, we beseech thee to keep thy Church and household continually in thy true religion; that they who do lean only upon the hope of thy heavenly grace may evermore be defended by thy mighty power; through Jesus Christ our Lord. Amen.

This is the Gregorian Collect for this Sunday, and it is very similar to the Collect for Trinity XXII. In translation, however, the words 'Church and' were added in the invocation, and the word 'mighty' in the petition.

This Collect is among the few that directly mention the Church, which is likened here to a household, as in Ephesians: 'You are fellow citizens with the saints and members of the household of God.'[1] The word household is a particularly important Old Testament word. There a household was much more than a mere family, or even an extended family. It was above all a religious entity. Its origins are in the call of the patriarchs, and the special destiny of the Jewish people. 'Shall I hide from Abraham what I am about to do, seeing Abraham shall become a great nation and in him all the nations of the earth shall be blessed?'[2] Abraham, Isaac and Jacob were the leaders of households in this religious sense, seeds from which a greater household, the Church, was to grow.

The religious significance of the word is made all the clearer by its subsequent association with the Passover. The Passover recalled the Exodus, which was just as crucial for the creation of the Israelites as a people set apart for God's special purposes, as was the call of the patriarchs. The story of the founding of the Passover is told in Exodus 12. There we read how Moses divided the Israelites into households for the purposes of keeping the Passover. These Passover households were, therefore, the primary units of the people of Israel that God was recreating by rescuing

1   Eph 2:19   2   Gen 18:17-18

them from their bondage in Egypt. These households were not simply ordinary family units, because it was the Passover that governed the size of each household. 'They shall take a lamb for a household, and if a household is too small for a lamb, then a man and his neighbour shall take one according to the number of persons.'[3] A household, consequently, had a technical religious meaning, as well as an ordinary social meaning. It was a word to describe a gathering of people keeping the Passover, and Jesus and his twelve apostles meeting in the Upper Room for Passover were just such a gathering. They were also the Church in embryo, conceived but not yet born.

What the Passover was to the Jewish household, the Eucharist became to the Christian household. The New Testament shows that Christian households or house-churches, centred round the Eucharist, were vital features of the Church's early life. A Christian household was called a church; that is an accredited unit of the Church. So we hear of the church in Nymphas' house and the church in the house of Aquila and Prisca.[4] The letter to Philemon is addressed to him, Apphia, Archippus and 'the church in his house'.

The idea of the Church as a whole being a household, as implied in our Collect and in Ephesians, is a special theme of the Epistle to the Hebrews. There we are to consider 'Jesus, our great high priest', who is favourably compared with Moses, who, though he was great, was great only as a servant within God's household. Jesus, however, is far greater, for now and forever he presides over God's household as a Son. And we are all part of this divine household, 'if we hold fast our confidence and pride in our hope'.[5] In Hebrews we are taught how the old covenant with the house(hold) of Israel is superseded by the new covenant with the household of Jesus, whose mysterious and eternal ministry as both Priest and Victim is creative of and central to its existence and continuing life. In him alone there is life and truth, and on him, therefore, we must 'lean', if he is going

3 Ex 12:3-4   4 Col 4:15, 1 Cor 16:19   5 Heb 3:1-6

to be able to keep 'his Church and household continually in his true religion'.

Another aspect of the Old Testament household was that its origins were nomadic. Abraham, Isaac and Jacob were wanderers from well to well and from one pasture to another. But their stories depict them as religious pilgrims, and not simply wandering nomads. They were men whom God guided and guarded in their travels. They were men of faith, who 'went out, not knowing where they were going'.[6] This was indeed a measure of their faith. This was also the truth behind the wanderings of the house(hold) of Israel under Moses and Aaron. We get a fine picture of this guidance by God of his people in Numbers. He revealed his guiding, guarding presence to them in a cloud, and we are told 'sometimes the cloud remained from evening until morning: and when the cloud was taken up in the morning they set out. At the command of the Lord they encamped and at the command of the Lord they set out'.[7]

The Church, as the new household of Israel, is also a pilgrim body. The Holy Spirit rests upon the Church as the cloud overshadowed the Israelites, and by the Holy Spirit the Church is guided and guarded on its journey. As the Collect stresses, we are to 'lean only' upon him, and we can, because he 'continually keeps' us. And, according to our Collect, it is in his 'true religion' that we are continually kept.

'True religion' refers to the faith and practice of the Church. Through Moses God not only guided the Israelites to the Promised Land, but also gave them the laws and ceremonies that they were to keep continually when they got there. The tragedy of the Jews, however, was that these laws and ceremonies given by God became in time a barrier that separated them from God. Instead of keeping them in the way of true religion, the keeping of them

6   Heb 11:8   7   Num 9:21-23

became the way of a false religion. 'The very commandment which promised life proved death to me',[8] says St. Paul. The Pharisee Saul faithfully kept the law, and became God's enemy. The Christian Paul, however, faithfully followed Jesus, and became the great champion of God's true religion. Consequently a pilgrim Church must have a religion that will not ossify into a mere code of laws and ceremonies, suitable only for those living in unchanging circumstances. (See also commentary on Trinity VII.)

For the new Israel the Promised Land is never reached in this world and in this life time. Always we are to remain pilgrims with only 'heavenly grace' to 'lean upon'. But in our pilgrimage God's power is 'mighty' to defend all who put their trust in him. A pilgrim Church must expect change and be ready to face the unexpected. Moreover the pace of its journey will not be uniform. Sometimes it must remain in one place, as it were, till guided to move on, as was the experience of the Israelites in the desert. Then suddenly it will be required to move quickly, when it finds itself living in an era of rapid change, as is the case today. Whatever the situation it must never lose heart, but 'lean only' and wholeheartedly 'upon the hope of thy heavenly grace', after the spirit of this Collect. Amid the current sense of uncertainty concerning the faith and practice of the Church, and the present noise of theological disagreement within the Church, this Collect seems to be a particularly topical prayer, which we can use with gratitude for its obvious relevance. Moreover we should especially notice how it has been strengthened in translation by the addition of the word 'mighty'. It is a prayer of hope as well as of commitment. 'Is anything too hard for the Lord?'[9] As Jesus said, when it comes to coping with change, and the need to change, God has the power to help us to think and achieve the apparently impossible, dissolving enmities and creating fellowship and peace.[10] It is this conviction that strengthens and also enables us pilgrims to journey always in hope. (See also commentary on Trinity XVI.)

8 Rom 7:9-12   9 Gen 18 : 14   10 Mk 10 : 27

EPIPHANY VI

O God, whose blessed Son was manifested that he might destroy the works of the devil, and make us the sons of God, and heirs of eternal life; grant us, we beseech thee, that, having this hope, we may purify ourselves, even as he is pure; that, when he shall appear again with power and great glory, we may be made like unto him in his eternal and glorious kingdom; where with thee, O Father, and thee, O Holy Ghost, he liveth and reigneth ever one God, world without end. Amen.

This Collect, probably by Bishop Cosin, was written for the 1662 Prayer Book. In the early Sacramentaries, the Sarum Missal, and the first two Prayer Books no provision was made to keep this Sunday, which only occurs occasionally, and when it did occur the Proper for Epiphany V continued to be used.

As is so common in Collects written for the 1662 BCP, it was constructed out of the themes of the Epistle and the Gospel. It has an unusual trinitarian ending, but see earlier comment in the Introduction.

The Collect starts by stating a very archaic sounding reason for the Incarnation, 'to destroy the works of the Devil'. These words are taken directly from the Epistle,[1] and they remind us of the Catechism, where we are required to promise that we will renounce 'the Devil and all his works'. How, we may ask, are we nowadays to conceive of the Devil? Are we obliged to conceive of him at all? Is not a belief in a personal Devil too primitive a concept for modern Christians to subscribe to, something akin to the biblical teaching of a flat earth and a three decker universe, which we may, indeed must, discard?

[1] 1 Jn 3:8

The biblical evidence, however, when set against this reasoning, is disconcerting. The fact is that a belief in the Devil is not primitive, as one might expect, but of late origin. It is not in the Bible an aspect of theology that becomes weaker and less significant as the centuries passed by, but the reverse. The Devil, for instance, played no part in the theology of Moses and the earlier prophets. He emerges for the first time in the post-exilic writings. It is suggested indeed that the whole idea of the Devil is an importation from the dualistic religion of Babylon. In the Old Testament, however, he remains a shadowy figure playing no prominent role in its theology, whereas, in marked contrast, in the New Testament, in the Gospels, the Epistles and the Book of Revelation, the Devil takes centre stage. Strange as it may seem, the Devil is someone whom we must above all associate with Jesus.

He is there at the start of his ministry in our Lord's temptations, but after they were over we are expressly told that the Devil only left him temporarily, awaiting 'an opportune time'.[2] The Devil and his associates, the demons, feature prominently in so many of the Gospel stories. They dog his steps, and his healing miracles were seen as mighty victories over them.[3] Then, again, at the end the Devil makes his presence felt, as Christ's admonishment of Peter makes plain, 'Simon, Simon, behold Satan demanded to have you that he might sift you like wheat, but I prayed for you that your faith may not fail.'[4] That Jesus saw his passion as a final confrontation with his lifelong adversary is made plain by his cryptic comment at the time of his arrest, 'This is your hour and the power of darkness.'[5] When Jesus speaks to his disciples of the Devil, he calls him Satan, and the translations always print the name with a capital S, even though the Reformers declined giving him a capital D in this Collect.

When we turn to the Epistles the prominence given to the Devil is in no way lessened. All warn us against him and the subtlety of his ways. Yet all assert that in Christ we are safe from his power.[6] Finally, in Revelation St.

2   Lk 4:1-13   3   Mk 1:23-25 et al   4   Lk 22:31-32
5   Lk 22:53   6   Eph 6:12, 1 Pet 5:8, Jas 4:7, Jude 9, 1 Jn 2:18-22 et al

John prophesies the ultimate destruction of the Devil and all his works at the end of the age. Meanwhile, however, while this age still runs, the Devil will remain powerfully active on earth, all the more so in fact because he knows that his days are numbered and his power through Christ is broken.[7] On this evidence it seems impossible for us to simply eradicate all reference to the Devil and retain an undiluted Gospel. There is, however, one most prominent example of how the Church has, wittingly or unwittingly, contrived to remove him from the central position he held in the mind of Jesus. He has been removed from the Lord's Prayer! There is no denying that, according to the longer version in St. Matthew that we all use, the Greek demands that we pray, 'Deliver us from the Evil One.'[8] The presence of the article makes the evil Jesus had in mind personal rather than impersonal, and our modern translations acknowledge this. Belief in a personal Devil may indeed be difficult for us, but are there not difficulties of a deeper kind inherent in our refusing to share the recorded beliefs of Jesus? It is one thing to say that the doctrine of the Incarnation involves the acceptance that Jesus was a man with the essential limitations of his time, and therefore his theological understanding would naturally include such errors as believing that David wrote all the Psalms and Moses all the Pentateuch. It is surely quite another to say that his understanding of the nature of good and evil was similarly flawed and limited. May we for this reason doubt his perception of God as being 'Abba', our loving Father? It was a radical teaching. And what of his teaching about the Sabbath? In this, and other spiritual perceptions, he showed himself to be no ordinary man of his time. Why then should we doubt his perception of the real nature of the power that is in rebellion against God as being personal, the Evil One? Such a belief does not demand a dualistic doctrine of God who remains one and sovereign. At all events we must record that the whole of the New Testament agrees with this Collect, even if we may be tempted (by whom?) to skim over the opening words with our tongue in our cheek.

---

7 Rev 12:7-12   8   Matt 6:13 cf Lk 11:4

Jesus came also, the Collect says, to make us 'sons of God and heirs of eternal life'. But are we not all naturally 'sons of God'? Is not that our natural spiritual state as human beings? In what way then can we say that Jesus has made us God's sons? According to liberal theologians, among whom Harnack is probably the most famous, the essence of Christ's Gospel is the declaration of the simple message of the Fatherhood of God and the brotherhood of man. But to proclaim such a Gospel Jesus surely did not need to mount such an uncomfortable pulpit as the Cross! The New Testament, moreover, does not support such an interpretation of the Gospel. Would that it did! How simple our faith would be! It declares rather that to become truly the children of God men and women need not simply to be created, but also to be redeemed and sanctified. This is the far less comfortable truth that it proclaims. Such is the grip, it declares, that evil has upon all creation, including and especially upon all mankind, and so serious is the consequence of human sinfulness, that nothing less than a divine intervention was required to save us all from death and destruction. Men and women, though made in the image of their Creator, have lost that image, become separated from him, and are 'in bondage to decay' to use St. Paul's dramatic phrase.[9] Therefore an act of divine redemption was necessary; nothing else could save us. So in Jesus God acted; this is the essence of the Gospel.[10]

Only, therefore, through Jesus can God truly become our Father. This is because only he is truly the Son of God, 'the only begotten Son'. Equally only through him do we all become in any true sense of the phrase 'brothers and sisters'.[11] Naturally, because of sin, we are as separated from each other, living as rivals and enemies, as we are separated from God. Sin has created this dual disastrous separation, which makes such a sad mockery of all easy definitions of the Gospel. This is the consistent teaching of the New Testament, but nowhere is it put more starkly then in St. John, Chapter 8 where Jesus says, 'You are of your father the Devil, and your will is to do

---

9   Rom 8:21   10 Jn 3:16   11 Mk 3:31-35

your father's desires'. [12]

But through Christ we are redeemed from the Devil's grasp. This is the Good News. He also says, 'I came that they might have life and have it abundantly'.[13] Through Christ the power of evil is broken and 'the works of the Devil' destroyed. Through Christ our hopes concerning the Fatherhood of God and the brotherhood of man do become a reality or, as the Collect puts it, we may indeed become 'the sons of God and heirs of eternal life'. But only through Christ. Again it is St. John who puts this truth with uncompromising directness and clarity. 'He who believes in the Son of God has the testimony (of the Gospel) in himself . . . And the testimony is this, that God has given us eternal life, and this life is in his Son. He who has the Son has life; he who has not the Son of God has not life.'[14]

That all this should come true for us is, as the Collect says, the Christian hope. But if we truly hold this hope, we will do more than just enjoy it; we will be inspired to seek to imitate Jesus and 'to purify ourselves even as he is pure'. All the great Christian virtues, faith, hope and love are dynamic, because they are only present within us by virtue of his indwelling Holy Spirit. The indwelling of the Holy Spirit does not destroy our freedom of will, but it does direct it and inspire it. How mysterious is this joining of our spirit with God's Spirit! Canon Masterman reminds us that St. Augustine comments on the passage (1 John 3 : 1-8) which inspired this Collect, like this, 'See how he does not do away with free will, for he says, "purify himself." Who purifies us but God? Yet God does not purify us if we are unwilling. Therefore, in joining your will to God, you purify yourself.' It is as if God wants to give us all the credit for what he does for us! It is surely equally important that we should not let this happen, lest we pride ourselves on what is not in truth ours, but to give all the glory to God. We may take the credit for washing our hands, but not for purifying our

12 Jn 8:44   13 Jn 10:10   14 1 Jn 5:11-12

hearts. For the latter, unless God works his will within us such work cannot be done. 'Make me a clean heart, O God, and renew a right spirit within me'[15] was the cri-de-coeur of the Psalmist. There is not that power within us naturally that can do such a blessed thing. We regularly acknowledge this truth whenever we attend Matins or Evensong, and pray the versicle and response, 'O God, make clean our hearts within us, and take not thy Holy Spirit from us.'

Finally, we pray, 'that, when he shall appear again with power and great glory, we may be made like unto him in his eternal and glorious kingdom'. First, we pray that we may be like him in the purity of his human life, then we pray that we may share hereafter in the glory of his divine life. St. Peter opens his second Epistle with words that sum up the aspirations of this Collect perfectly, but they are words that perhaps most of us will want to read a few times before we can grasp their full significance. 'His divine power has granted us all things that pertain to life and godliness through the knowledge of him that called us to his own glory and excellence, by which he has granted to us his precious and very great promises, that through these we may escape from the corruption that is in the world because of passion, and become partakers of the divine nature.'[16]

This is a stupendous assertion. It is the ultimate Christian hope, and the New Testament makes it clear that the fervour with which this hope was held was the special inspiration of the earliest Christians. They lived expecting Christ's second coming at any time, and consequently an intense excitement sustained their fellowship and worship. What wonderful things the second coming would mean for all who were in Christ![17] 'To be made like unto him'. 'To become partakers of the divine nature.' Appropriately the New Testament ends with these excited words, 'He who testifies to these things says, "Surely I am coming soon". Amen. Come, Lord Jesus.'[18]

15 Ps 51:10   16 2 Pet 1:3-4   17 1 Thess 4:13-18   18 Rev 22:20

Although the centuries come and go, the Christian hope remains, and this Collect catches something of that hopeful excitement that should characterise our spiritual lives, as we look to the ultimate future. We do not celebrate the Eucharist only in thanksgiving for what Christ has done, but also in expectation of what he will do, 'until his coming again'.[19] This Collect similarly recalls what Christ's first coming has achieved, and reminds us of what his second will achieve. Such thoughts are to inspire us to more earnest endeavours to purify our lives, for in his glorious kingdom there is a place prepared for us where 'the pure in heart shall see God'.[20]

19 Prayer of Consecration   20 Matt 5:8

SEPTUAGESIMA

O Lord, we beseech thee favourably to hear the prayers of thy people; that we, who are justly punished for our offences, may be mercifully delivered by thy goodness, for the glory of thy Name; through Jesus Christ our Saviour, who liveth and reigneth with thee, and the Holy Ghost, now and ever. Amen.

This is the Gregorian Collect with the important addition of the phrase 'by thy goodness' introduced in its translation.

The season of the 'Gesimas' was a preparation for Lent started by St. Gregory the Great (540-604) at the time of the collapse of the Roman Empire. This was a time of chaos. An age was ending and another was in the pangs of birth. In this time of great change the Church, thanks very largely to the leadership of St. Gregory, was to play a crucial role, and was able to establish its pre-eminent position in the new medieval civilisation that emerged in western Europe. Nonetheless, this was a time in which war was destroying what had been thought indestructible, and this Collect, and the next, reflect the desire of Christians to discover God's hand in the evils of the times, and their longing for deliverance from them.

The main petition in this Collect highlights what appears to be two contrasting activities of God, his just punishment of sinners and his merciful deliverance of them. They are, however, to be understood not so much as contrasted as related activities, and the Collect leads us to recognise this. Although divine mercy does not do away with the need for divine justice, it does, as St. James says, 'triumph' over it.[1] The words 'by thy goodness,' which are additions to the medieval Collect, should be allowed to govern our 'just punishment', as well as 'our merciful deliverance'. To do so makes all the difference.

1   Jas 2:13

If we look at the Bible, both Old and New Testaments teach that God is personally involved in both of these activities. In Isaiah the prophet reveals how God is at work in the political events of his time, both meteing out just punishment and bringing in merciful deliverance. He warns his hearers that, because their sins are so grievous, God's just punishment will not pass quickly. After each section of his prophecy he ends with the refrain, 'For all this his anger is not turned away and his hand is stretched out still.'[2] But nevertheless it is God's will also to save Israel. So Isaiah reveals how God will in his own good time break the punishing yoke of foreign oppression, and then war will make way for peace and chaos for order. His agent in this merciful deliverance will be called 'Prince of Peace, and of the increase of his government and of peace there will be no end...The zeal of the Lord of Hosts will do this.'[3] What Israel must do in response to this word of God is to repent, accept the just punishment of God, and wait in faith, hope and obedience for his merciful deliverance. This prophecy of Isaiah was later seen to refer to Jesus, and is now one of the passages we specially love to hear read at Christmas time.

The story of David and Bathsheba, in which we see God's dealings with an individual rather than the nation, makes similar points. David is treated with both just punishment and merciful deliverance. The king accepts that he has sinned deeply, and recognises the justice of the divine punishment proclaimed by the prophet Nathan. What is decreed takes place, but, because it is accepted in penitence, the outcome of this evil episode in David's life is not disastrous. Divine favour is not withdrawn from him and his house, and his kingdom becomes strengthened and his throne established. It is because he accepts that he is being 'justly punished for his offences' that he is also 'mercifully delivered by God's goodness'.[4]

In the New Testament this theme is present in many of the Epistles (Romans, 1 Peter, James, Jude), but perhaps especially in Hebrews. There we are told that, if God did not indeed punish us for our offences, it would

---

2   Is 9:12   3   Is 9:7   4   2 Sam 11 & 12

show that he did not really love us. His punishment reveals his love just as surely as does his mercy, and therefore both must be welcomed by us. 'God is treating us as sons; for what son is there whom his father does not discipline (that is if he loves him). If you are left without discipline...then you are illegitimate children and not sons...For the moment all discipline seems painful...but God disciplines us for our good that we may share his holiness.'[5]

This is the attitude towards divine punishment that this Collect accepts, and how important it is that we accept it too. We are to take God's side against our own sin, knowing that the consequences for those who do so will in the end be good. It will be then for us, as it was for the Psalmist, who said, 'It is good for me that I have been in trouble, that I may learn thy statutes.'[6]

This Collect does not ask the question, "Why does God punish?", or query how he punishes. Following the Bible the Collect simply accepts that he does, and declares that his punishments are just. It is easy to believe that God is just, but perhaps less easy to believe that God inflicts punishments. And in particular, how can we believe that he inflicts punishments, if war, disaster, sickness and death are to be accepted as divine punishments, as they certainly are in the Bible? If we must accept the proposition that God punishes, perhaps it is easier to conceive of divine punishment as being something inherent within all sin. Sin then becomes its own punishment. Moreover, we can see the presence of mercy as well as justice in such a theory. As the pain caused by the hot embers warns the child not to advance into the flames, so an inherent theory of divine punishment can be seen as a warning device to warn, and thereby save, sinners of the consequences of their ways. Nor is justice offended by this theory of consequential punishment. We reap what we sow, says St. Paul, lest a righteous God is mocked by unrighteous men.[7]

5   Heb 12:7-11   6   Ps 119:71   7   Gal 6:7

Unfortunately experience has a way of making nonsense of all such tidy reasoning. The fact is that sin is not a merely personal thing with merely personal consequences. We are so united in the bonds of our common humanity that 'if one member suffers, all suffer together.'[8] Not only are the sins of our fathers visited upon us[9], but the sins of our children and our neighbours are also. And our own sins so obviously affect our children and our fellow men. No one can keep his own just punishment to himself, even if he should want to. How unfair the biblical teaching seems, and it is indeed challenged within the Bible. Ezekiel declared that God in future would only mete out individual punishment.[10] But the realities of life continue to be, at least for the great majority, both unjust and unmerciful in their consequences, presenting us with a moral dilemma, as well as physical sufferings to cope with.

God's answer is the Cross. In the Cross God in his justice and his mercy takes his place both with those who are justly and with those who are unjustly punished, seeking to redeem them all. And in the Gospel we are called to take up our cross and follow him, which means to become involved in this divine work of redemption through suffering. We are in him to fulfil what he has accomplished. St. Paul writes to the Colossians, 'In (Christ) all the fullness of God was pleased to dwell, and through him to reconcile to himself all things... making peace by the blood of his cross... I (for my part therefore) now rejoice in my sufferings for your sake, and in my flesh I complete what is lacking in Christ's afflictions.'[11] Through the Cross and our willing involvement in the redemptive suffering of Christ in the context of our own lives and the lives of others, the corporate consequential suffering for sin that is the sad lot of men is, as it were, turned upside down, and becomes no longer a means of just punishment, but a means of merciful deliverance. In Colossians St. Paul goes on to stress the mystery and the glory of what Christ has done, and in which we are privileged to share. It is nothing less than the redemption of the world. In the Cross just

8   1 Cor 12:26   9   Ex 20:5   10   Eze 18   11   Col 1:19-24

punishment and merciful deliverance have been fused into one, and the result is glorious. This, too, this Collect emphasises.

'Glory' is the word that the New Testament uses to describe what happened on Good Friday. Indeed if we called that day 'Glorious Friday' such a title would have a much more biblical ring about it! Although we associate such teaching particularly with St. John, all agree that his crucifixion was Christ's glorification.[12] There he was crowned 'King of Glory'.[13] The Collect confirms this, stressing that all just punishment and all merciful deliverance of sinners redounds to the glory of God. God is glorious and God is love, and the Cross reveals that the true heart of love, in which the greatest glory resides, is (in earthly terms) redemptive innocent suffering. So, if we would share in Christ's glory hereafter, we must be willing to share in his redemptive suffering here. And it is to this that we are called. So St. Peter says, 'Rejoice in so far as you share in Christ's suffering. In so doing you are blessed, because the spirit of glory and of God rests upon you.'[14]

It is undeserved suffering that alone has within it the power to redeem the world from sin. Hence its supreme value. It is through such suffering, borne gladly and willingly for the glory of God's Name after the example of Christ, that 'mercy triumphs over judgement' without destroying it. This Collect, therefore, traces a spiritual progression that ends in glory. The penitent acceptance of our just punishment leads us on to accept willingly a share in the redemptive suffering that brought about in Christ our merciful deliverance, and so to a share in 'the glory that shall be revealed'.[15] This is a Collect that takes us to the very heart of the Gospel.

12 Jn 7:39, 17:1-5   13 Te Deum   14 1 Pet 4: 12-19   15 Rom 8:18

SEXAGESIMA

O Lord God, who seest that we put not our trust in any thing that we do; mercifully grant that by thy power we may be defended against all adversity; through Jesus Christ our Lord. Amen.

This Collect, like the last, comes out of the turbulent times of St. Gregory the Great. The western half of the Roman Empire was being overrun by Germanic tribesmen, and the Emperor, whose capital was Constantinople, not Rome, was powerless to provide protection to the disintegrating western half of his Empire. It was also a time of famine, pestilence and poverty, and by dint of his wisdom, energy and charity St. Gregory, who was Bishop of Rome, became the recognised leader of the peoples in the West. Although personally seeking to keep on friendly terms with the Emperor, he crossed a political rubicon of great significance when he made an independent peace with the advancing Lombards without imperial permission. From his action flowed the later claims of the Papacy to independence from all controls by Emperors or Kings, which in turn was an important contributing factor in the yet more important claim to the role of divinely ordained teacher both of Emperors and Kings, and all those they ruled, in all matters, whether political or religious. The claim of the Papacy to this supreme authority became the dominant factor in, and characteristic feature of, all life in western Europe for the next 1000 years.

The connection between these considerations and this Gregorian Collect is that in the Latin the Collect says 'by the protection of the teacher of the nations', instead of 'by thy power'. Did the original, however, refer to the Church or, perhaps, the Pope, rather than to God? It could have, especially considering the thinking and circumstances of the time and, if so, the Reformers made a significant change in their translation in a direction more congenial to protestant sentiments. At all events there is now no possible ambiguity in the Collect's meaning.

The Collect opens with a phrase that requires scrutiny, if not justification. Do we distrust ourselves so much? Is it right that we should? When we look at the way that Jesus taught and dealt with individuals, we notice how often he encouraged his hearers, and those to whom he ministered, to think for themselves and to make their own decisions. He was a great challenger. He never took away people's moral independence. His regular ending to a parable was, 'He who has ears to hear, let him hear', and by implication, act.[1] ' "Teacher," said a lawyer, "what shall I do to inherit eternal life?" Jesus said to him, "What is written in the law? How do you read?" '[2] He made the man think for himself and answer his own question. Jesus was not the kind of teacher that encouraged his disciples to reply timidly to a query, "Master, you tell me." In the parable of the talents the servant that did nothing with the talent given to him was roundly condemned, whereas those who used their initiative were warmly praised.[3]

Yet, in St. John's Gospel, we hear Jesus telling the parable of the Vine and the Branches. 'I am the vine, you are the branches...and apart from me you can do nothing.'[4] On several occasions he rebuked his disciples for their foolish actions and their worldly attitudes in words calculated to make them most distrustful of their own powers. 'You are a hindrance to me, for you are not on the side of God but of men.'[5] This may have been said directly to St. Peter, but St. Mark makes it clear that Jesus had all his disciples in mind as he said it.

So there is a balance to be kept here. On the one hand, we must put our whole trust in God as we go on our way in life, whereas, on the other, the nature of our trust in God is not to be such as to drain us of all ability to decide and act for ourselves. Indeed, the opposite is to be the case. Putting our whole trust in God, if properly conceived, is the way to the fullest possible release of our natural energies and abilities. We are not certainly to be seekers after our own will, but rather agents of God's will; but very active agents.

1   Mk 4:9   2   Lk 10:25   3   Matt 25:14-30   4   Jn 15:5
5   Matt 16:23. Mk 8:33

The biblical virtue that characterises this kind of trust that leads to action is, perhaps surprisingly, meekness. It is a virtue in the Bible that leads on to successful action and positive results. 'The meek,' said Jesus, 'shall inherit the earth.'[6] This is an unlikely outcome, however, if we understand meekness in its contemporary sense, where it has been shorn of those strong, energetic undertones that characterise its biblical meaning. This change in its meaning is well illustrated by the reading that Moses (of all people) 'was the most meek of all men'.[7] What an unexpected paragon of this particular virtue!

We have had occasion to mention St. Gregory the Great, and he too makes an excellent example of a meek man in the biblical sense. Almost single-handed he rescued the Church from the overwhelming disaster that befell it in what are rightly called the Dark Ages. His energy and wisdom re-organised and revitalised it, starting from Rome. Then with the aid of the monks of the Benedictine Order, which was founded in those dark days, he set about turning back the tide of paganism and heresy that was enveloping the Church, and set it on its successful way of re-evangelising western Europe. It was he who sent St. Augustine to England in 596. Yet he was a man of the simplest faith and the greatest gentleness. It is meekness that combines such trust and gentleness with dynamic energy and fearless zeal.

So this prayer is not one that should leave us fearful of deciding and acting for ourselves. Rather it should be such as to inspire us to face up to adversity, and to be active in our own defence. 'I will trust and will not be afraid.'[8] A true trust in God leads to power from God. 'They who wait for the Lord shall renew their strength.'[9] We put our whole trust in God, and not at all in ourselves, but in that whole trust we are to live positively and, if need be, take steps by word or deed to defend ourselves, and others, 'against all adversity'.

---

6 Matt 5:5   7 Num 12:3   8 Is 12:2   9 Is 40: 31

However, we should perhaps pause to ask what is meant by 'against all adversity'. There are surely some forms of adversity against which God is clearly not going to defend us. We cannot sensibly pray for immunity from the common lot of men, especially as Jesus chose to share it. Just as we have felt, therefore, that it is necessary for us to understand the negative 'we put not our trust in anything that we do' in terms of the positive 'we put our whole trust in God', if we are to understand properly the opening of this Collect, we find ourselves needing to change the negative 'defend us against all adversity' into the more positive 'deliver us in all adversity' truly to understand its ending. Without doubt, as we go forward trusting God, we are going to meet adversity, and the kind of defence we need against it is such as to enable us to continue to go forward. St. Paul was fearless in his desire to preach the Gospel, and never drew back from any adversity in the fulfilling of his vocation. He was able to witness, however, to the power of God to defend him in the midst of all adversity. To Timothy he wrote from his prison in Rome, 'At my first defence no one took my part...but the Lord stood by me and gave me strength...so I was rescued from the lion's mouth. And the Lord will rescue me from every evil and save me for his heavenly kingdom. To him be the glory for ever and ever, Amen.'[10] To St. Paul this deliverance, and others that he experienced, was not so much 'against all adversity' as in the midst of adversity, and was positive in its ultimate purpose.

To trust God, then, is to accept his manner of 'defence against all adversity', and the Bible and Christian experience both suggest that this takes the form of strength to cope with and use for good, adversity of all kinds, as well as to be rescued from it. In this way what may seem to us to be a barrier in our path can become a door that opens the way to better things, and the adversity, against which we pray to be defended, becomes a means of grace and blessing. Such is the mystery of God's power 'to defend us against all adversity' of which this Collect speaks.[11]

10 2 Tim 4:16-20   11 Ps 27:1-7

QUINQUAGESIMA

O Lord, who hast taught us that all our doings without charity are nothing worth; send thy Holy Ghost, and pour into our hearts that most excellent gift of charity, the very bond of peace and of all virtues, without which whosoever liveth is counted dead before thee; Grant this for thine only Son Jesus Christ's sake. Amen.

This Collect is one of the finest to come from Cranmer's pen. It is an adaption of the medieval Collect, but particularly differs from it in omitting that Collect's mention of Sacramental Confession, which was so customary at this season. (The title 'Shrove Tuesday' means Confession Tuesday.) The theme of this Sunday, however, continues to be with preparing us for Lent, with its Collect emphasising the positive virtue of love, as both the beginning and the end of the spiritual life. Church discipline must lead to love, if it is to be worth anything in God's eyes, for without love there is no real life in us.

This is such a beautifully worded Collect that its hard edge may at first glance escape our notice. The general sentiments appear so readily acceptable. Do we not all agree upon the supreme importance of love, which is, of course, the word that we would prefer to 'charity' these days? The world at large would certainly agree that it is love that really gives worth to what we do. But if we pray this prayer, rather than just read it, its cutting edge cannot be denied. And very disturbing it is too, as is so much of the New Testament's teaching about love. This Collect accurately reflects this teaching.

However, before we proceed to comment on this Collect we must make an important point about the English word 'love' as it is used in the New Testament. There it is used to translate three separate Greek words, and therein lie the seeds of misunderstanding. These three words are eros, philia and agape, and it is essential that we understand the difference between these three Greek words. Eros is love based on physical attraction, whereas philia is love arising from a common mind and spirit, and may well be described as friendship. Both eros and philia describe natural human feelings common to us all, and there is no special virtue in either. However, both can be most beautiful in their expression, as the Bible makes plain in some memorable passages.

'Jacob loved Rachel', says the Scripture with approval, and 'served seven years for her, and they seemed to him but a few days because of the love that he had for her'.[1] And Elkanah, we are told, loved his barren wife Hannah, and sought by his love for her to comfort her for her inability to have children. His love for her was in no way dependent on her providing children. 'Why is your heart sad?' he asks, 'Am I not more to you than ten sons?', for surely she was to him.[2] Then, who is not moved by the classic descriptions of friendship between Ruth and Naomi, and David and Jonathan? 'Entreat me not to leave you', says Ruth to her mother-in-law, 'Where you go I will go... Your people will be my people and your God my God... May the Lord do to me, and more also, if even death part me from you.'[3] And when David heard of his friend's death he sang in his famous lament, 'I am distressed for you, my brother Jonathan; very pleasant have you been to me; your love to me was wonderful, passing the love of women.'[4]

However, although they can be feelings expressed with beauty and heroism, both eros and philia can be, and sadly often are, expressed with both lust and cruelty. This, too, is faithfully recorded in Scripture. David's erotic love for Bathsheba was real enough and proved no passing fancy, but it made him both a murderer and an adulterer.[5] The bond of deep affection between the three sons of Zeruiah was famous and strengthened the cause of David's kingdom, but it led Joab to commit a revengeful murder, which brought with it a curse upon him.[6] Out of such human love, therefore, can

1   Gen 29:20   2   1 Sam 1:8   3   Ruth 1:16-17   4   2 Sam 1:26
5   2 Sam 11   6   2 Sam 3:17-32

come evil as well as good, for both eros and philia can operate to their fullest measure apart from God. But this is not so with agape, and it is with agape that this Collect is exclusively concerned. Agape is of God and not of us. He who loves with agape, says St. John, 'is born of God and knows God, for God is agape'.[7] It is not natural for us to love in this manner, and if we do so, it is evidence of God in our lives. St. John again; 'God is agape, and he who abides in agape abides in God and God abides in him'.[8] Nothing like this can be said of eros and philia.

It is because agape is wholly of God that we must pray for it. The Collect describes it as a divine gift, and bids us pray the Holy Spirit to pour it into our hearts. He is the giver of agape, as he is of life. 'God's love has been poured into our hearts through the Holy Spirit, which has been given to us.'[9] It is uncertain in the context of this saying whether St. Paul is writing of God's love for us or of our love for him, but the distinction is immaterial, for all agape is altogether of God. When we love God with agape, then, the love with which we love him is, as it were, God's love returning to himself. For this reason Jesus speaks of himself and the Father coming to 'make their home' with those who love with agape.[10] Agape is indeed the life of the Trinity, and has its eternal reality within 'the home' of the Father and the Son. When we love with agape, therefore, whether it be God or our neighbour that we love, we share in the heavenly home life of the Father and the Son, or rather they share their home life with us.

The Collect agrees with St. John in stressing the primacy of divine action in all aspects of agape. We pray here that the Father may send his Holy Spirit to 'pour into our hearts' his gift of agape. St. John says, 'In this is love, not that we loved God, but that he loved us.'[11] The Collect for Trinity VI underlines the same truth with similar words, 'Pour into our hearts such love towards thee.' The words of both Collects remind us inevitably of

7 1 Jn 4:8   8   1 Jn 4:16   9   Rom 5:5   10 Jn 14:23
11 1 Jn 4:10

Pentecost and the outpouring of the Holy Spirit upon the Apostles. This outpouring continues to our day upon the Church and through the Church. And one is reminded again of Johannine teaching as we pray this prayer, 'From his fulness we have all received, grace upon grace,'[12] and 'it is not by measure that he gives the Spirit'.[13]

––––––––––––

Agape in our Collect is described as 'the very bond of peace and of all virtues'. St. Paul confirms this assertion. It is agape that holds all together, for even the best of virtues are rendered ineffective and even perverse without agape. To the Colossians he spells out this truth. 'Put on then, as God's chosen ones, holy and beloved, compassion, kindness, lowliness, meekness and patience, forbearing one another, and if any has a complaint against another, forgiving each other...and above all else put on agape, which binds all together in perfect harmony.'[14] In Ephesians he makes the same point. After an even longer description of Christian behaviour and morals, he stresses the supreme virtue of agape. 'Therefore (to sum up) be imitators of God, as beloved children, and walk in agape, even as Christ loved us.'[15]

But best known of all St. Paul's writings on the subject of agape is his poem in 1 Corinthians 13. The words of that famous passage are echoed in the opening clause of this Collect, and it is the Epistle for this Sunday. 'All our doings without agape are nothing worth' sums up St. Paul's teaching on the subject; even our worship, our theological understanding, our penitence, our almsgiving and our service in God's name are made subject to this acid test.

––––––––––––

So agape in our Collect is linked with all aspects of living the true life. All must be inspired by it. But it goes further and declares that without agape

12 Jn 1:16   13 Jn 3:34   14 Col 3:12-13   15 Eph 5:1-2

we cannot be deemed to be in reality alive at all, for without it 'whosoever liveth is counted dead' before God. Now, does not this sound a harsh saying? Herein lies the hard edge to this Collect, to which reference was made at the beginning of this commentary. One feels bound to ask, also, if there is biblical justification for such an assertion. Does it not conflict with the belief that God himself is agape?

We have had occasion to stress the closeness in thought between this Collect and the Johannine writings, and it is there that we read, 'He who does not love abides in death. Anyone who hates his brother is a murderer, and we know that no murderer has eternal life abiding in him.'[16] There, love and life on the one hand, and hatred and death on the other, are linked together. Not having love is described as 'abiding in death'. God is agape, and God is the only source of life. The life that he gives is agape-filled life, and therefore life drained of agape is essentially a dead existence, something that is 'counted dead before God'. So, far from the truth that God is agape invalidating this teaching, it makes it logically inevitable. To live, then, is to love, and to love is to live. These two words, so close in their spelling, are as close in their real meaning. Therefore 'let all that you do be done in love'.[17]

16 1 Jn 3:14-15   17 1 Cor 16:14

ASH WEDNESDAY

Almighty and everlasting God, who hatest nothing that thou hast made, and dost forgive the sins of all them that are penitent; create and make in us new and contrite hearts, that we worthily lamenting our sins, and acknowledging our wretchedness, may obtain of thee, the God of all mercy, perfect remission and forgiveness; through Jesus Christ our Lord. Amen.

This is another Collect composed in 1549. It is said throughout Lent until Maundy Thursday, according to the rubric in the 1928 book.

The title Ash Wednesday comes from the ancient custom of anointing worshippers with ash, made from the palm crosses kept from last year's Palm Sunday. The meaning of the ceremony is to remind us that physically we are mere matter, to be reduced at death, from 'earth to earth, ashes to ashes, dust to dust.'[1] Spiritually, too, without divine redemption eternal death awaits us. The call of Lent is for us to remember this, and to resolve to live on the level of the spirit and not merely on the level of the flesh. The anointing of the ashes is done on the forehead in the sign of the cross, and should move us to remember our anointing at Baptism with water with the sign of the cross, for there sacramentally we died to sin and rose again to eternal life through Jesus Christ.

This Collect starts, as does that for Quinquagesima, with one of those negative clauses so beloved of Cranmer, which sound so well in liturgical prayer. The opening of both these Collects, which are said together for the first four days of Lent, may also be compared in meaning as well as in style. They emphasise the same truth. That for Quinquagesima makes it plain that, although man may act without love, God certainly never does, and

1 B.C.P. Burial Service

that for Ash Wednesday declares that God hates nothing that he creates; and since such negatives are a way of emphasising the opposite to themselves, they both positively affirm God's love for all creation.

The Bible, however, does not portray God as being devoid of all ability to hate. Certainly all forms of evil, and especially idolatry, are an abomination to him.[2] Moreover, if we love God, we too are to be sure to 'hate the thing that is evil'.[3] Such impersonal hatred by God is exactly what one would expect, and indeed desire of him. How awful it would be if God were indifferent to evil! Divine hatred, therefore, is an aspect of divine wrath, which is the reverse side of, and not the opposite of, divine love. It is indifference to either good or evil, which is its true opposite, for true love has a passionate nature, to which even we sinners can testify from our own experience.

There is trouble, however, for our Christian susceptibilities when the Bible appears to attribute to God, not only a general hatred of evil, but also a personal hatred of evil-doers. It is, we believe, just that ability to hold the former, without indulging the latter, that is so characteristic of God, as opposed to ourselves. In the Passion of Jesus we see this truth so clearly exemplified. Jesus may have condemned his enemies, the Pharisees and Sadducees, but he did not hate those who hated him. He may have driven out the money changers and the sellers of pigeons for desecrating the Temple, but that action in no way implied any hatred of them as individuals. In the Old Testament, however, there are texts, notably 'Jacob I loved, but Esau I hated',[4] that seem to suggest that God does hate individuals who opposed his will, and that therefore it is right and proper for us to hate evil-doers, as well as evil in general. This certainly was the interpretation that the spiritual leaders of our Lord's day put upon those texts, but we should note that Jesus was at pains to repudiate their teaching. We, he stressed, are not to hate our enemies; on the contrary we are to love them, and in so doing we are to reveal ourselves as being true children of God, who sends

2   Is 1:12-15, Jer 7:1-20   3   Ps 97:10   4   Mal 1:3, Rom 9:13

his sunshine and rain on the just and the unjust alike.[5] Hatred, taught St. Paul, is one of the works of evil to which the Holy Spirit is constantly opposed,[6] and St. John warned that, since the spirit of the world hates God, in this wicked world Christ's faithful followers will experience hatred too.[7] But we are never to return it. 'Be angry but do not sin; do not let the sun go down on your anger, and give no opportunity to the Devil.'[8] said St. Paul.

Some confusion, however, has been caused by the way in which the word 'hate' is sometimes used in both the Old and New Testaments to mean reject, or not to choose. This is indeed its proper meaning in that text already quoted in Malachi, where the prophet is saying that God chose Jacob, but did not choose Esau, in the working out of his covenant relationship with the Jewish people. The doctrine of divine election is central to the biblical revelation. God chose the Jews with whom he made a covenant, the Old Testament, and he chose not to include other nations in that covenant. However, as St. Paul makes clear in Romans 9-11 this election of the Jews was all part of God's loving purpose for all that 'he had made.' It was not a sign of divine favouritism, which was how the Jews mistakenly interpreted their election. Through Christ, St. Paul teaches that all mankind are to become part of God's elect, for Christ came to open a new covenant, the New Testament, which was to embrace all creation.[9] This new covenant was established by Christ in his life, death and resurrection, but it is the special calling of the Church to fulfil it down the ages, until it is made complete in Christ's coming again. It is revealed as a work of cosmic redemption, no less, for God 'hateth nothing that he has made.'

This use of the word 'hate' to describe rejection for a good purpose is also used by Jesus in the same characteristically biblical fashion, when talking of the cost of Christian discipleship. He said, 'If anyone comes after me and does not hate his own father and mother and wife and children and brothers and sisters, yes, and even his own life, he cannot be my disciple'.[10] St.

---

5   Matt 5:43-48   6   Gal 5:20   7   Jn 15:18-24   8   Eph 4:26
9   Eph Chapters 1-3   10 Lk 14:26

Matthew rephrases this to read, 'He who loves father or mother more than me is not worthy of me.'[11] If we are to help forward, and not hinder, the loving purposes of God, we too must be prepared to choose only the best, and in so doing accept the cost of rejecting anything, even that which is good, that interferes with that choice. In the doing of God's will we do not always have before us the easier choice of rejecting the bad for the good, any more than Christ himself had. He had to lay down his life upon the Cross, even as we may have to. The good can be the enemy of the best.

Although God 'hatest nothing that he has made' and is 'the God of all mercy', he nevertheless requires penitence of us, because without penitence his forgiveness cannot really reach our souls. God loves and forgives: he 'desireth not the death of a sinner, but rather that he may turn from his wickedness and live.'[12] Yet without repentance on our part, involving a change of direction in both thought and deed (in Greek 'metanoia') 'his mercy and loving kindness towards us' is blocked off from us. Sin creates a barrier between us and God, and it is part of his love for us that he requires that we repent, so that this barrier may be removed. Because he so greatly desires this, he himself gives us his grace to this end; 'by grace you have been saved.'[13] In Christ he meets us in our sinful state; he does not withdraw himself from us because we are sinners. However, repentance is required of us, indeed he calls us to it.[14] It is through repentance that we become fellow-workers with God in our own salvation, and are made able to know the joy of God's forgiveness, for the end of God's forgiveness is that 'we may come to his eternal joy.'

Such necessary things cannot be achieved in a short time. Metanoia is certainly the work of a life-time, and surely of longer duration even than that. For though we may hope that the process of metanoia, which is so essential for our eternal redemption, may continue beyond death, it still remains vital that we enter upon that spiritual activity of change while we

11 Matt 10:37   12 Prayer of Absolution in Morning and Evening Prayer
13 Eph 2:8   14 Mk 1:15

are here. This Collect, however, makes plain the greatness of the spiritual task involved, when it speaks of the need for us to acquire a new, as well as a contrite, heart.

Nevertheless, it is another of those absolutely central doctrines of the Gospel that this is indeed possible. Jesus spoke of the experience of being 'born again' and of its necessity to Nicodemus[15], and he does not ask of us the impossible. St. Paul confirms this teaching, when he declares that nothing counts for anything in the spiritual life 'but a new creation'.[16] To the Colossians, also, he talks of us putting on the 'new nature' that we have been given through Christ,[17] and to the Corinthians he says, 'If anyone is in Christ, he is a new creation (or new creature): the old has passed away, behold, the new has come.'[18] It is the ultimate work of Christ to make all things new, even to the creating of 'a new heaven and a new earth'.[19] Into this new creation Christ calls us, and the way we are to respond to this call is by faith and repentance. It is by faith that we apprehend the new, and by repentance that we slough off the old. By faith and repentance we can acquire a new, as well as a merely contrite heart.

According to the Collect, what we are to obtain is 'perfect remission and forgiveness.' If we translate 'perfect remission' as perfect release from sin's bondage, we can contrast remission with forgiveness. They are two sides of one whole, and it is certainly very important to realise that there are two sides to the matter of our forgiveness. There is the objective and the subjective side: we must be forgiven, and we must accept and experience that forgiveness. In our dealings with God the second is the problem. Such is God's love that his willingness to forgive us is certain and sure, but just because his love is so marvellous, our own sin against him looms that much larger. The greater the goodness of him whom we offend, the greater will be our fault. When we sin against another sinner, there is usually, as we

15 Jn 3:1-5   16 Gal 6:15   17 Col 3:10   18 2 Cor 5:17
19 Rev 21:1-7

may say, half-a-dozen of one and six of the other. But when we sin against God the fault is wholly and completely on our side. For this reason our guilt is much greater, and the difficulty for us to receive and experience forgiveness that much harder. 'Be of sin the double cure', wrote Toplady in his famous hymn.[20] What we need is both God's forgiveness and the inner conviction of it. Only then may we know the true joy of forgiveness. Jesus said, 'There is more joy in heaven over one sinner who repents than over ninety-nine righteous persons who need no repentance.'[21] This heavenly joy can only be ours too if we are able really to accept God's forgiveness, and so appreciate the wonder of it, free, gracious, undeserved, and given at such infinite cost to God. But first we must 'truly and earnestly repent',[22] and this too has its difficulties.

How can we best be helped to experience this double cure, which our Collect describes as 'perfect remission and forgiveness?' The traditional way is through the sacrament of Confession and Absolution before a priest. It is a proven way, used by very many. Although it is not necessary for all, it may be that many may never find the joy of 'perfect remission and forgiveness through Jesus Christ our Lord' any other way, and only ignorance of this sacrament is preventing them from discovering this for themselves. In the B.C.P. the use of sacramental confession is taught particularly in the section entitled 'The Visitation of the Sick', but it is also referred to in the rubric that is printed as part of the service of Holy Communion. In both places there is sensitive recognition of our spiritual need for 'a quiet conscience', and also wise counsel is given as to how we may experience it. The Anglican position on Sacramental Confession is summed up in the saying, 'All may, none must, and many should'. It is a time-honoured means of grace and a sacrament for which all who use it are deeply grateful. In the Church of England it is probably too little used, and there are numerous troubled souls who need to discover it. Ash Wednesday is a very traditional day for using this sacrament.

20 'Rock of Ages' by A M Toplady   21   Lk 15:7
22 Invitation to Confession in Holy Communion Service

The Collect speaks of us 'worthily lamenting our sins and acknowledging our wretchedness.' These words take us to the heart of the matter. We must come to grips with the fact that we are sinners, and with the nature of our own particular sins. We are much too prone to look at the evils of the world, and our own wrong doing in particular, with anger and frustration rather than with repentance. The tendency these days is to rationalise evil in general and our sins in particular, and to believe that to analyse them is to cure them. The Psalmist teaches us more wisely when he says of his sin, 'Against thee only have I sinned and done this evil in thy sight.'[23] We must regain a clear perception of the spiritual dimension in all the evils of the world, and the sins we personally commit. It is to God that we must go, for all our sins are sin against him, and only he can make our hearts clean and renew our spirits. The old prayer of the Psalmist is never outdated. 'Make me a clean heart, O God, and renew a right spirit within me'.[24] It is, as the Collect says, only from God, 'the God of all mercy', that we may 'obtain perfect remission and forgiveness.' Consequently the growth in the work of well-meaning but unbelieving counsellors and of unbelieving psychiatrists contains great spiritual dangers for those who put their trust in them. It is such an important truth that 'only God can forgive sins',[25] and therefore it is only from him that we can 'obtain (that) perfect remission and forgiveness', which our troubled souls so earnestly desire. (See also the commentary on the Collect for Trinity XXIV.)

23 Ps 51:4   24 Ps 51:10   25 Lk 5:21

LENT I

O Lord, who for our sake didst fast forty days and forty nights; give us grace to use such abstinence, that, our flesh being subdued to the Spirit, we may ever obey thy godly motions in righteousness, and true holiness, to thy honour and glory, who livest and reignest with the Father and the Holy Ghost, one God, world without end. Amen.

This is another Reformation Collect composed in 1549. As mentioned earlier, this is one of the two Sunday Collects to be addressed to Jesus. The other is that for Advent III.

First, we recall the forty days and nights of our Lord's temptations. This length of time appears quite frequently in the Bible, as does also the span of forty years. Perhaps we should not take either of them too literally. However, since the old Scriptures point to Christ, we should recognise the prophetic connection between the forty days and nights that Noah spent in the Ark, Moses on the mountain and Elijah in the wilderness with our Lord's temptations. In each God preserved these earlier men in their dangers, from water, fire and hunger, as he did Jesus from the Devil. So it is that the Church's season of Lent lasts for forty days.

In this Collect we hear of the need for the 'flesh' to be 'subdued to the Spirit'. In the New Testament the word 'flesh' (sarks) has usually a spiritual, rather than a physical meaning, in the same way as the word 'world' has. 'Flesh', therefore, should usually be understood as 'the spirit of our body', just as the 'world' should be understood as 'the spirit of the world'. So 'to set your mind on the flesh is death'[1] may be likened to 'if anyone loves the

1 Rom 8:6

world, the love of the Father is not in him'.[2] In the B.C.P. the flesh and the world are linked with the Devil as our great spiritual enemies, and they mean, when we speak of them together, the spirit of our bodies, the spirit of the world and the spirit of evil. The purpose of abstinence and fasting is to subdue the spirit of our bodies, our 'flesh', to the Spirit of God, so that we live lives that are obedient to his 'godly motions in righteousness and true holiness'.

We need to bear this biblical understanding of the word 'flesh' in mind, when, for instance, we say the Prayer of Humble Access before coming up to receive Communion. It also makes sense of that difficult, but important, passage in John 6, on which that prayer is obviously based. 'Truly, truly I say to you, unless you eat the flesh of the Son of Man and drink his blood, you have no life in you; he who eats my flesh and drinks my blood has eternal life, and I will raise him up at the last day... He who eats my flesh and drinks my blood abides in me, and I in him'.[3] It is the Spirit of the body of Jesus that we take to ourselves in Communion to become in us the spirit of our bodies. The Spirit of Jesus's body, his flesh (and blood), was wholly obedient to the Spirit of God. In this he was clearly different to us. Our flesh is a constant source of sin, and the Prayer of Humble Access rightly speaks of our 'sinful bodies'. In Jesus, however, his flesh was always obedient to the Spirit, through whom his body of flesh and blood had been miraculously conceived in the womb of Mary. His, therefore, was a life of 'true holiness', one wholly obedient in body and soul to the godly motions of the Spirit. So we 'eat the flesh of thy dear Son Jesus Christ' in Holy Communion in order that 'our sinful bodies may be made clean by his body', or in the words of this Collect, in order that 'our flesh may be subdued to the Spirit'.

Yes, it is mysterious and difficult! Perhaps it is no wonder we read, 'Many of his disciples, when they heard this, said, "This is a hard saying, who can listen to it?"[4] Nevertheless it is this teaching that alone makes sense of the Holy Communion Service. Through our partaking of Christ's 'flesh and

2   1 Jn 2:15   3   Jn 6:53-56   4   Jn 6:60

blood' we are being remade, body and soul, 'after the image of (the) Son, in order that he might be the first-born among many brethren'.[5] In so doing we are preparing ourselves, body and soul, for our life in heaven. In Baptism we were born again 'into Christ', body and soul; and in Communion we are renewed 'into Christ', body and soul, which are thereby both being 'preserved unto everlasting life'. Meanwhile our flesh must be 'subdued to the Spirit', and through these two great Sacraments we receive the grace, that we pray for in this Collect, to enable this to happen. (See also commentary for Easter III.)

In the Sermon on the Mount three of the main elements of the Jewish spiritual life are mentioned; fasting, prayer and almsgiving. Fasting has been recognised by religious men from time immemorial to be conducive to spiritual activity and is found in all religions. Prayer and fasting are described by Christ as the proper means of casting out evil, according to one version of the healing miracle that he performed after his Transfiguration.[6] Even so, it was the particular criticism levelled at Jesus by the Pharisees that he was lax in keeping the rules of fasting.[7] In his answer, however, he foretold that the time would come when his disciples would fast, and in the Acts of the Apostles there are several references to the practice.[8] The custom in our Lord's day was to fast on Mondays and Thursdays, and these would have been the two days in the week referred to by the Pharisee, who prayed in the temple.[9] No doubt in the earliest days of the Church this custom would have been retained. However, before long, as the gulf between Christians and Jews widened, Wednesdays and Fridays became the Christian days of fasting; Wednesday because it was the day of the betrayal, Friday because it was the day of the Crucifixion.

In the history of the Church fasting has played a prominent part, and in certain areas, especially in the East, it has been kept with special strictness. In the West a distinction between fasting and abstinence came into

---

5   Rom 8:29   6   Mk 9:29   7   Mk 2:18   8   Acts 10:30, 13:3
9   Lk 18:12

being in medieval times and was retained after the Reformation in England. Abstinence forbids one to eat certain foods, but does not require one to reduce the amount of food one eats. Fasting requires one to eat less than usual. In the 1928 revision of the Prayer Book the only days of genuine fasting enjoined are Ash Wednesday and Monday to Saturday in Holy Week. In addition, however, the season of Lent, the Ember Days, Rogation Days and the eves of five special festivals, which included Christmas and Whitsunday, and all Fridays that are not festival days, are all to be kept as days of abstinence. Nowadays, it must be said, although Ash Wednesday and Good Friday are kept by many as days of fasting, and the season of Lent, and perhaps Fridays, as times of abstinence, the other days enjoined in the Prayer Book have been largely forgotten.

With regard to the keeping of Lent, new ideas have largely replaced abstinence from meat, which was particularly mentioned in earlier times, even to the extent of being the subject of an Act of Parliament in 1548, by abstinence from other things, which may not necessarily include food or drink. This would seem to be exactly in keeping with the spirit of this Collect. We pray that we should 'use such abstinence' as is needed to subdue the cravings of the flesh to the demands of the spirit. To attack in ourselves a potential addiction to smoking or television watching, as well as such things as alcohol, sweets, chocolates or biscuits, by abstaining from them throughout the comparatively long period of Lent, and regularly on Fridays, would seem to be very much to the point. Moreover, since to do so, especially if these things are greatly enjoyed, will be hard, we will certainly need the grace of God to persevere. And it is especially for this grace that we pray in this Collect.

In Romans St. Paul puts before us another reason for abstinence; 'It is right not to eat meat or drink wine or do anything that makes my brother stumble'.[10] This text weighed particularly heavily on Christian consciences in the last century when drunkenness was such a major problem among the poor of our cities. Consequently Christians ministering or working in them pioneered the setting up of Temperance Societies throughout the land. In our modern society, however, we see two different versions of this abiding principle gaining ground. First, there is the regular call to Christians to fast for charity's sake, by the giving up of a meal in order to give the price of it to those who starve in other parts of the world. Fasting of this kind also shows clearly how fasting ought to be linked with prayer and almsgiving, a legacy from the Old Testament that our Lord confirmed.[11]

Secondly, because there is a growing feeling among Christians that many modern farming methods are cruel, some have become vegetarians, or at least abstainers from meat produced under factory farming methods, in order to make a Christian witness against what they believe is wrong. Nor is it only the fate of farm animals that distresses so many today. The long term effect of the use of pesticides and chemical fertilisers is such as to alter the nature of the soil and to create serious pollution problems, even though they have greatly increased yields. So they are moved to buy only what is organically grown. The Bible makes the important point that food and drink must primarily be accepted as God's gifts, and only secondarily as the reward of man's labour. Psalm 104 in particular speaks of this truth. First, we are to 'wait all upon (God)', who gives us our 'meat in due season', and, secondly, we are 'to go forth to (our) work and to (our) labour.' To abstain therefore from food gained in defiance of such spiritual insights is perceived increasingly to be a necessary Christian witness. It is seen to be not only necessary for conscience sake, but also as a prophetic gesture, since what is happening is full of danger for the future. 'As for sinners, they shall be consumed out of the earth',[12] for it will not support them. Moreover poisoned ground will bring forth poisoned food, just as surely as 'a bad tree will bear evil fruit'.[13]

---

10 Rom 14:15   11 Matt 6:16-18   12 Ps 104:23-35   13 Matt 7:17

The ultimate motive for fasting and abstinence is that we should 'obey thy godly motions in righteousness and true holiness to thy honour and glory.' St. Paul also links these two virtues: 'Put on the new nature created after the likeness of God in true righteousness and holiness.'[14] However, the voice of God guiding us in righteousness and holiness can only be heard when we have quietened the clamorous demands of the body. Of some in Philippi St. Paul said, 'Their god is the belly'[15], and we all know the temptation to obey our bodily demands before those of God. Self-indulgence is one of the greatest enemies of the spiritual life. Our physical nature is of God, but it is hard to dedicate it to him, and we usually only realise how self-indulgent we are when we try to assert authority over our bodies. St. Paul points to the struggles of athletes with admiration and commends their example to us,[16] and they merely struggle for earthly rewards.

The emphasis on our fasting and abstinence being to deepen our relationship with God, rather than to enhance our standing in the eyes of others, should be particularly noted. Jesus warned us against the kind of fasting that feeds our self-conceit, and, perversely, the truth is that the more faithfully we fast, the more likely it is that our fasting will feed our pride! 'They have their reward'[17] was our Lord's sad comment. The true test of its value in our lives is if it unites us more closely to God, as it does in the lives of the Saints. A true asceticism is one motivated only by obedience and love. In this matter it is particularly true that 'the written code kills, but the Spirit gives life.'[18] The text 'Let your light so shine before men, that they may see your good works and give glory to your Father who is in heaven'[19] can be thoroughly misleading, unless we fully realise we cannot fulfil it self-consciously. All we can consciously do is to live disciplined and obedient lives. Then the Spirit, which shines with its own secret light, and which always seeks to glorify the Father, will enable our lives to shine. 'When you fast, anoint your head and wash your face, that your fasting may not be seen by men, but by your Father, who is in secret; and your Father, who sees in secret, will reward you,'[20] is how our Lord put it on another occasion.

14 Eph 4:24   15 Phil 3:19   16 1 Cor 9:24-27   17 Matt 6:16
18 2 Cor 3:6   19 Matt 5:16   20 Matt 6:17

LENT II

Almighty God, who seest that we have no power of ourselves to help ourselves; Keep us both outwardly in our bodies and inwardly in our souls; that we may be defended from all adversities which may happen to the body, and from all evil thoughts which may assault and hurt the soul; through Jesus Christ our Lord. Amen.

This is a translation, with some changes, of the Gregorian Collect. One, however, is significant. The Latin Collect spoke of us being 'destitute of all virtue.' This has been rendered 'that we have no power of ourselves to help ourselves.'

Both our utter weakness and our dependence on God's strength is an often repeated theme in the Collects (eg. Epiphany IV). By implication this belief pervades all the Collects. God is strong, we are weak. This is the firm foundation on which the prayers of the Church are built, and we are not ashamed to declare it. Indeed, we glory in this truth, and we know that it is folly to imagine anything else. 'Let anyone who thinks that he stands take heed lest he fall.'[1] We rely on God for everything, and the root of sin is the refusal to recognise this, and to seek to be independent of him.

From the first pages of the Bible,[2] this truth is emphasised. Perhaps the famous story of the Prodigal Son expresses it best of all.[3] 'Father, give me the share of the property that falls to me... Then he gathered all he had and took his journey into a far country.' This desire to be independent of God is the root cause of our troubles. We are made free, but not independent of God. Our freedom is given us as a gift, so that we in turn may freely give our wills to God, and spend our bodies gladly and willingly in his service. If we do so, we shall experience the peace and joy of conscious dependence

1 1 Cor 10:12   2 Gen 3   3 Lk 15:11-32

on God. But foolishly we use our freedom to attempt to escape from God's loving protection and wise control. The prodigal, therefore, looks out at us from our mirrors for, from time to time, in one way or another, we have all sought to take that journey away from the Father. We need, however, to 'come to ourselves' and return declaring, 'Father, I have sinned against heaven and before you.' This recognition 'that we have no power of ourselves to help ourselves' is, therefore, something that we all must learn, and probably often relearn, as we go through life.

It is, perhaps, more difficult than it has ever been to learn this vital spiritual lesson today, because of the power science and technology puts into our hands. In stressing, as we do in this Collect, that we need God to 'keep' and 'defend' us, we seem to push up against the whole weight of the spirit of the age. We should notice, however, that the Collect declares that it is God, rather than we, who sees this truth so clearly! And this should comfort us. Indeed, this is the truth that guarantees the Gospel. It is because God always knew of our need that he sent his Son, a knowledge that he revealed beforehand in the Old Testament.[4] His knowledge of all our needs is the basis of God's compassion and mercy towards us. 'Your heavenly Father knows that you need them all'.[5] The whole Bible declares that God certainly sees that we have needs, both physical and spiritual, and is concerned that we are helped in all of them. However, in order that we may receive God's help, two spiritual attitudes are required of us, faith and repentance. We can only pray this Collect, therefore, with sincerity, if we do so in a spirit of faith and repentance. The Gospels show that Jesus was unable to help some 'because of their unbelief'.[6] Equally, 'if we say that we have no sin we deceive ourselves'.[7] Without faith and repentance we block the way for God 'to keep us both outwardly in our bodies and inwardly in our souls'.

The main petition twice contrasts body and soul, while at the same time emphasising their mutual importance. As we have already stressed, God

4   Jer 31:31-34   5   Matt 6:32   6   Mk 6:5-6   7   1 Jn 1:10

is concerned for the needs of both. It is through the body that the spirit is made active. St. Paul instructs us 'to present our bodies as a living sacrifice, holy and acceptable to God, which is our spiritual worship.'[8] To live clean, disciplined lives physically is part of 'our spiritual worship.' Our bodies affect our souls, just as surely as our thoughts and beliefs govern our actions and affect our health. Wholeness and holiness are related words, and much good has come from the modern emphasis on this truth.

It is possible, however, to misrepresent this truth. It is wrong to so stress the connection between physical wholeness and spiritual holiness as to make them identical. Some do so to the extent of making those that are physically handicapped feel they must be guilty of sin, perhaps unrealised, to be so afflicted, and more especially is this so if, after prayer, they are not healed. Certainly Jesus declared that some sickness is the result of sin, and this is obviously the case. So to the man he healed at the Sheep Gate he said, 'See, you are well. Sin no more, that nothing worse befall you.'[9] But he also taught how affliction need have nothing to do with sin; indeed, he looked on it rather as an opportunity out of which God might be glorified. To the question, 'Rabbi, who sinned, this man or his parents, that he was born blind?', he answered, 'It was not that this man sinned or his parents, but that the works of God might be made manifest in him.'[10]

The main value of good health is that it enables us to serve God and our neighbour actively. It can, therefore, only be properly appreciated in its context as part of the life that God wants us to live. Health is no different from wealth in this respect. To obtain it and keep it is not an end in itself, but only a means whereby a greater end may be served. That greater end is the glory of God, for that is the purpose of all creation. The premise of S. Ignatius Loyola is right. 'Man', he writes in the opening words of his Spiritual Exercises, 'was created to praise, reverence and serve God.' Everything finds its true value in the extent to which it fulfils its part in this overriding purpose. Bodily health and human happiness are no

8 Rom 12:1   9 Jn 5:14   10 Jn 9:2-3

exceptions. To a non-Christian, health and wealth are obviously and absolutely good; sickness and poverty are obviously and absolutely bad. Christians, however, cannot view these things in this simplistic way.

To live out the true balance between the physical and the spiritual in our life, however, is not easy. That our religious convictions can make us sometimes cruel and unloving is well exemplified by the Pharisees's opposition to Jesus healing on the sabbath day. It can make us look foolish too! 'You hypocrites!' said Jesus. 'Does not each of you on the sabbath untie his ox or his ass from the manger and lead it away to water it? And ought not this woman....... whom Satan has bound for eighteen years be loosed from her bond on the sabbath day?'[11] Yet that Jesus put our spiritual welfare before our physical welfare as a matter of principle is also plain. 'If your right eye causes you to sin', he said, 'pluck it out; it is better for you to enter into the kingdom of God with one eye than with two eyes to be thrown into hell'[12]

Such teaching is confirmed by St. Paul, who, though a healer, not only taught, but was himself taught by God, the limited value of bodily health and physical well being. He tells us graphically of how he asked God to heal him of some serious affliction that appeared to be grievously hindering his ministry, but was clearly told that it was not God's will that he should be healed.[13] Then, of his trials in prison he wrote, 'I want you to know, brethren, what has happened to me has really served to advance the Gospel', so he rejoices at them. 'Yes, and I shall rejoice'.[14] St. Paul's teaching on slavery is also relevant to this matter: 'Were you a slave when called? Never mind. But if you can gain your freedom, avail yourself of the opportunity'.[15] After the same token we can say, "If you are sick, never mind, but get well if you can. It is all a matter of how best you can serve God." In the final analysis nothing else really matters.

---

11 Lk 13:15-16   12 Mk 9:47   13 2 Cor 12:8-10   14 Phil 1:12-19
15 1 Cor 7:21

We pray as we approach Holy Communion, 'Cleanse the thoughts of our hearts.' The 'evil thoughts' that matter are of the heart. An evil thought does not harm us unless it is welcomed into the heart. It may knock on the heart's door, but while it remains outside it is merely a temptation. At all costs we must not welcome it in, and let it stay there. Only 'what comes out of a man is what defiles a man.'[16] So long as we keep it out, it cannot defile us. Then we can 'draw near with a true heart in full assurance of faith, with our hearts sprinkled clean from an evil conscience.'[17] And what a comfort that is!

However, this is not easily done. As we recognised in this prayer, we do not have sufficient power of ourselves to protect us from all the powers of evil. All the time we need God's help and protection, and such self-knowledge motivates this wise prayer. As we pray it, therefore, we must lay a proper emphasis on those familiar closing words, 'through Jesus Christ our Lord'. (And is there not a temptation whenever we pray the Collects to fail to do this?) It is Jesus who must be 'the guardian of our souls'[18], and the glorious truth is that he delights to be so. Our task is to co-operate by faith and obedience. He 'stands at the door' of our souls 'and knocks'[19], but he cannot be truly the guardian of our souls while he remains outside. We do not need him simply in the role of a sentry to warn us from outside our lives. We need him deep within ourselves, acting as our Lord. So we must let him in, right in, and if we do so we know he will gladly enter, and, as he says, 'sup with us'. To our ears the reference here to Holy Communion is unmistakable. It is in that blessed mystery that we take Jesus into ourselves, so that he may be 'our great Redeemer, our Friend and Brother'[20]. This is the truth that makes regular reception of Holy Communion so essential to our lives. Through it Jesus comes to save us from all 'that may assault and hurt the soul', for which protection we are praying here. This is the mysterious way that he himself has chosen to 'keep us' and 'defend' us.

---

16 Mk 7:20   17 Heb 10:22   18 I Pet 2 : 25   19 Rev 3 : 20
20 The Prayer of St. Richard

This Collect particularly stresses the unity of body and soul, as we have said. If we keep this unity firmly in mind we will not only be helped to react properly to human problems such as sickness and misfortune, but also to understand the great theological doctrines that concern Christ. The unity of body and soul in him is of crucial importance to the truth of the Incarnation, the Crucifixion, the Resurrection and the Ascension. All must have been physical as well as spiritual events, if they were really human events. To maintain the unity of body and soul in Christ is just as vital as to maintain it in ourselves. To do so will save us from heretical beliefs about him. The Athanasian Creed puts the truth succinctly. Jesus is 'perfect God and perfect man, of a reasonable soul and human flesh subsisting'.

This unity of body and soul in both Christ and us also makes all the difference to our understanding of life after death. We believe in 'the resurrection of the body,' and not just in the living on of our souls in some disembodied state. Like Christ, we shall have after death a resurrection body, that is a body suitable for the requirements of life then, whatever they may be.[21] In the service for Christian Burial it is stressed that what is taking place as we inter or cremate our loved ones is being done 'in sure and certain hope' that there is a resurrection experience awaiting them beyond death, because of what Jesus has done for us. We particularly mention there the changing of 'our vile body that it may be like unto his glorious body, according to the mighty working, whereby he is able to subdue all things to himself'.

However, neither in life nor in death are we primarily, let alone exclusively, concerned for our bodies. Our spirits are supremely what matter, and they too can be 'vile'. Can they be made like unto his glorious Spirit? That surely is what above all we hope for 'according to his mighty working'. The Gospel does undoubtedly give us this hope, for the power of God is such as it can 'subdue all things to himself'. Such great thoughts help us to anticipate our own death in a spirit of hope, as well as comfort us as we bury those we love.

21 1 Cor 15:44

It is also apposite to recall here that when we receive the elements in Holy Communion the priest prays that through them Christ may preserve our 'bodies and souls unto everlasting life'. This prayer, therefore, that God may 'keep us both outwardly in our bodies and inwardly in our souls' is a prayer that has meaning for our life in both this world and the next.

LENT III

We beseech thee, Almighty God, look upon the hearty desires of thy humble servants, and stretch forth the right hand of thy Majesty, to be our defence against all our enemies; through Jesus Christ our Lord. Amen.

This Collect is Gregorian, and it may be noticed that it is very similar to that for Epiphany III and for Trinity III. The words 'against all our enemies' were added in translation.

Look upon the hearty desires of thy humble servants', we pray. This means, of course, the desires of our hearts, and it is perhaps likely that none of us really wants them to be too closely scrutinised! A far more natural prayer would seem to be that with which we start Holy Communion, 'Cleanse the thoughts of our hearts.' 'Our hearty desires' are the truest indication of who we are, for, as Bishop Philip Loyd has said, 'Our hearts are a workshop in which our characters are forged.'[1] That on which we set our hearts has immense power over us, even creative power. In the end it makes us whatever we become.

'What person knows a man's thoughts, except the spirit of the man which is in him.'[2] We can know our own hearty desires because we are spiritual beings. We have the ability to look at ourselves and analyse ourselves and, therefore, to repent and believe, 'to refuse the evil and choose the good'.[3] We are self-creating beings in the sense that we can form our own characters by choosing on what to set our hearts. This is the measure of our responsibility to our Creator for what we think about and for what we desire. 'Keep your heart with all vigilance, for from it flow the springs of life.'[4] (See further commentary for Trinity III.)

---

1 The life according to St. John, by Philip Loyd   2 1 Cor 2:11
3 Is 7:16   4 Prov 4:23

Next, we pray that into this situation God will come to help us. 'Stretch forth the right hand of thy Majesty', we pray. At God's right hand is Christ; he is 'the man of thy right hand',[5] and he is the Word of God incarnate. 'The Word of God is living and active, sharper than any two-edged sword, piercing to the division of soul and spirit... and discerning the thoughts and intentions of the heart.'[6] It is the Word of God in the person of Jesus that must come and speak to our hearts and cleanse the desires that form there, which in their turn form us.

The special condemnation of Jesus was for those who had hardened their hearts. This was his condemnation both of the Pharisees and the Apostles alike. Both were perversely uncomprehending. They refused to accept and understand him, because they had set their hearts upon having a false Messiah. They would not do what he said, because they believed in false ideals and selfish hopes. Again and again it was this perversity that saddened Jesus, and which made him condemn those he loved. 'Do you not yet perceive and understand? Are your hearts hardened? Having eyes do you not see, and having ears do you not hear? And do you not remember?'[7] As God looks on us and into the desires of our hearts, must he not say the same? Like those who knew the Lord in the days of his earthly ministry, we too look at his deeds and words in the Gospels and refuse to apply the lessons that they teach us, because of our hardness of heart. 'To-day if ye will hear his voice, harden not your hearts.'[8] We must recognise the note of urgency in the Psalmist's words. They are sure to have relevance for us.

What we must learn to do is to lay our heart close to the sacred heart of Jesus, and to seek, as it were, to adjust our heart-beat to his. The heart of Jesus is a divine, yet a human heart. He too ' learned obedience by the things which he suffered.'[9] His heart is not too high for us, for he bids us come to him, 'and learn of me, for I am meek and lowly in heart.'[10] We are

5 Ps 80:17   6 Heb 4:12   7 Mk 8:17-18   8 Ps 95:8
9 Heb 5:8   10 Matt 11:29

invited to know the fellowship of the heart of Jesus, that is the fellowship of his inner spirit. St. Paul said to the Philippians, 'I have you in my heart.'[11] Jesus says the same to us, and what joy if we will say the same to him! 'My heart is ready, my heart is ready; I will sing and give praise with the best member that I have.'[12] This best member is our heart. 'Where your treasure is, there will your heart be also,'[13] said Jesus.. Our treasure is in fact Jesus himself, and if he really is, we will have him in our heart. It is these thoughts and truths that lie at the heart of the age-old devotion to the Sacred Heart of Jesus.

The result of our union with the sacred heart of Jesus is that we are defended from the spiritual enemies that attack us. St. Paul talks about divine protection in terms of putting on armour. To love as Jesus loves, to want what Jesus wants, and to have the hearty desires for ourselves that Jesus has for us is to know an inner protection, a protection at depth that is the surest of all armour. The prayer of Jesus in John 17 is for all his disciples, those who knew him by sight and us who know him by faith alone. 'I am praying for them.'[14] It is a wonderful inspiration that we should be borne upon the heart of Jesus to the Father. The author of the Epistle to the Hebrews writes with supreme confidence of the power that flows from those loving prayers to defend us 'against all our enemies.' 'Consequently he is able for all time to save those who draw near to God through him, since he always lives to make intercession for them.'[15] So we have confidence because we know that 'the hearty desires' of Jesus, set at the right hand of God's Majesty, are that we may be defended from all our enemies. (See also commentary for Trinity III.)

This defence, however, is not such as will leave us with no battles of our own to fight. The devotion to the Sacred Heart of Jesus does have a tendency towards a quietism that has no place in the New Testament. 'I do not pray

11 Phil 1:7   12 Ps 108:1   13 Matt 6:21   14 Jn 17:9
15 Heb 7:25

that thou shouldest take them out of the world, but that thou shouldest keep them from the Evil One.'[16] The desire of Jesus is that we should know the joy of real victory. He enters our life to help us win what will be our victory, although without him we could not win it. 'This is the victory that overcomes the world, our faith. Who is he that overcomes the world, but he that believes that Jesus is the Son of God?'[17] Coming close to Jesus is not simply to shelter within the protection of his power and his love. It is rather to be sent out in new power and with new love to overcome our enemies, not simply to be defended from them. 'Above all taking the shield of faith with which you can quench all the flaming darts of the Evil One.'[18]

In this Collect then we ask God to look upon our hearty desires. Those hearty desires must be that we keep close to the sacred heart of Jesus. From it, broken for the sins of men, pours, however, the infinite power of his love. That will defend us and strengthen us and bring us to everlasting life. 'Let not your hearts be troubled, neither let them be afraid.'[19] 'You have sorrow now, but I will see you again and your hearts will rejoice, and no one will take your joy from you.'[20]

16 Jn 17:15   17 1 Jn 5:4-5   18 Eph 6:16   19 Jn 14:27
20 Jn 16:22

LENT IV

Grant, we beseech thee, Almighty God, that we, who for our evil deeds do worthily deserve to be punished, by the comfort of thy grace may mercifully be relieved; through our Lord and Saviour Jesus Christ. Amen.

From early times this Sunday was known as Refreshment Sunday, and it was marked by a relaxation of the Lenten rule. The well-known modern term, Mothering Sunday, comes from the Epistle, where we are taught that the Church is 'the mother of us all.' This Collect, which is similar to that for Septuagesima, is basically the Gregorian Collect for this Sunday. In translation, however, two changes were made. In 1549 the adjective 'evil' was added, and in 1662, more importantly, the verb 'deserve'. So in the composition of this Collect we can trace an interesting progression of thought. The Gregorian Collect in the Sarum Missal acknowledged that 'we were worthily punished for our behaviour'; in 1549 Cranmer amended this to read 'which for our evil deeds are worthily punished'; then finally Cosin guides us now to acknowledge that 'for our evil deeds (we) worthily deserve to be punished'. In this case each small additional amendment has improved the prayer.

First, we declare before God that we 'worthily deserve to be punished.' This surely is a remarkable admission that merits our careful consideration. We have, however, already considered the theme of divine punishment in the Collect for Septuagesima. The wording of the opening relative clauses in both Collects is very similar. There is little difference in declaring that we are 'justly punished' and that we 'worthily deserve to be punished.' Behind both admissions lies the realisation that it would be a very bad thing for us, if we were saved from all punishment for our sins, but not saved from sin itself. God, however, being loving and wise as well as just, will not allow this to happen. He punishes us lest we be confirmed in our sins, and for this we should be grateful. His punishment is part of his redeeming activity, not in conflict with it. Such truths are the justification for, and the proper purpose of, all punishment.

It is, however, all part of our sinfulness that our natural reaction to punishment is quite different to the attitude adopted in this Collect. No ordinary person welcomes punishment! 'For the moment all discipline seems painful rather than pleasant; later it yields the peaceful fruit of righteousness to those who are trained by it.'[1] That is the point; we must allow ourselves to learn our lesson. This willingness to be 'trained by it' is a vital ingredient in repentance, which should lead us on to amendment of life. It is not Christian penitence, either to resent punishment, or to bear it with resignation like the hardened criminal, who will do his sentence, and then, when occasion arises, return to his old ways, hoping to get away with it this time. Such attitudes characterise worldly sorrow, which is simply the sorrow of being caught out in wrongdoing.

True repentance leads us to accept any punishment for sin with humility, even gladly. When we recognise our guilt and are truly sorry for our sin, we confirm in our hearts the sentence passed upon us. This is St. Paul's point when he writes, 'Let God be true though every man be false, as it is written, "That thou mayest be justified in thy words and prevail when thou art judged." If our wickedness serves to show the justice of God, what shall we say? That God is unjust to inflict wrath upon us? By no means.'[2] Rather, he seems to say, that it would be better that we should all perish and that God remain just. If God is false, the very foundations of true life have crumbled. Therefore none should hope for the kind of forgiveness that would be at the expense of God's justice.

However, such arguments do seem what one can only describe as heavily theological. Romans 3 does not make heart-warming reading! Even as we

1   Heb 12:11   2   Rom 3:4-5

accept God's justice, we cannot but hope for his mercy, especially if we believe that God's justice is part of his love. Indeed we can only accept God's justice willingly, if we believe that it is. Moreover, in the end, as we consider God's inevitable judgement upon our lives, we must all approach it in the hope of mercy, rather than the hope of justice. No doubt we should in penitence accept God's justice, knowing that for 'our evil deeds we worthily deserve to be punished', but the Gospel also encourages us to hope for a mercy that will 'triumph over justice'.[3] The prodigal did well to approach his father so humbly, but even as he did so, did he not secretly hope for more than he asked for, even if what he received was beyond his wildest dreams? Cannot we do the same? This Collect encourages us to do so.

The second part of our Collect speaks of 'the comfort of thy grace.' Grace is the power of God operating in us to change us into the kind of people he would have us be. If we were so changed, we would cease to 'worthily deserve to be punished.' This grace of God is at work in all who turn to him in faith and repentance. It is at work in us both to help us repent of our sins and avoid evil, and also to embrace that which is good and so become good. It enables us to 'hate the thing that is evil'[4] and to love, as well as 'think on', whatever is true, honourable, just, pure, lovely and gracious.[5] In all this there is great comfort for those guided by God's grace. It is then as the Psalmist says, 'His soul shall dwell at ease.'[6]

But the grace of God will lead us into uncomfortable activities also. As we, through the grace of God, become less and less deserving of punishment, we will be called to be concerned for those who are, and even to share in their fate. This is an aspect of the demand that we take up our cross, which is part of Christ's Cross. The Crucifixion of Christ shows us how the punishment for our sin falls upon God, as well as upon us. Because God is love, this must be so. Loving parents suffer, if they have to punish their

3   Jas 2:13 A.V.   4   Ps 97:10   5   Phil 4:8   6   Ps 25:12

children for wrongdoing, and the more loving the parents and the more grievous the wrongdoing, the more real will be the parents' pain. So love always involves suffering if opposed by evil, even to the point where love will desire to take the punishment upon itself, rather than allow the objects of its love to perish on account of their evil deeds. Is it not this truth that we see in operation in the Crucifixion, when 'the Son of man gave his life as a ransom for many'[7] and 'bore our sins in his body on the tree'[8]?

So the grace of God drives us out to share the fate of sinners, and to serve them in so doing. It does not only make us hate sin, but also helps us to love sinners. Through the operation of God's grace we are called to share in his redeeming work. There is much comfort to be had in answering this call, even though it can, in a most literal sense, involve us in great discomfort. Essentially this is a spiritual comfort, felt chiefly because we are bringing comfort to others. It is described by St. Paul to the Corinthians in all its essential paradox. 'Blessed be... the Father of mercies and God of all comfort, who comforts us in all our afflictions, so that we may be able to comfort those, who are in any affliction, with the comfort with which we ourselves are comforted. If we share abundantly in Christ's sufferings, so through Christ we share abundantly in comfort too.'[9]

Lastly, we pray that, although we deserve to be punished, nevertheless we may yet 'mercifully be relieved.' The Latin word 'respiremus', here translated 'be relieved', means more literally 'be given a breathing space' or, as we might say colloquially, a breather, a rest. It is from this word, and also from the Gospel for the day, which is the story of our Lord feeding the five thousand, that we get the traditional title for this mid-Lent Sunday, Refreshment Sunday. We know that it is as much a necessity of God's mercy that we be relieved, as it is a necessity of God's justice that we be punished.

7   Mk 10:45   8   1 Pet 2:24   9   2 Cor 1:3-5

So it is that the Collect and the Gospel both point to the Eucharist. There we are to find our refreshing food. It is food suitable for sinners 'who worthily deserve to be punished.' He came to us in our 'sinful flesh', though he lived in it without sin. He was 'made sin, who knew no sin',[10] and he shared our punishment. And now he continues to come to us in the Eucharist. In it we go to him, meet him there, and receive him into ourselves. As we do so we may use words of St. Paul and adapt them to our need. 'By God's will I may come to you and be refreshed'.[11] From his altar throne Jesus holds his arms out wide in welcome to all who know that they 'worthily deserve to be punished', and who now seek 'the comfort of his grace' in penitence and faith. 'Come unto me all that are in travail and are heavy laden, and I will refresh you'[12], he says to us. Then he bids us go forth in faith and bring 'the comfort of his grace' to others. 'Through Christ (God) reconciled us to himself and gave us the ministry of reconciliation... so we are ambassadors for Christ, God making his appeal through us'[13] is how St. Paul describes this truth. We, therefore, who pray here 'mercifully (to) be relieved through our Lord and Saviour Jesus Christ' must accept that the main way this prayer will be answered for us is for us in turn to share our sense of comfort and our faith with others.[14]

10 2 Cor 5 : 21   11 Rom 15:32   12 Matt 11:28 (A.V.)
13 2 Cor 5 : 18, 20   14 Matt 28 : 18-20

LENT V

We beseech thee, Almighty God, mercifully to look upon thy people; that by thy great goodness they may be governed and preserved evermore, both in body and soul; through Jesus Christ our Lord. Amen.

This is a loose translation of the Gregorian Collect. (See commentary) It is not very distinctive of Passion Sunday, and in 1689 a substitute was written by Bishop Patrick, which was never, however, authorised. In other Anglican Provinces this Collect has been changed for one considered more appropriate for the day. As this was the Collect in the Sarum Missal it was used by Cranmer.

———————————

'We beseech thee, Almighty God, mercifully to look upon thy people.' A frequent petition in the Collects is that God should look upon us. 'Look upon our infirmities,' (Epiphany III) we pray, and 'look upon our hearty desires'. (Lent III) The idea that God looks upon us all is basic to our faith. 'The Lord looked down from heaven, and beheld all the children of men; from the habitation of his dwelling he considereth all them that dwell on the earth.' His glance is penetrating, for 'he fashioneth all the hearts of them, and understandeth all their works.'[1] He looks on us with love. 'And Jesus, looking upon him, loved him.'[2] But he looks with sorrow, for he knows what we have done and how we have failed. 'And the Lord turned and looked upon Peter.'[3] Yet he looks also upon us with hope, knowing of what by his grace we are capable. 'And Jesus, looking upon them said, 'With men it is impossible, but not with God.'[4]

God looks upon us, then, with eyes of understanding, love, sorrow and hope. We in our turn are to keep our gaze fixed upon him, for 'in thy light, shall we see light.'[5] 'I will lift up mine eyes unto the hills, from whence cometh

1 Ps 33:13-14   2 Mk 10:21   3 Lk 22:61   4 Mk 10:27
5 Ps 36:9

my help. My help cometh even from the Lord, who hath made heaven and earth.'[6] 'Looking to Jesus, the pioneer and perfector of our faith'[7] we are to be like Moses, who journeyed on, 'for he endured as seeing him who is invisible.'[8] We ask God to look upon us so that he may govern and preserve us, both in body and soul. We look to him so that we may be obedient to his least wish, knowing that our salvation depends upon the readiness with which we do his will. 'Behold, even as the eyes of servants look unto the hand of their masters, and as the eyes of a maiden look unto the hand of her mistress; even so our eyes wait upon the Lord our God.'[9] Our safety is in the doing of God's will. We are so often tempted to be content with lesser standards, with solutions that are the result of mere expediency. We know really that to do this is fatal. 'Lord, what wilt thou have me to do?'[10] This is the real question that we should be constantly and instinctively asking, and it will only be natural for us to do so, if we look constantly and instinctively towards him.

'Governed and preserved'; God's goodness is such that the one follows naturally on the other. In the Latin the idea of being governed is linked only with the body and of being preserved only with the mind. In translation the two verbs are united, and consequently so are we, the word 'soul' being preferred to 'mind'. This surely is an improvement. If God governs our unruly wills and affections, he will also preserve and protect us. We are protected, first, from ourselves. The prodigal returned to his father and desired to work for him under his orders, for he no longer trusted himself. 'Treat me as one of your hired servants.'[11] It was not only as a punishment, we may suppose, that he wanted to be demeaned, but as a protection against further folly. How greatly we need this protection! Evil is a form of madness, as the Gospel stories make plain. 'I do not understand my own actions. For I do not do what I want, but I do the very thing I hate.'[12] A heavy drinker handing the key of the pantry over to his wife is only doing what we must do to God, as we hand over our will freely to him, for we have come to realise that 'in his service is perfect freedom.' There is no safety for body and soul, except in conscious and constant dependence on 'his great goodness.' 'I know that his commandment is eternal life.'[13]

Secondly, we are protected from all the powers of evil. 'Lord save me.'[14] 'Save, Lord, we are perishing.'[15] The story of Jesus rescuing his disciples on the sea of Galilee makes vivid and visible the cry of the Psalmist: 'Save me, O God, for the waters are come in, even unto my soul. I stick fast in the deep mire, where no ground is: I am come into deep waters, so that the floods run over me.'[16] 'The goodness of God endureth yet daily,'[17] and it reaches out to us, like the hand of Jesus to save Peter from drowning. Nothing can harm us, if we keep looking to God for help and protection. We have reached solid ground, and the floods can batter against us as they will. 'Everyone then, who hears these words of mine and does them, will be like a wise man, who built his house upon the rock; and the rain fell, and the floods came and the wind blew and beat upon that house, and it did not fall, because it had been founded on the rock.'[18]

What we ask for ourselves, we ask for the whole people of God. In the Latin (familia) the word translated 'people' in this Collect is really 'family'. It is so translated in the Collect for Good Friday, but for no obvious reason it has been changed here. The people of God are members of his family, made members through faith in his only Son. Rule within this family, as within every good family, is maintained by love, and protection also is afforded through the love that we feel for one another. In our unity we are governed and preserved. Love, then, is both the law and the unifying spirit governing and preserving God's people. 'Speaking the truth in love, we are to grow up in every way into him, who is the head, into Christ, from whom the whole body, joined and knit together by every joint with which it is supplied, when each part is working properly makes bodily growth, and upbuilds itself in love.'[19]

13 Jn 12:50   14 Matt 14:30   15 Mk 8:25   16 Ps 69:1-2
17 Ps 52:2   18 Matt 7:24-25 19 Eph 4:15-16

Such a text inevitably points us to the Eucharist. There we are all joined to Christ, there we recognise his headship of the family of God and his lordship over ourselves, and there the principle is established that what we do as individuals we also always do as members of a family. The words of the prayer of oblation in the B.C.P. are particularly illustrative of this point. 'And here we offer and present unto thee, O Lord, ourselves, our souls and bodies, to be a reasonable, holy and lively sacrifice unto thee; humbly beseeching thee that all we who are partakers of this Holy Communion may be fulfilled with thy grace and heavenly benediction.' Our offering is personal and corporate. The sacrifice of Christ that avails for us is both personal and corporate. Nowhere is this truth more vividly demonstrated than in the Eucharist. We pray in this Collect that God may preserve us 'both in body and soul'. Such language sounds so very personal, and yet the prayer here is specifically a corporate prayer for 'thy people', the family of God. This family is seen then as having a 'body and soul' of its own to whose life and health we all contribute. It is especially in and through the Eucharist that 'the great goodness' of God, that is his grace, is enabled to 'govern and preserve' the family of God 'both in body and soul,' and all of us who are members of it, for we are the Body of Christ.

The fact that our thoughts on this Collect have led us to the Eucharist, where we claim the eternal benefits that derive from Christ's sacrifice on the Cross, show that the words of this Collect are not really so inappropriate for Passion Sunday after all. On this Sunday we look with special devotion at the Cross. We are reminded not only how our salvation was won, but also of our Lord's demand that, if we are to follow him, we must be willing and eager to take up our cross too. If we are to be 'governed and preserved evermore, both in body and soul' obedience is required both of his family and of all the members of it. This sacrifice of obedience is the 'lively sacrifice' of 'ourselves, our souls and bodies' about which the prayer of oblation speaks. Only as we make that sacrifice of obedience can we as

138

individuals, and the Church as a family, be sure to live in safety under God's rule and protection, 'governed and preserved evermore' by him.

The word 'evermore', however, leads us to consider how ultimately what we want is humanly speaking impossible, for we want protection from death. Death is our last and apparently ever-victorious enemy, but the glorious truth is that in Christ we may even know protection in it, if not from it. 'Then comes the end', says St. Paul, 'when Christ delivers the kingdom to God the Father after destroying every rule and every authority and power. For he must rule until he has put all his enemies under his feet. The last enemy to be destroyed is death.'[20] One of the greatest truths of the Gospel is that death has been defeated or, rather, 'death is swallowed up in victory'.[21] There can be no consideration more appropriate for Passion Sunday than to consider how Christ has transformed totally the truth about death.

So it is that we may approach death no longer as an 'enemy' but now as a 'friend', through which we may discover all that we are here praying for, which is to be 'preserved evermore, both in body and soul'. Rupert Brooke, who served in the Great War, like so many others had to face the reality of sudden death, and indeed soon after he wrote these beautiful lines it claimed him.

> War knows no power. Safe shall be my going,
> Secretly armed against all death's endeavour;
> Safe though all safety's lost, safe where men fall,
> And if these poor limbs die, safest of all.

They movingly express a Christian's confidence as he faces his last enemy, even though the writer did not actually claim to be one.

---

20 1 Cor 15:24-26   21 1 Cor 15:54

THE SUNDAY NEXT BEFORE EASTER

Almighty and everlasting God, who, of thy tender love towards mankind, hast sent thy Son, our Saviour Jesus Christ, to take upon him our flesh and to suffer death upon the cross, that all mankind should follow the example of his great humility; Mercifully grant that we may both follow the example of his patience, and also be made partakers of his resurrection; through the same Jesus Christ our Lord. Amen.

This is the first Sunday in which the Sunday Collect derives from the Gelasian Sacramentary, though in the Sarum Missal it followed the version in the Gregorian Sacramentary. In translation two significant changes were made. In its opening the phrase 'of thy tender love' was added, and the repetition of the word 'follow' in the petition, as well as the invocation, was not in the original. Both changes, however, add greatly to the Collect's beauty and devotional force. (See commentary).

This Sunday nowadays is always referred to as Palm Sunday, rather than its rather cumbersome official title. The title Palm Sunday is medieval, even though the medieval Proper emphasised the Passion and made no mention of the particular events of the day, which were read as the Gospel for Advent Sunday; and the B.C.P. follows this arrangement. The Sunday owes its title to the ancient custom of carrying palms in procession and using them for decoration, and it was some of these palms that were later to provide the ashes that were used on the following Ash Wednesday.

Palm Sunday is the fortieth day after Ash Wednesday, and so the official end of Lent. Holy Week, therefore, is really a mini-season on its own, although usually thought of as part of Lent. Throughout it the Collect for Palm Sunday is used, until Good Friday. One must say, however, that it is a great pity the B.C.P. provides no special Collects for the other days in

Holy Week, particularly Maundy Thursday. The American B.C.P. does so to its enrichment.

The motive of 'tender love towards mankind', that is ascribed to the Father for sending the Son, comes as an addition to the Latin Collect, and is surely a welcome one. Our atonement was the consequence of God's tender love for us. It is right that this is stressed at the start of Holy Week. 'For God so loved the world that he gave his only Son that, whoever believes in him should not perish, but have eternal life.'[1] That is, perhaps, the best known text in the Bible. The love of God precedes our faith, and our faith responds to it. Our atonement is not caused by our love for God, but by his love for us. 'In this is love, not that we loved God, but that he loved us and sent his Son to be the expiation for our sins.'[2]

The Collect says that God 'sent his Son, Jesus Christ, to take upon him our flesh.' The tender love of God is seen just as much in the Incarnation as in the Passion of Christ. 'To take upon him our flesh' was the condescension of God entering into mankind, for which he had such tender love. 'To suffer death upon the cross' was the humiliation of that flesh that the Son of God had taken. The one follows upon the other. There is a sense, then, in which the Incarnation was the greater sacrifice, since it was the initial one. 'When thou tookest upon thee to deliver man thou didst not abhor the virgin's womb' is how this truth is expressed in the Te Deum. So it is that we pray in this Collect that we may follow the example of his great humility, and this refers as much to his coming among us, as to his dying for us. 'Have this mind among yourselves, which you have in Christ Jesus, who though he was in the form of God did not count equality with God a thing to be grasped, but emptied himself, taking the form of a servant, being born in the likeness of men.'[3] We are moving into Holy Week, and our eyes are fastened upon the Cross, but let us not, as this Collect stresses, forget the Incarnation. It was in his infancy that his death was prophesied, when the wise men

1 Jn 3:16   2 1 Jn 4:10   3 Phil 2:5-7

brought their gift of myrrh, and the holy Simeon foretold his passion; and throughout his ministry he knew how it would end. 'And he began to teach them that the Son of man must suffer many things, and be rejected... and be killed.'[4]

The first step that we take down some eventful path is often taken unheedingly. We do not always realise the significance of what we have done or said. For good or ill, however, one thing leads to another, and soon a situation has occurred, the consequence of which we must go through with to the end. It is unlikely that Zaccheus foresaw the marvellous consequences for him, when he climbed that sycamore tree in his effort to see Jesus,[5] and it is central to the parable that Dives did not realise the dread consequences of his attitude towards Lazarus.[6] Jesus, however, always knew what was his destiny. 'I have a baptism to be baptised with, and how I am constrained until it is accomplished'.[7] If we are to follow the example of his great humility and his patience, then we need to be aware of what the consequences will be. But we must not let them deter us. 'No one who puts his hand to the plough and looks back is fit for the kingdom of God.'[8] Moreover in this case the price is infinitely worth paying. 'Truly, truly I say to you, you will weep and lament... but your sorrow will be turned into joy... and no one will take your joy from you.'[9] Nonetheless, it will be hard to keep faith with Jesus, even though his emphatic promise (truly, truly ...) is greatly encouraging. We are in Holy Week, and the Cross with all its challenge cannot possibly be evaded. This Collect, however, points us towards how we may acquire that spirit of discipleship that will rise to any challenge, however testing it may be.

We should notice that twice in this Collect we use the word 'follow'. It is a word that was frequently on the lips of Jesus. 'And Jesus said, Follow me.'[10] 'And he said to him, 'Follow me.'[11] 'And come, follow me.'[12] It is like a refrain.

4 Mk 8:31   5 Lk 19:1-10   6 Lk 16:19-31   7 Lk 12:50
8 Lk 9:62   9 Jn 16:20-22   10 Mk 1:17   11 Mk 2:14
12 Mk 10:21

Here it is stressed that the call to follow is along the way of humility and patience. Implicit in both words is self-denial, and the New Testament leaves us in no doubt that hard things will be required of those who would be Christ's disciples. 'For to this you have been called, because Christ also suffered for you, leaving you an example that you should follow in his steps.'[13] The Collect exactly echoes such a text.

In this, however, two truths help us particularly. First, we are following an example. In the Upper Room, having washed the Apostles' feet, Jesus said, 'I have given you an example that you also should do as I have done to you'[14] Sometimes it is the divinity, and sometimes the humanity of Christ, that is the truth about him that is most inspiring and helpful. Here it is the realisation of his humanity that especially comes to our aid. He asks us to do only what he has shown us can be done. He knew sorrow and loneliness, physical weakness and fear. 'Because he himself has suffered and been tempted, he is able to help those who are tempted.'[15] He faced all these common frailties successfully; 'he has been tempted as we are, yet without sinning.' [16] So we are following one who has been victorious in the struggle.

The second truth that makes all the difference is that Christian discipleship means present companionship with Christ. We do not follow a past and distant Christ. Discipleship is for us essentially what it was for St. Peter and St. Mary Magdalene. This is the mystery of his continuing presence; he is for us too 'a very present help in trouble.'[17] He is not an absentee master; 'Lo, I am with you always.'[18] This is the truth that makes us 'more than conquerors through him who loved us',[19] because even now we may be 'partakers of his resurrection.' We follow the risen Christ, who mysteriously remains our companion. We do not, like Moses, simply endure, looking for a future reward.[20] We may experience a definite foretaste of that reward now. There will, however, be more to come, as St. John says, 'See what love the Father gives us, that we should be called children of God; and so we are... Beloved, we are God's children now; it does

13 1 Pet 2:21   14 Jn 13:15   15 Heb 2:18   16 Heb 4:15
17 Ps 46:1   18 Matt 28:20   19 Rom 8:37   20 Heb 11:26

not yet appear what we shall be, but we know that... we shall be like him.'[21]

So the Collect leads us to pray that we may be 'partakers of his resurrection' now. How wonderful! But we can only experience this truth as we follow faithfully in humility and patience, after the emphasis in this Collect. If we do, we will experience through our devotion to Christ, whose living presence is something we have become conscious of, the strength to combat besetting sins, deep-seated fears and longstanding temptations. Our lives will be changed. We will look out on people and events with different eyes. The reason for such an outcome will be the presence of Christ in our lives. For St. Paul he became such a dominant presence that he could say, 'Christ lives in me; and the life I now live in the flesh I live by faith in the Son of God, who loved me and gave himself for me.'[22] To have such an experience of Christ is indeed to be a 'partaker of his resurrection.'

21 1 Jn 3:1-2   22 Gal 2:20

GOOD FRIDAY

Almighty God, we beseech thee graciously to behold this thy family, for which our Lord Jesus Christ was contented to be betrayed, and given up into the hands of wicked men, and to suffer death upon the cross, who now liveth and reigneth with thee and the Holy Ghost, ever one God, world without end. Amen.

Almighty and everlasting God, by whose Spirit the whole body of the Church is governed and sanctified; Receive our supplications and prayers, which we offer before thee for all estates of men in thy holy Church, that every member of the same, in his vocation and ministry, may truly and godly serve thee; through our Lord and Saviour Jesus Christ. Amen.

O merciful God, who hast made all men, and hatest nothing that thou hast made, nor wouldest the death of a sinner, but rather that he should be converted and live; Have mercy upon all Jews, Turks, infidels and hereticks, and take from them all ignorance, hardness of heart, and contempt of thy word; and so fetch them home, blessed Lord, to thy flock, that they may be saved among the remnant of the true Israelites, and be made one fold under one shepherd, Jesus Christ our Lord, who liveth and reigneth with thee and the Holy Spirit, one God, world without end. Amen.

The B.C.P. provides three Collects. The first two are taken from the numerous extra prayers appointed to be said in the Sarum Missal during Holy Week. The first is Gregorian and was said as a special final prayer at the end of Mass on the Wednesday in Holy Week. The second is Gelasian, though altered slightly in the Gregorian Sacramentary, in which form it was in the Sarum Missal. It is one of several special prayers appointed to be said there after the Gospel on Good Friday. The third was composed in 1549, but is a conflation of three prayers said for non-Christians on Good Friday in the Sarum Missal. In 1928, however, this prayer was amended so as to pray that God's mercy may embrace the Jews 'and all who have not known thee, and who deny the faith of Christ crucified' — an obvious improvement.

'We beseech thee graciously to behold this thy family.' The vision of us being members of God's family is expressed specifically in Ephesians. 'For this reason I bow my knees before the Father, from whom every family in heaven and on earth is named, that according to the riches of his glory he may grant you to be strengthened with might through his Spirit in the inner man, and that Christ may dwell in your hearts through faith.'[1] It is a thought that is basic to the whole Gospel. Through Christ we are made truly God's children. 'He has destined us in love to be his sons through Jesus Christ.'[2] But without Christ it is a very different matter. Words, which in their context refer specifically to Gentiles as opposed to Jews, are more or less descriptive of the non-Christian and unbeliever. 'You are strangers to the covenants of promise, and without hope and without God in the world'.[3] It is only 'through him that (all) have access in one Spirit to the Father'.[4] It is Christ who introduces man to God as Father, and who bids us pray to him as such. And because of our new relationship with God, who can now be called by us what Christ called him, 'Abba, Father', we are all brethren, committed to loving each other as Christ and the Father love us all. 'Because you are sons, God has sent the Spirit of his Son into our hearts crying, Abba, Father.'[5] And of course, 'he who loves God should love his brother also.'[6]

The true family of God entered mankind when Christ was born. Then God's only Son was born of a human mother. We thought of what this meant at Christmas time. Mary is the spiritual foster-mother of Christians, just as

1   Eph 3:14-17   2   Eph 1:5   3   Eph 2:12   4   Eph 2:18
5   Gal 4:6   6   1 Jn 4:21

Joseph is the foster-father of Jesus. We by grace and faith are adopted into the family that started at Bethlehem. 'When the time was fully come, God sent forth his Son, born of a woman... so that we might receive adoption as sons.'[7] Christ, then, is more than just our Lord and Saviour; he is also our Brother. In St. Richard's lovely words, he is 'our great Redeemer, our Friend and Brother.' What this amounts to is not fully perceived until we have grasped the truth of God as Holy Trinity. The eternal life of God is essentially a family life, and through Christ and the Holy Spirit we are being drawn to share in the eternal family life of God. (See Trinity Sunday).

At the Crucifixion we see the family that is being broken up by death being recreated by grace. One of the most moving moments in the Gospel story is when the mother of Jesus makes her way to the foot of the Cross to be with her Son as he dies. We may imagine how the news reached her. No doubt her friends would have debated whether to tell her. Might it not be too much for her to bear? So much is conjecture; all we know is that Mary resolutely made her way to Jesus, as he hung on the Cross. We hear of others, who did not dare to come so close. 'All his acquaintances, and the women who had followed him from Galilee, stood at a distance and saw these things.'[8] Only Mary and John and Mary's sister and Mary Magdalene are mentioned as having been brave enough to have come right up close to Christ to be with him as he died.[9] Maybe the courage of the others was not sufficient, or maybe their love was not deep enough to suffer the agony of that sight. For those four, however, both their courage and their love were sufficient. Yet although the love of all of them for Jesus was, no doubt, infinitely deep, without doubt it is Mary that dominates the little party. They came with her; she was not brought by them. And as she stands before her Son, who is her Lord, he sees her. Mary had walked the path of obedience and love to the end, and it was indeed a bitter end. As Simeon had prophesied, a sword was now being driven through her own soul also.[10]

7   Gal 4:4-5   8   Lk 23:49   9   Jn 19:25   10   Lk 2:35

What had started with an act of glad and willing faith, 'Behold, I am the hand-maid of the Lord; let it be to me according to your Word,'[11] had ended down this terrible cul-de-sac.

Then Christ recreated the family that at his death was disintegrating. 'He said to his mother, "Woman, behold your son." Then he said to the disciple, "Behold your mother." And from that hour the disciple took her to his own home.'[12] The official birthday of the Church is Whitsunday. But the conception of the Church is on Good Friday. Mary and John go away to live together, and in that home we see the pattern of Christian fellowship. How precious they must have been to each other! How sacred and tender must have been the love they felt for each other! All would be for Jesus' sake, for he had given them to each other. The same must be true for our love for each other in the Church. We are brothers and sisters, because Jesus has given us to each other. All our work together and our fellowship together must be for Jesus Christ's sake. We have not chosen each other. We have been given each other by Christ himself, just as Mary was given John, and John was given Mary.

The Church, then, is the family of God for which Christ 'was contented to be betrayed, and given up into the hands of wicked men'. In that agony and humiliation, as we too draw near, recognising there the love of God for us, we suddenly become aware of many more, who have also gathered around the Cross, and are, like us, looking up into the face of Christ. From the Cross Christ bids us look to right and left, and says, 'Here are your brothers and sisters'.[13] Is not this truth made physically real for us when we kneel at the altar-rail to receive Communion? Spiritually we look up to him on the altar, and then he bids us notice that there are others kneeling on either side of us. It is as he says. They are our brothers and sisters. For his sake we must be careful to recognise them as such.

---

11 Lk 1:38   12 Jn 19:26-27   13 Mk 3:35

As a result of Christ's death, two things happen. Many families will be divided. 'In one house there will be five divided, three against two and two against three; they will be divided, father against son, and son against father, mother against daughter and daughter against mother, mother-in-law against daughter-in-law and daughter-in-law against mother-in-law.'[14] But also many new families will be created. These are families that the Spirit of God creates, families 'not born of blood nor of the will of the flesh nor of the will of man, but of God.'[15] 'Truly I say to you there is no one, who has left house or brothers or sisters or mother or father or children or lands for my sake and for the Gospel, who will not receive a hundredfold now in this time, houses and brothers and sisters and mothers and children and lands, with persecutions, and in the age to come, eternal life.'[16] The Church is a family, and every Diocese and every Parish are families within that family.

As the second Collect suggests, life within the family is to be a busy one. Everyone is to have 'his own vocation and ministry.' We are called into the Church, and we can all find work to do there, and a special part to play there. The analogy of the Church which is best known is that of the Body of Christ. St. Paul sees the Church as a single body inspired by one Spirit. Christ is the head, and we are obedient and healthy limbs, performing the functions required of us by him. Each must fit in with the work of others, without fuss or confusion. 'There are varieties of gifts, but the same Spirit; and there are varieties of service, but the same Lord.'[17] To find our niche in our own Parish is essential for every Christian. Co-operation is never easy, and it is from the common experience of communion with Christ crucified that we will find the inspiration to work together. 'A family that prays together stays together'. This saying is even more obviously relevant to a spiritual family in a Parish than it is to a natural family in a house. And the peculiar corporate prayer of the family of God is the Eucharist, where we kneel before the mysterious truths of Christ's Crucifixion and Resurrec-

14 Lk 12:52-53   15 Jn 1:13   16 Mk 10:29-30   17 1 Cor 12:4

tion, and realise the presence of our Saviour with us. It is out of that family sacrament especially that we all find the inspiration to fulfil our special 'vocation and ministry', and become to each other 'your servants for Jesus' sake.'[18]

The third Collect is specially for non-believers and those who, though they are religious men and women, are sincerely wrong in their beliefs. 'Take from them all ignorance, hardness of heart and contempt of thy Word.' How obviously these words fit many in our country. Certainly we do not have to think only of 'Jews and Turks'. Sadly in large measure they fit Christians as readily as unbelievers, especially the last two phrases. 'Father, forgive them, they know not what they do', was the first of our Lord's words from the Cross.[19] It covers so many in its generous love. But what of those, who cannot claim to be ignorant of what 'hardness of heart and contempt of his Word' mean to God? What of those, who know that it was such things that crucified Christ and hurt the passionate love of God? Indeed what of us who would pray this prayer? We have not got the screen of ignorance to hide behind, and yet our hearts are still so often hard, and we too are so often disobedient of his Word.

It is surely significant that the bitterest opponents of Christ were religious and, in large degree, good men. Judas, Caiaphas and even Pontius Pilate come into this category. Religion wrongly directed, however, is a particularly deadly form of ignorance, involving hardness of heart and contempt of God's Word. The effort needed to discard wrong ideas of God is greater even than the effort needed to discard wrong ways of behaviour. Firm in their false doctrines, the religious leaders of Judaism rejected their Messiah, and destroyed him with hatred. 'You are of this world. I am not of this world. I told you that you would die in your sins, for you will die in your sins, unless you believe that I am he.'[20] Spiritual pride is the sin against the Holy Spirit, which, while it remains, forbids forgiveness.[21] To

---

18 2 Cor 4:5   19 Lk 23:34   20 Jn 8:24   21 Mk 3:29

be passionately and utterly convinced that one is right, when one is wrong, makes repentance and faith impossible. The need for a true faith, therefore, can hardly be over-emphasised. 'He who believes in the Son has eternal life; he who does not obey the Son shall not see life, but the wrath of God rests upon him.'[22] Ignorance, like love, may cover a multitude of sins, but ignorance must be in the end acknowledged and the truth reign. 'If you were blind you would have no guilt; but now that you say, "We see", your guilt remains.'[23] The Gospels do not consist only of comfortable words.

The words of Jesus hardly encourage us to believe that all religious men are going the same way. It matters what one believes, and especially what God one believes in. 'We know that the Son of God has come, and has given us understanding to know him who is true; and we are in him who is true, in his Son Jesus Christ. This is the true God and eternal life. Little children, keep yourselves from idols.'[24] Such were St. John's last words to the Christians committed to his charge, and the relevance of his concern has a very modern ring about it. Love of our neighbour does not include encouraging him to continue to believe in that which is false. Indeed the opposite is true. However difficult it may be to act upon this truth, is it not a particularly relevant one for the Church to address during its Decade of Evangelism in our pluralist society?

The third Collect, however, ends on the note that is so firmly struck in the first. The prayer emphasises that brotherhood within one family is God's will for all mankind, because God is the Father of all. 'Fetch them home', we pray. 'In my Father's house are many rooms', said Jesus. [25] The 'many' here has the same force as it has in the text, which we particularly remember on Good Friday, 'the Son of Man came... to give his life as a ransom for many.'[26] There is no limit to God's mercy and loving kindness. Scripture declared that it is the Father's will that all, not just many, shall come to know him,[27] and to this end from the Cross his love embraces all, and also in heaven there is room for all. We are praying here that all shall

22 Jn 3:36   23 Jn 9:41   24 1 Jn 5:20-21   25 Jn 14:2
26 Mk 10:45   27 1 Tim 2:4

find their way to that welcoming place prepared by the Father for his children and by the Son for his brethren,[28] and that our Lord's prophecy shall be completely fulfilled, for he said, 'I, when I am lifted up from the earth, will draw all men to myself'.[29] Most certainly we are all called through Christ to share in the eternal family life of God the Holy Trinity, such is the wonder of our vocation as human beings created in God's image. That all mankind attain to this life with God must be our constant prayer and our chief concern. This is the burden of the Good Friday Collects. It is also the essential purpose of the Gospel.[30]

EASTER EVEN and EASTER DAY

EASTER EVEN

Grant, O Lord, that as we are baptised into the death of thy blessed Son our Saviour Jesus Christ, so by continual mortifying our corrupt affections we may be buried with him; and that, through the grave and gate of death, we may pass to our joyful resurrection; for his merits, who died, and was buried, and rose again for us, thy Son Jesus Christ our Lord. Amen.

EASTER DAY

Almighty God, who through thine only-begotten Son Jesus Christ hast overcome death, and opened unto us the gate of everlasting life; We humbly beseech thee, that as by thy special grace preventing us thou dost put into our minds good desires, so by thy continual help we may bring the same to good effect; through Jesus Christ our Lord, who liveth and reigneth with thee and the Holy Ghost, ever one God, world without end. Amen.

Easter Collect added in 1928.

O God, who for our redemption didst give thine only begotten Son to the death of the cross, and by his glorious resurrection hast delivered us from the power of our enemy: Grant us so to die daily unto sin, that we may evermore live in him in the joy of his resurrection; through the same Jesus Christ our Lord. Amen.

Our Easter Day Collect is the Gregorian Collect that was used in the Sarum Missal. This Collect is a revision of the earlier Gelasian Collect, but not, one must say, an improvement on it. The invocations in both are the same, but the earlier Collect's petition, by mentioning our Lord's Resurrection and our own rising from death to life, was clearly so much more appropriate for Easter Day than our petition now. St Gregory's revision, therefore, is hard to comprehend and harder still to approve; however, see commentary.

In the 1549 Prayer Book two separate Propers were provided, an arrangement that was discontinued in the 1662 revision. However the Collect for the second Proper was retained for use on Easter I, where it was also expected to be used in the 1549 Book.

The Collect for Easter Even was written by Bishop Cosin for the Book of 1662.

In the revision in 1928 an additional Easter Collect was provided. This was the prayer used in the Sarum Missal as part of a devotion to precede the first Mass of Easter, and retained in the 1549 Prayer Book as part of a special devotion to precede Matins on Easter Day. This special Easter devotion was omitted in the 1662 Book, but since this Collect is perhaps more distinctive of the season than the official Easter Collect its return to our Prayer Book is most welcome.

In the Collect for Easter Even we are reminded that what must be put to death are our 'corrupt affections' before there is any hope for our rising to newness of life. The victory that Jesus has won for us is not simply over death, but also and primarily over evil. His triumphant rising to life on Easter Day is the consequence of his victory over evil on Good Friday. It is vital to appreciate the dependence of Easter upon Good Friday, otherwise Easter Day is a mere tour de force by God without moral significance. The Resurrection of Jesus is to be seen as the outward sign of his atoning sacrifice on the Cross, by means of which he slew evil as he lay down his life. He 'cancelled the bond which stood against us... nailing it to the Cross.'[1] Evil had Christ by the throat, but it was Christ who overcame evil with good, and who triumphed in the power of divine love. 'God raised him up, having loosed the pangs of death, because it was not possible for him to be held by it.'[2] Since death and sin are connected, his victory over the one

1   Col 2:14   2   Acts 2:24

meant that his victory over the other was assured. Since sin had been conquered, 'death no longer had dominion over him.'[3]

This victory of Christ over sin and death has 'opened unto us the gate of everlasting life', but on the same terms. First, we must face our present enemy, evil, and then we may face confidently our last enemy, death. We are not encouraged to hope for eternal life as a result of Christ's victory automatically. He did not die for us in any cheap substitutionary fashion. He did not win the victory over evil so that we may sin with impunity. 'Are we to continue in sin that grace may abound? By no means!'[4] His victory was only for us in the sense that we may take advantage of it, if we will. 'Brethren, what shall we do? And Peter said to them, 'Repent...'[5] He has paved the way, but we must proceed along that narrow, yet victorious path, that alone gives us hope of everlasting life. 'I set before you an open door.'[6] He has not given us a blank cheque.

By our faithful and penitent response to what God in Christ has done for us, we are to enter into Christ's victory and experience a sharing in it. This is, moreover, to be a continuing experience. The 1928 Collect bids us pray that this may happen 'daily'. We are reminded by that word of Christ's command that we take up our cross 'daily',[7] and of the Christmas Collect, in which our renewal in the Holy Spirit, through the experience of being 'born again in Christ', is also seen to be something we experience daily. What a challenge to us as Christians is this word 'daily' ! There are numerous activities that must be done daily, and we get used to their continuing demands on us. Without too much trouble we allow them to become part of our permanent daily routine; we should also allow spiritual activities to have an equally regular part in our everyday lives. By our daily acts of repentance and faith we are 'to die daily unto sin', and 'daily be renewed in the Holy Spirit'. The rewards for such a routine will be infinitely great. By this means we are to live day by day, and even for ever, 'in Christ in the joy of his Resurrection.'

---

3 Rom 6:9   4 Rom 6:1   5 Acts 2:37-38   6 Rev 3:8
7 Lk 9:23

There is an unexpected practicality about the Easter Collect. It seems to forget about Christ's Resurrection as soon as it is mentioned, and goes on to pray for God's 'continual help' for us to live a good life here. The Epistle for Easter Day is similarly down to earth; almost disconcertingly so. There the change of tone is very abrupt. 'When Christ, who is our life, shall appear, then shall you also appear with him in glory. Mortify, therefore, your members which are upon the earth: fornication, uncleanness, inordinate affection...'[8] From the sublime, we are brought down, if not to the ridiculous, then to the lowest of the low.

There is a temptation for us to revel in Easter in a false and cosy way. Many still go to Church on Easter Day; few go on Good Friday. This is a sign of shallowness. But then it is surely a national disgrace that Good Friday is not a public holiday. It is a national disclaimer of its importance. This increases the temptation just to enjoy the spring flowers, the message of good news, the idea that it all ended well and Jesus lives happily ever afterwards. It would be nice to think that after all sin does not matter, and that what sin means, namely the Crucifixion of the Son of God, was merely a tragedy that had a happy ending. Talk of 'fornication, uncleanness, inordinate affection, evil concupiscence and covetousness, which is idolatry', grates badly on our ears, if we come to worship on Easter Day in an unrepentant frame of mind. The Epistle indeed ends in even more uncomfortable fashion with a solemn warning about the wrath of God coming down upon the children of disobedience. Those who have taken no part in the solemn rites for Maundy Thursday and Good Friday, and have not sought to understand the meaning of Gethsemane and Golgotha, may even find Easter rather like a fairy story, enjoyable, unreal and easily forgotten. If so, how sad!

However, it cannot be denied that all too few of the crowds in Church at Easter and Christmas are regular weekly worshippers. (*Sunday School teacher*: What does C of E stand for? *Little boy*: Christmas and Easter). The

8   Col 3:4-5 A.V.

real joy of Easter must inevitably pass us by, if we have felt no sorrow for Christ's passion. 'If we have been united with him in a death like his, we shall certainly be united with him in a resurrection like his.'[9] The 'if' is important. It is repeated. 'If we died with Christ, we believe that we shall also live with him.'[10] But what if the condition is not forthcoming? What if we are not united in his death in any way at all? Can we hope, as if by magic, that we are washed clean of sin, and are therefore assured of happiness in eternal life? Commonsense and Scripture combine to warn us, 'do not be deceived, God is not mocked.'[11] The Resurrection of Jesus is not the same sign of hope to those who resist God's Spirit, and refuse wilfully to obey his laws, as it is to those who believe and repent. 'You were called to freedom, brethren; only do not use your freedom for an opportunity for the flesh... The works of the flesh are plain... I warn you, as I warned you before that those who do such things shall not inherit the kingdom of God.'[12] The Gospel has its hard side to it. The Collect and the Epistle for Easter Day stress this hard side.

But to those, who repent and believe, and have been baptised in Spirit and in truth, it most certainly is such a sign. 'For you have died, and your life is hid with Christ in God. When Christ who is our life shall appear, then you also will appear with him in glory.'[13] Our prayer, therefore, is that God, who through faith and repentance and membership of his Church has us already in his keeping, will 'put into our minds good desires', and by his continual help 'bring the same to good effect.' We are his. May we live as such. We are still beset by temptations and many natural weaknesses. We live in Christ, but we know ourselves too well not to realise how false we can yet be. 'I therefore.. beg you to lead a life worthy of the calling to which you have been called, with all lowliness and meekness, with patience, forbearing one another in love.'[14]

---

9 Rom 6:5   10 Rom 6:8   11 Gal 6:7   12 Gal 5:13-21
13 Col 3:3-4   14 Eph 4:1-2

Easter's glorious message, then, is surprisingly practical, unexpectedly stern, uncomfortably down to earth. It gives us a sign that assures us that good is stronger then evil, that death can be swallowed up in life, but, although it declares that eternal life is the free gift of God to all his children, it is a gift that must be received. This directs our thoughts instinctively towards the service of Holy Communion, for that is the God-given way in which we may receive this 'inexpressible gift.' Moreover, Easter is preeminently the day appointed for Anglicans to receive their communion, as the rubric after the Holy Communion Service makes plain.

Nearly all the resurrection stories in the Gospels have an eucharistic element in them. ('Jesus appeared to the eleven as they sat at table'[15] ... 'He took the bread and blessed and broke it and gave it to them.... he was known to them in the breaking of the bread'.[16] ... Jesus came and took the bread and gave it to them'.[17]) It is in the Eucharist that the risen Christ, bringing with him the divine gifts of forgiveness and eternal life, the gifts he won for all mankind in his death and resurrection, makes himself known to us in the breaking of the bread. In obedience to his command we 'do' the Eucharist, and receive him, his body and blood, his divine yet human life, into ourselves as we eat and drink the bread and wine. It is through Holy Communion very especially that we experience his 'special grace preventing us.' It is by regular Communion very particularly that we experience his 'continual help.' Just as every Sunday is a little Easter, so every service of Holy Communion takes us to that Upper Room, where the first disciples were made 'glad when they saw the Lord,' and heard him say, 'Peace be with you,' and where he breathed on them and said, 'Receive the Holy Spirit'.[18] Every service of Holy Communion, therefore, is a new resurrection appearance of Jesus to his disciples.

---

15 Mk 16:14   16 Lk 24:30-35   17 Jn 21:12   18 Jn 20:20-21

158

In the Collect of Easter Even we pray that 'we may pass to our joyful resurrection, for his merits who died, and was buried, and rose again for us.' Our resurrection will not be identical to his. Jesus rose in bodily form to reappear on earth, having died and been buried. Such will not happen to us. That it happened to him, however, is of the first importance for us. It shows that our resurrection will also be a bodily one, though our resurrection body will be a spiritual body.[19] The essential truth of our bodily resurrection is that beyond death we retain our individuality. We stay ourselves, and death does not snap the essential link between this life and the life we live hereafter. 'See my hands and my feet, that it is I myself,'[20] said Jesus to his bewildered disciples. His hands and feet were specially to be noticed, because they still carried the marks of his Crucifixion, so that the disciples, though 'disbelieving for joy and wondering', might reassure themselves that what they saw was no disembodied spirit , but their Lord and Master alive again. In a way we cannot now fully understand, we, too, will just as completely and individually be alive again when ' we pass to our joyful resurrection.' This is the force of the article in the Apostles creed, ' I believe in the resurrection of the body.'

This truth, also, has relevance for the article in which we declare our belief in 'the Communion of Saints.' Beyond death we will have fellowship one with another, just as we have fellowship one with another here. It is part of our Christian faith that beyond death we shall know each other, and be able to love and serve each other. Above all, we will be with Christ, who has gone before us to his 'joyful resurrection' 'to prepare', as he said, 'a place for us, so that where he is we may be also.'[21] There we are to 'evermore live with him in the joy of his resurrection'. To live with him is to live with 'a great multitude, which no man could number' [22]. Like us, they know that through Christ God has 'overcome death and opened unto us the gate of everlasting life'. The visions of heaven in the Book of Revelation are all of corporate joy. There we are not only at one with God, but are also at one with each other, which makes our joy complete.

19 1 Cor 15:44, 53-54   20 Lk 24:39   21 Jn 14:3-4
22 Rev 7:9-10

EASTER I

Almighty Father, who hast given thine only Son to die for our sins, and to rise again for our justification; grant us so to put away the leaven of malice and wickedness, that we may always serve thee in pureness of living and truth; through the merits of the same thy Son Jesus Christ our Lord. Amen.

This Collect was composed in 1549, and until 1662 was used for the second celebration on Easter Day and for all the weekdays in Easter week, as well as this Sunday. In 1662, however, Propers were set for the Monday and Tuesday in Easter week only, for which the Easter Collect was used, and this Collect was confined to this Sunday.

This Sunday is commonly called Low Sunday in contrast to Easter Day, which is High Sunday, and ends the Easter octave.

———————————

The opening of this Collect is unique for an unexpected reason. Remarkably it is the only Sunday Collect that starts by addressing God directly as Father. The third Collect for Morning Prayer does so, and the Collects for Advent III, Epiphany VI, Lent I, Trinity IV and Trinity XXIV have endings in which the Father is mentioned, but what one would imagine was the most natural of all ways to start a Christian prayer is not normally used by the composers of our Collects, whether they be men of the medieval or the reformation Church. Moreover, strange as it may seem, neither 'Almighty Father' nor 'Father Almighty' is precisely scriptural, although the sense and implication of such an address most certainly is. We hear Jesus addressing God as, 'Father, Lord of heaven and earth'[1] and 'Holy Father'[2] and often simply 'Father'. That the early Christians prayed to God as Father in accordance with our Lord's teaching is indicated plainly in the

1 Lk 10:21   2   Jn 17:25

Gospels[3], and confirmed by the Epistles, where St. Paul stresses that it is also the Holy Spirit, and not only Jesus, that insists that we address him in this intimate manner.[4] Nevertheless, the evidence from Acts and the Epistles, such as it is, suggests that the early Church, no less than the medieval Church and our reformation Church, did not usually address God as Father in formal corporate prayer.

In Acts we twice hear of the Apostles praying at an official gathering of the earliest Christians. At the first before the election of Matthias, God is simply addressed as 'Lord, who knowest the hearts of all men,'[5] a form of address typical of our Collects (see Whit Sunday), and then later when they met after their interrogation by the Sanhedrin, they addressed God as 'Sovereign Lord, who didst make the heaven and the earth and the sea and everything in them,'[6] an address more typical of Jewish worship.[7] Then we notice that in the formal prayerful endings to Romans, Hebrews and Jude God is not called upon as Father. The two paeans of praise to God, which start both Ephesians and 1 Peter, are perhaps particularly interesting. Both start in identical fashion, which may suggest that that form of words was often used to start a formal time of prayer, perhaps at the consecration of the Eucharist. There God is certainly called Father, but only specifically Father of Jesus, not our Father. 'Blessed be the God and Father of our Lord Jesus Christ.' [8]

Too much cannot be made, of course, of such very slender evidence, especially as St. Paul always speaks of God as 'the Father' or 'our Father' in his short prayerful openings to all his Epistles. 'Grace to you and peace from God our Father and the Lord Jesus Christ.'[9] But it does nonetheless, give some scriptural support to this convention that has controlled the style of our Prayer Book Collects, and the medieval Collects on which they are so often based, with this one exception. Which prompts the further query, why on this Sunday? Is not Low Sunday a peculiar Sunday on which to break the mould?

---

3   Matt 6:9, Lk 11:2   4   Rom 8:15, Gal 4:6   5   Acts 1:24   6   Acts 4:24
7   2 Chron 6:14   8   Eph 1:3, 1 Pet 1:3 - also 2 Cor 1:3   9   Rom 1:7 et al

The probable answer is that there is no special reason why Cranmer acted differently when he wrote this Collect. Yet one may fairly observe that such a way of addressing God would be particularly appropriate at Eastertide. It was then that Jesus stressed the Fatherhood of God to his disciples. To Mary Magdalene he said, urging her to use such words when she met the other disciples, 'I am ascending to my Father and your Father.'[10] It was particularly then that God revealed himself to be our 'Almighty Father, who has given his only Son to die for our sins and to rise again for our justification.'

We meet in this Collect the important biblical word 'justification', which is also not found elsewhere in the Collects. Its meaning is central to Pauline theology. It means "being put into a right relationship with God". In this Collect it is linked expressly with Christ's Resurrection, and, although the words of the Collect are taken from Romans 4 : 25, they are not typical of St. Paul's normal teaching. He usually links our justification either with the sacrificial death of Christ, or our faith in the saving power of that death, for instance, 'Since all have sinned and fall short of the glory of God, we are justified by his grace as a gift, through the redemption which is in Christ Jesus, whom God put forward as an expiation by his blood, to be received by faith.'[11] St. Paul perceived that sin had created such a gulf between God and man, that no earthly thing, not even the law, could bridge it. The law could not bridge this gap because no one was able to keep the law, not even in the letter, let alone in the spirit. The law, he said, was 'holy and just and good,'[12] but nonetheless because of man's sin 'the law brings (only) wrath.'[13] If man and God, therefore, were ever to be in a right and loving relationship with each other, at one with each other, something besides the giving of the law was required. And that something only God could do. So God acted again. He sent his Son that we may be saved from our predicament, from being for ever separated from him, and instead 'be justified', so that we may be for ever united with him. This God effected 'as a gift' through Jesus

10 Jn 20:17   11 Rom 3:23-25   12 Rom 7:12   13 Rom 4:15

Christ, 'who was put to death for our sins and rose again for our justification.' This is the Gospel.

According to St. Paul, however, there must be a response by us to what God has done for us 'by his grace', if our 'justification' is to be sealed, so St. Paul can also say 'we are justified by faith.'[14] This does not take away his emphasis on the divine initiative in this process. It is still true that we 'are justified by his grace as a gift', but that gift must be received by faith. Our free-will is preserved. Moreover this gift must be retained and not later rejected. The faith, therefore, that justifies is no static once for all affair, but a spiritual reality that grows and deepens. It will have a starting point certainly, which will naturally be an unrepeatable event, to which we may look back in gratitude. This may be something unperceived at the time, such as our Baptism in infancy, or it may be an experience, of which we are very conscious. But the vital thing is that this justifying faith must continue and develop, or it may wither and die.

In Romans 4 : 25, on which this Collect is based, the process of justification is linked specifically with the Resurrection of Jesus, and, as we have said, this is not typical. However, in so doing St. Paul is stressing the continuing nature of justification in our lives. It is his risen life that must indwell us, and this will be indeed the case, if we continue to live 'believing in him that raised from the dead Jesus our Lord.' [15] Our justification is therefore just as dependent on the risen life of Christ, as it is on the sacrificial death of Christ. He died for our sins once, an event that remains in the past; he rose again for our justification, an event that does not remain in the past, but continues for ever. On this risen life we must draw by faith to keep us justified, and so continue to be in a right relationship with God both through Christ and in Christ.[16]

———————————

The Collect goes on to talk of 'the leaven of malice and wickedness' that

14 Rom 5:1   15 Rom 4:24   16 Rom 5:10-11

must be put away by the indwelling of Christ, through whom and in whom we are justified. We recall St. Paul's teaching in 1 Corinthians 5. There he contrasts the 'old leaven of malice and wickedness'[17] not with new leaven, but with 'the unleavened bread of sincerity and truth', which is Christ himself. We are talking here about our growth in the spiritual life. There is both an inner and outer corruption, 'malice and wickedness', that must be purged and done away. The whole of us must be cleansed. As we have said, the law could not achieve this necessary spiritual cleansing. Only something utterly radical and new could achieve this vital inner baptism. Through Christ, who 'died for our sins and rose again for our justification', we too may die to sin and rise again to newness of life in him. This is what is necessary, nothing less, a spiritual death and resurrection. 'You must consider yourself dead to sin, and alive to God in Christ Jesus'.[18]

It is the specific purpose of the sacraments of Baptism and Holy Communion to effect this complete spiritual transformation, and to maintain it in our lives. 'Do you not know', says St. Paul, 'that all of us, who have been baptised into Christ Jesus, were baptised into his death? We were buried therefore with him by baptism into death, so that as Christ was raised from the dead by the glory of the Father, we too might walk in newness of life.'[19] It is this newness of life that we continue to receive as we partake of Holy Communion, 'feeding upon Christ by faith with thanksgiving.' In this way we can hope 'to put away the leaven of malice and wickedness' from our lives, and keep it at bay.

The purpose of this putting away of 'malice and wickedness' is that we may serve God in 'pureness of living and truth.' St. Paul in Corinthians 5 has 'sincerity' rather than 'pureness of living', but the meaning surely is the same. Sincerity and purity are both transparent qualities, through which the light of truth may shine. Where else can they be found but in Christ? He is the truth, and we must become pure, in order to receive him and

17 1 Cor 5:8 A.V.   18 Rom 6:11   19 Rom 6:3-4

reflect him. The pure in heart see God, and through them others may come to see him too. That is why Christ could say, 'he that has seen me has seen the Father', [20] for he was truly pure in heart and pure in deed. The Father, as it were, showed through in all he did and in all he was. So for us, it all amounts to our living in Christ and following his example. There is no realistic hope that we may be able 'to serve God in pureness of living and truth' any other way, but nonetheless 'everyone, who thus hopes in him, purifies himself even as he is pure.'[21] Therefore, however much we recognise the need for Christ to indwell our lives and to give us his grace, if we are to be justified and serve God faithfully we must still make our own contribution of conscious effort. Christian faith in what God in Christ has done for us is no easy option, but a call to costly discipleship.

It would, however, be ending this commentary on what is an Easter Collect on a false note if we leave the emphasis there. The Gospel is much more full of encouragement than of warning. It is not our faithfulness on which we may depend but God's.[22] Moreover, since to live a good life is really our innermost heart's desire[23], it is true that we will find it 'an easy yoke' to be joined to Christ, as he said. As we accept this 'yoke' we shall, as promised, and as we long for, 'find rest for our souls'. It is this intimate relationship with Christ that enables us to make lasting sense of our troubled, transient lives. Certainly from time to time, and for some most of the time, 'we labour and are heavy laden'. But if we are willing to 'learn' from Christ by being yoked to him in spirit all is transformed. The necessary 'burden' of costly discipleship does become 'light', for mysteriously it becomes not so much something that we carry, but something that carries us.[24] Suddenly nothing that must be done becomes too difficult for us to do.[25] Because Christ has conquered we also may become, as St. Paul says, 'more than conquerors through him who loved us'[26], and who is always with us. Now, such a thought does make an appropriate ending to our consideration of this prayer that brings the Easter octave to its close.

---

20 Jn 14:8   21 1 Jn 3:3   22 1 Thess 5:24   23 Rom 7:22
24 Matt 11:28-30   25 Phil 4:13   26 Rom 8:37

EASTER II

Almighty God, who has given thine only Son to be unto us both a sacrifice for sin, and also an ensample of godly life; give us grace that we may always most thankfully receive that his inestimable benefit, and also daily endeavour ourselves to follow the blessed steps of his most holy life; through the same Jesus Christ our Lord.

This is another 1549 Collect based on the Epistle. This Sunday is known as Good Shepherd Sunday, a title taken from the Epistle and Gospel.

In the Epistle St. Peter speaks of Christ's death in words taken from Isaiah 53. This was one of the main proof texts of the early Church to show 'that Christ died for our sins in accordance with the Scriptures.'[1] His death was a vicarious sacrifice, 'full, perfect and sufficient, for the sins of the whole world.'[2] There was no accident about it. It was prophesised long before. Moreover Christ said of his death, 'I lay down my life... no one takes it from me, but I lay it down of my own accord.'[3] He did this because it was the Father's will that he, the Messiah, should 'give his life as a ransom for many.'[4] This giving of himself in sacrifice is called here God's 'inestimable benefit', which we are to 'most thankfully receive.' Our means of receiving it is faith. The way we show we have received it is obedience in discipleship.

In the Epistle St. Peter also warns us that, just because we are Christians, we are 'called' to trials and tribulations, and that we are not to consider this strange or even unwelcome. Rather we are to acknowledge this as a necessary testing of our faith, which elsewhere St. Peter describes as more precious than gold. 'If, when you do right and suffer for it, you take it patiently, you have God's approval. For to this you have been called.'[5] Christ himself has shown us the way. 'When he was reviled, he did not

1   1 Cor 15:3   2   Prayer of Consecration in Holy Communion Service.
3   Jn 10:18   4   Mk 10:45   5   1 Pet 2:20-21

revile in return; when he suffered, he did not threaten; but he trusted to him who judges justly.'[6] We must follow, for he has left us 'an ensample of godly life.' So the sacrifice and the example are linked in this Collect, as they are in the Epistle, and in the Gospel too. There, also, Christ is the one that 'lays down his life.' He does so as a faithful shepherd, and in the Palestine of those days shepherds were leaders, not drivers, of sheep. Sheep followed their shepherds. So we must follow our 'good shepherd, who lays down his life for the sheep.'[7]

This combination of ideas in this Sunday's Collect, Epistle and Gospel, the receiving of Christ's atoning sacrifice and the following in the way of his sacrificial life (and, if need be, death) is central to our understanding of the great sacraments of Baptism and Holy Communion. He has died for us. We believe in what he has done for us. We receive this 'inestimable benefit', through which we are forgiven and offered the gift of eternal life, with repentance, faith and thanksgiving. We do this once for all in Baptism, and repeatedly in Holy Communion, but as we do so, we also pledge ourselves (or in Baptism others may pledge it for us) that we shall 'endeavour ourselves to follow the blessed steps of his most holy life.' The receiving and the following are inextricably linked, even as faith and works are linked. This, we may note, is also the theme of the Palm Sunday Collect.

Two small words in this Collect may require underlining, lest they be overlooked. They are 'always' and 'daily'. We have stressed the unity of the Collect's petition; the receiving and the following are not to be separated. These words add greatly to the flavour of both these necessary spiritual activities. Our thanksgiving for what God has done for us in Christ must be a constant aspect of our spiritual life, and our efforts to follow Christ must be a conscious daily act of obedience.

This combination of constant thanksgiving and daily endeavour is very

6   1 Pet 2:23   7   Jn 10:11

much the theme of the long prayer with which St. Peter starts his first Epistle, from which the Epistle for this Sunday is taken. He speaks of the result of Christ's death and resurrection as 'an inheritance which is imperishable, undefiled and unfading, kept in heaven for us,' and our constancy in thanksgiving is to match the certainty of this inheritance. We are to 'rejoice with unutterable and exalted joy.'[8]

Our thanksgiving, however, is to be a spur to action. Day by day, we are to follow with equal constancy him whom we love, even though we have not seen him in the flesh. We are to be 'as obedient children', 'loving one another from the heart', and 'putting away all malice and all guile and insincerity and envy and all slander', for 'we have tasted the kindness of the Lord.'[9] 'New every morning is the love our wakening and uprising prove',[10] so we are to reply, 'My mouth shall daily speak of thy righteousness and salvation, for I know no end thereof'.[11] God faithfully provides all our daily needs, and we must as faithfully renew our obedience day by day. 'Today if you will hear his voice', said the Psalmist,[12] do not be deaf and disobedient. Today is where we are, and where we 'must take up our cross and follow Christ.' [13] Tomorrow will present us with further challenges to faithful obedience; meanwhile we are to ignore them, and concentrate on 'the day's own troubles'. [14] They will be sufficient for us to cope with, and for our coping God will provide sufficient grace. We may notice that this thought is also an important element in the Collect for Christmas Day.

This Collect's reference to Christ as our example in 'godly' living, and its call to us to follow him in 'holy' living, points us towards the subject of evangelism.[15] In the light of the Church's declaration of a Decade of Evangelism, and the general uncertainty in what evangelism today consists, this Collect may seem to have a special relevance. It can, perhaps, be prayed with this important consideration particularly in mind.

8 1 Pet 1:3-9   9 1 Pet 2:1-3   10 J. Keble – The Christian Year   11 Ps 71:13
12 Ps 95:8   13 Lk 9:23   14 Matt 6:34   15 Jn 13:15, 1 Pet 2:21

168

There can be no denying our call as Christians to witness to our faith by setting 'an example in speech and conduct', as St. Paul puts it.[16] However, it is also clear that there are difficulties and dangers, both physical and spiritual, for us in this vocation. Those of a spiritual nature are, perhaps, particularly well illustrated by the Pharisees, even though they were our Lord's opponents. They, too, believed they were called of God to be 'a guide to the blind, a light to those in darkness, a corrector of the foolish and a teacher of children.'[17] They became, however, 'blind guides, straining at the gnat and swallowing the camel'[18], and so become for us a warning rather than an example. As the Church accepts the challenge and responsibility of evangelism afresh we must beware of their flawed spirituality, remembering that none could have been more sincere than they.

Some guiding principles clearly emerge from Scripture in this matter of evangelism. First, although we are called by Christ 'the light of the world' (even though he also claimed that title particularly for himself), any effective shining we may do for the good of others will be unselfconscious, since its purpose and outcome must only be to 'glorify God'.[19] We do have a 'light', but that 'light' is not of ourselves, even though it is to be in ourselves. So we notice how it was finely said of the Apostles that others 'recognised that they had been with Jesus'.[20] Their discipleship showed 'in speech and conduct'. It was clear to all who was their Lord. And, although they did not cease their opposition, even their opponents were impressed.

Secondly, this same story makes plain that the primary purpose of evangelism is not to make converts, but to witness to the lordship of Christ and to glorify God. When this is done faithfully, however, wonderful results will be forthcoming and converts will be made, but these desirable results will be of God, rather than of us. The Apostles certainly met with great success, as well as much opposition, in their evangelism. Their word had power, because it was the word of God. They experienced what Jesus had promised they would experience, for he had said, 'They will deliver you

16 1 Tim 4:12   17 Rom 2:19-20   18 Matt 23:24   19 Jn 8:12, Matt 5:14 - 16
20 Acts 4:13

up…but you are to say whatever is given you in that hour, for it is not you who speak, but the Holy Spirit.'[21] So St. Luke in Acts describes their success as the work of God rather than of the Apostles. 'The Lord added to their number day by day'.[22]

Thirdly, the New Testament makes it clear that the work of evangelism is not to be considered the sole prerogative of the Church's ordained leaders. All are to be involved, and part of the leaders' task is to educate and encourage all to be involved. Especially this is true in the area of setting a Christian example in the ordinary spheres of life, which is so particularly the theme of this Collect. Not all are called to be prophets and martyrs, but all are called to do 'the work of an evangelist'.[23] So the circumstances of our lives should always be allowed their full weight. The saying, 'Be as wise as serpents and innocent as doves'[24], is apropos here. Just as there are differences of vocation, so there are different ways and means in evangelism. St. Paul and St. Peter, for instance, fully understood the special problems facing those who were married to non-Christians, or who had to work in an unsympathetic or dangerous environment. They both taught that often just to be faithful spouses and loving parents, good citizens and helpful neighbours, and obedient subjects that conscientiously served the community, all done for Christ's sake and with prayer, was both acceptable to God and full of converting power.[25] The phrase 'daily endeavour' in this Collect is suggestive of this scriptural teaching.

However, the sterner side of evangelism, the danger as opposed to merely the difficulty of it, is not absent from this Collect, since it reminds us of our Lord's 'sacrifice for sin'. The number of the martyrs and confessors of the Church is still being added to today. Mercifully our Lord's warning of 'floggings, imprisonment and death'[26] are not going to be our lot as we in this country 'daily endeavour' to set a Christian 'example in speech and conduct' in this Decade of Evangelism, but we can be sure that it will be the fate of some in other parts of the world. Still in some places for some people

21 Mk 13:9-11   22 Acts 2:47   23 2 Tim 4:5   24 Matt 10:16
25 1 Cor 7:16, 8:7-13, 9:22, 1 Pet 2:13 - 17 et al   26 Matt 10:17 - 22

'to follow the blessed steps of his most holy life' means a genuine via dolorosa, and this Collect can be well used as an intercessory prayer for them. However our prayer for them can also be one of thanksgiving, for a light always shines brightest in the darkness and their great reward is assured.[27]

27 Matt 5:11-12

EASTER III

Almighty God, who shewest to them that be in error the light of thy truth, to the intent that they may return into the way of righteousness; grant unto all them that are admitted into the fellowship of Christ's religion, that they may eschew those things that are contrary to their profession, and follow all such things as are agreeable to the same; through our Lord Jesus Christ. Amen.

This Collect derives from the Sacramentary of St. Leo, but was slightly changed by St. Gregory by the addition of the words 'of righteousness' in the invocation. This is the form it took in the Sarum Missal, and what Cranmer translated.

The opening invocation reminds us that it is all too easy to be in error about the true meaning and purpose of 'Christ's religion.' In the Old Testament the prophets were constantly at odds both with the religious leaders of their time, and the general public to whom they preached. It was their divinely given task to show them the error of their ways, 'to the intent that they may return into the way of righteousness.' They were not thanked for 'the light of God's truth' that they shed upon the errors of understanding and practice that prevailed in their times. They were rather rejected and persecuted. It is unfortunately man's way to allow religion to settle into a static liturgical system and to make it merely a matter of keeping precise rules. But such is not the true 'way of righteousness.' Isaiah is very fierce when he speaks of God's abhorrence at such activities and attitudes masquerading as true religion. 'When you come to appear before me, who requires of you this trampling of my courts? Bring no more vain obligations... Your new moons and your appointed feasts my soul hates; they have become a burden to me... Even though you make many prayers, I will not listen... Remove the evil of your doings from before my eyes. Cease to do evil, learn to do good; seek justice, correct oppression, defend the fatherless, plead for the widow.'[1] And Micah puts it all with splendid simplicity; 'He has showed you, O man, what is good; and what does the Lord require of you, but to do justice and love kindness and to walk humbly with your God.'[2]

In this Jesus was the true heir of the prophets. When he came to the Temple, he drove out those who were turning God's house of prayer into a 'den of thieves',[3] and the Pharisees hated him, because he showed up their injustice and hypocrisy.[4] But we do well to admit to ourselves that it is all too easy to be similarly 'in error' about the true meaning and purpose of Christ's religion. When Jesus spoke of it to his own disciples, we notice how confused they were. 'Do you not yet perceive or understand? Having eyes do you not see, and having ears do you not hear? And do you not remember?'[5] Even at the very end of his life, having been 'so long time with him', they remained as perplexed as ever. 'We do not know what he means,' they all said'.[6] 'Christ's religion' is not easily comprehended by sinful men. Does not the opening invocation therefore apply to us? And if so, in what ways?

Both the Church as an organisation, and we as God's children, must be constantly concerned lest we take a wrong turning in our religious life. That this is possible, and that the consequences are most serious, is emphasised by Jesus in his parable of the two ways.[7] Indeed the sad implication of that parable is that in this vital matter there is more failure than success. So we must be repeatedly turning and returning to God in a humble and enquiring spirit. 'In thy light shall we see light',[8] said the Psalmist. And that we should never cease to live by that light, 'the light of thy truth', is the main burden of this prayer.

Christ's religion is called here 'the way of righteousness'. This can be taken in two ways, depending on which word one lays the emphasis. If it is on

---

1 Is 1:12-17   2 Mic 6:8   3 Matt 21:13 (A.V.)
4 Mk 7:1-13, Matt 23   5 Mk 8:17-18   6 Jn 16:18   7 Matt 7:13-14
8 Ps 36:9

'righteousness', it emphasises behaviour; if on 'way', it suggests a spiritual journey. So the phrase underlines the truth that 'Christ's religion' is both a 'way of life' and a 'way to life'. If we stress the latter, we highlight the truth that it is a journey of discovery, in which we follow Christ, in order to find God. The word 'religion' means 'binding together' God and man. Jesus saw his 'religion' in these terms. 'I am the way, the truth and the life', he said. 'No man comes to the Father but by me'.[9] That we should come to the Father is what matters, and we follow Christ to reach him. This is 'the way of righteousness', that is a way to the righteous God, who is the fount of all truth and life. Even to start along this way is to start to come truly alive. To find God, however, is to discover life in all its fullness, glory and truth.

This is a mysterious journey that we undertake, when we set out to follow Christ. The mystery of it, however, is such as we have to use language that, taken at face value, may appear nonsense! But the truth is that this journey is not just one that we undertake with Christ; it is also one in which we journey into him. Christ's religion is not simply a matter of following; it is also an experience of indwelling. When St. Paul spoke about the two great sacraments of Baptism and Holy Communion, he did so in a most peculiar way. We are baptised 'into Christ',[10] and in Holy Communion we eat and drink the bread and wine 'into' his remembrance.[11] The Greek for remembrance, anamnesis, means really 'a living presence brought into actuality by means of our memory'. The translation 'in remembrance of me', with which we are so familiar, does scant justice, therefore, to St. Paul's understanding of what is happening when we receive the consecrated elements, nor is it a literal translation of the Greek (eis tén emén anamnésin), which is 'into my anamnesis'. A.G. Hebert suggests that 'objective-remembrance' is about as close as we can get to translating this subtle word in English without using a long explanatory sentence.[12] This 'way' of Christ's religion, then, is mysterious indeed. It is a means whereby 'we may evermore dwell in him and he in us.' And since God was in Christ [13] this

9 Jn 14:6   10 Rom 6:3   11 1 Cor 11:24
12 A Theological Word Book of the Bible – See Memory.   13 2 Cor 5:19

indwelling is the way we do reach God, our journey's end. 'Your life is hid with Christ in God', said St. Paul.[14] If that is true for us, how mysterious that makes our lives!

If on the other hand we stress the word 'righteousness' in the phrase 'the way of righteousness', we stress the social and ethical implications of following Christ. And these are always going to demand our active attention, because as this Collect stresses, 'Christ's religion' is a fellowship, in which we must accept responsibilities and obligations towards our fellow Christians and towards the world at large. As John Wesley said, 'There is no such thing as a solitary Christian.'

'Fellowship' is one of the most important words in the New Testament (in Greek koinonia). Its root meaning is sharing, and what we are to share in this 'fellowship of Christ's religion' is primarily Christ himself, his righteous ways, and all the benefits that he has won for us. What are these? The Epistles constantly refer to them. They mention God's grace, the promises of the Gospel and the glory that is to come.[15] But we are also to share in Christ's sufferings and death, and if we do so, we shall share in his resurrection.[16] This sharing in the risen life of Christ means, also, a sharing in the Holy Spirit, and the divine nature itself.[17] Koinonia therefore, though linked specially with the Holy Spirit, means nothing less than fellowship with both the Father and the Son.[18] So the New Testament teaching on koinonia confirms the teaching that 'Christ's religion' is a spiritual journey to God in all his fullness.

But just as we cannot make this spiritual journey to God alone, neither can we have fellowship with God alone. Koinonia is also an experience of a new kind of fellowship with others. In Acts there is a famous description of what this fellowship meant for the first Christians. 'They devoted themselves to the apostles' teaching and fellowship, to the breaking of bread, and the

14 Col 3:3   15 Phil 1:7, Eph 3:6, 1 Pet 5:1   16 Phil 3:10-11
17 2 Cor 13:14, 2 Pet 1:4   18 1 Jn 1:3

prayers... All who believed were together and had all things in common; and they sold their possessions and goods and distributed them to all, as any had need.' It was both a spiritual fellowship, and a fellowship of practical help. It was one that called for sacrifice, but one, nonetheless, that was full of joy. 'Day by day they partook of food with glad and generous hearts, praising God, and having favour with all the people.'[19]

We are told that the start of this experience of koinonia was Baptism.[20] It was through that sacrament that the first Christians learned what it meant to be 'admitted into the fellowship of Christ's religion.' Since Easter was one of the great days for Baptisms, no doubt this Collect, coming so soon after Easter, was meant to remind the Church of the needs of the newly baptised. It should also remind us of our own Baptism, and the obligations that sacrament lays on us, that we should 'eschew those things that are contrary to our profession' as Christians, and to 'follow all such things as are agreeable to the same.'

Koinonia involves us in obligations and is, therefore, something that we must work at, but to this end we need God's grace. This is not only because to do so is going to call for many virtues, but also because this 'fellowship of Christ's religion' is not to become simply another human organisation, concerned mainly with its own members, as is the case, very properly, with other fellowships in the world. 'The fellowship of Christ's religion' is to be quite different to that, and one is reminded of Archbishop Temple's famous description of the Church, as being 'the only organisation that is primarily committed to promoting the good of those outside its fellowship'. But if the Church is controlled only by ordinary men and women, it will become like any other man-made and man-run organisation. So koinonia in the New Testament is especially linked with the person of the Holy Spirit, just as the concept of grace is especially linked with the person of Jesus. Yet they are united in their purpose, as in the familiar words of the Grace. [21] Indeed it is very difficult, even impossible, to separate the two in our spiritual

19 Acts 2:42-47   20 Acts 2:38   21 2 Cor 13:14

experience. Who can say where the fellowship of the Holy Spirit ends and the grace of our Lord Jesus Christ begins, or vice versa? What one can say is that koinonia is where both Jesus and the Holy Spirit equally make God's loving presence felt. So we are enabled to experience a new way of living, both with God and with others, 'the way of righteousness'.

This brings us to the final aspect of this Collect's petition which especially emphasises the outward aspect of Christ's religion. The Church's fellowship is practical as well as mystical. It is a real continuation of the life of Jesus, 'who went about doing good.'[22] In the Pauline Epistles the usual pattern is for the early chapters to be concerned with doctrinal and devotional subjects, and the later chapters to be concerned with practical considerations. Faith must be proved by works.[23] In this, as the Collect makes clear, there is a positive and a negative side.

First the negative; we are to 'eschew' what is contrary to our profession. In the Epistles the negative aspect of 'Christ's religion' is usually put in a positive way, as is done in this Collect; we are to 'eschew evil' says St. Peter quoting the Psalmist.[24] So positive words like hate, resist and fear are usually used. We are to 'hate what is evil', to 'resist the Devil', to fear the serious consequences of dishonesty and unkindness.[25] We are not just to avoid such things as 'fornication, impurity, passion, evil desire, and covetousness, which is idolatry'; we are to put all such things to death.[26]

In the main, however, the emphasis in the apostolic teaching on this matter is altogether positive. This is in line with a similar emphasis in our Lord's teaching in the Gospels. In the Sermon on the Mount St. Matthew was clearly depicting Jesus as a second but far greater Moses. Just as it was from Mount Sinai that Moses gave the Ten Commandments, so it is from the mountain[27] that Jesus taught that to keep them only in the letter was not sufficient for his disciples. An even fuller and truer goodness is

22 Acts 10:38   23 Jas 2:18   24 1 Pet 3:10, Ps 34:14
25 Rom 12:9, 1 Pet 5:9, Col 3:12-4:1   26 Col 3:5   27 Matt 5:1

therefore required of us. If one sets the Ten Commandments, which are largely negative, beside the wholly positive Beatitudes[28] one sees the difference. To attain to the holiness of the former one has certainly to believe and behave properly, but to attain to the holiness of the latter one must become a new person altogether.

So we find ourselves returning in thought to where we started. It is only as we enter into fellowship with Christ that we can hope to live out the demands of 'Christ's religion.' Therefore this religion is a spiritual journey to a new life in Christ. It is a way of following, a way of righteousness and a way to righteousness. St. Paul acknowledges the difficulty, inherent in such a journey, but he does so full of confidence that the desired end may be reached. 'Not that I have already obtained this end,' he says, but 'I press on to make it my own, because Christ Jesus has made me his own.' Therein lies our cause for hope too. Therefore we must press forward, forgetting the past and looking to the future, seeking 'the prize of the upward call of God in Christ Jesus.'[29] That prize is possible for us and 'all who have been admitted into the fellowship of Christ's religion', because God makes it possible through grace. 'Fear not, little flock, for it is your Father's good pleasure to give you the kingdom'.[30] 'He who calls you is faithful, and he will do it.'[31] 'He has made (us) his own.'

28 Matt 5:3-10   29 Phil 3:12-16   30 Lk 12:32   31 1 Thess 5:24

EASTER IV

O Almighty God, who alone canst order the unruly wills and affections of sinful men; grant unto thy people, that they may love the thing which thou commandest, and desire that which thou dost promise; that so, among the sundry and manifold changes of the world, our hearts may surely there be fixed, where true joys are to be found; through Jesus Christ our Lord. Amen.

This is a beautiful Collect, and a splendid example of liturgical prose. It is Gelasian, but has been changed in translation in a significant manner. The original opening, which was faithfully followed when first translated for the 1549 Book, was altered for the Book of 1662. Originally the opening read, 'Almighty God, who dost make the minds of all faithful men to be of one will...' In 1662 this idea of Christian unity, which, one can argue, detracted from the unity of the prayer, was eliminated. The prayer now focuses entirely upon the hope of heavenly joys without mention of any specific earthly blessings.

We are often reminded in the Collects of our absolute need for grace, (Advent I, Trinity XVII and XVIII) and our essential weakness of nature (Epiphany IV, Lent II). We are reminded of these truths again here. We are 'sinful men.' Our wills are 'unruly' and our affections perverse. Because of this weakness, brought about by our living with 'sin that clings so closely'[1] and, embracing it both gladly and willingly, we do not 'love the thing which God commandest, nor desire that which he doth promise.' Because of this evil that infects our 'wills and affections' we are living disorientated lives. A kind of madness has overtaken us. We have become 'futile in (our) thinking and (our) senseless minds have become darkened. Claiming to be wise (we) have become fools. (We) have exchanged the truth about God for

1   Heb 12:1

a lie', so 'God has given (us) up to dishonourable passions', and we have become 'filled with all manner of wickedness.'[2]

Our sin moreover is not only folly and wickedness; it is also misery. As a result 'there will be tribulation and distress for every human being who does evil.'[3] St. Paul speaks for all, when he not only perceived the error of his ways, but also the grip that sin had upon him. 'When I want to do right, evil lies close at hand. I delight in the law of God in my inmost being, but I see in my(self) another law making me captive to the law of sin.' In spite of repentance sin still ruled, and he could not of himself shake off its hold over him. So he cried out, 'Wretched man that I am! Who will rescue me?'[4]

This, then, is man's great predicament of being 'sold under sin'.[5] We are hearing again here the language of the slave market, that is so evident throughout the New Testament (See Trinity XIII). Sin has taken away our natural rights as God's children. We hear a lot about basic human rights these days, but those, about which we hear most, are really only peripheral. St. Paul goes to the heart of the problem. We are 'slaves to sin'.[6] We have lost 'the glorious liberty of the children of God'.[7] We must be redeemed, but 'we have no power of ourselves to help ourselves' in this matter. (Lent II) However, 'thanks be to God, through Jesus Christ our Lord,'[8] a power is present that 'canst order the unruly wills and affections of sinful men.' Through him we may be saved from the folly and misery of sin, from the kind of life that ends only in death. Because of God's love and power, we need not perish, but rather have eternal life.[9] So the opening of this Collect takes us to the very heart of the Gospel.

The main petition of this Collect is in two halves. The first half is a prayer that we may love what God commands and desire what he promises.

Jesus linked love and obedience. 'If you love me, you will keep my commandments.'[10] Obedience is as much the proof of love as works is of

2 Rom 1:21-32   3 Rom 2:9   4 Rom 7:21-24   5 Rom 7:14
6 Rom 6:20   7 Rom 8:21   8 Rom 7:25   9 Jn 3:16
10 Jn 14:15

faith. 'Thy commandments are wonderful, therefore doth my soul keep them.'[11] This is the spirit of one who is inspired by the Spirit of God's Son.[12] It is indeed the Holy Spirit, 'who proceedeth from the Father and the Son', who inspires us both to love and to obey. In the Collect for purity at the start of the Holy Communion Service we pray that the Holy Spirit may inspire us to 'perfectly love God', and we can only do this if we 'love the thing that he commands.'

Also in this prayer' desire' is linked to God's promises. On the one hand, 'love' is linked to our need to give obedience in the present, and we must not put off that obedience for a moment; on the other, however,' desire' is linked to promises that lie in the future, and it is not to matter how long we are to wait for them. We can wait patiently and hopefully, because these promises are guaranteed, first, through the arrival of Christ, 'All the promises of God find their 'Yes' in him'[13] is the quaint way in which St. Paul puts it, and they are confirmed a second time by the coming of the Holy Spirit, as Jesus said before his Ascension, 'I send the promise of the Father upon you.'[14] St. Paul puts it like this. We have been 'sealed with the promised Holy Spirit, which is the guarantee of our inheritance, until we acquire possession of it.'[15] Even so there is a need for much faith, hope and patience, as we wait to inherit all that is meant by the promises of God.[16] However, it is an active eager spirit with which we must wait, not a resigned passive one. It is to be for us as it was for the children of Israel, 'The secret things belong to the Lord our God; but the things that are revealed (i.e. the law) belong to us ... that we may do all the words of this law',[17] and do them gladly and willingly. It is 'scoffers', men of worldly spirit, says St. Peter, who disturb the faithful by asking, 'Where is the promise of his coming ?' We are not to listen to them, but 'according to his promise we (are to) wait for new heavens and a new earth in which righteousness dwells'[18] in a spirit of faith and obedience. (For further discussion on God's promises see Trinity XIV).

| 11 Ps 119:129 | 12 Gal 4:6-7 | 13 2 Cor 1:20 | 14 Lk 24:49 |
| 15 Eph 1:13-14 | 16 Heb 6:12 | 17 Deut 29:29 | 18 2 Pet 3:4,13 |

The second part of the petition takes us into those longed for 'new heavens and new earth' that God in Christ has promised. On earth all is change and decay. 'Here we have no lasting city, for we seek the city which is to come.'[19] Because the Evil One is the Prince of this world [20] it is a world in which death holds sway. All creation is 'in bondage to decay'. [21] We live 'among sundry and manifold change' and permanent uncertainty. 'You do not know what tomorrow will bring.' [22] But in spite of this we may know peace and joy. We may do so because 'we have built our house upon the rock', and that rock is God himself. [23] God never changes, [24] and we know that we are the objects of his everlasting love.[25] Therefore we are utterly persuaded that nothing whatsoever can separate us from him. [26] 'My heart is fixed, O God, my heart is fixed', wrote the Psalmist, therefore 'I will sing and give praise.' [27] Similarly St. Paul wrote, 'Rejoice in the Lord always; again I say rejoice.'[28] In spite of life's uncertainties, in spite of death's inevitability, 'our hearts may surely there be fixed where true joys are to be found.' This is the good news of the Gospel.

What are these 'true joys'? St. Paul said, 'Eye has not seen, nor ear heard, nor the heart of man conceived, what God has prepared for those who love him.' [29] Not all of the unknown is to be feared! Some of it is to be looked forward to with eager longing. Always the centre of Christian joy is the certainty that in the end we shall be with Christ. This is what transformed the future for the Apostles, this absolute certainty that beyond death they would be reunited with Jesus. They were filled with joy when he finally left them at the time of his Ascension, rather than being filled with dismay, because he had assured them that he went 'to prepare a place for them,' so that 'where he was, they may be also'.[30] That is why he could say to them that in the end and eternally they would know joy, and no one would take their joy from them.[31] It is this permanent relationship with Jesus, which starts here, that is the essential heart of all the 'true joys' that we may 'find' in heaven. (So we may recall the Sunday School way of spelling joy—J for Jesus, Y for you, and nothing in between).

19 Heb 13:14   20 Jn 16:11   21 Rom 8:21   22 Prov 27:1
23 Matt 7:24   24 Jas 1:17   25 Jer 31:3   26 Rom 8:38-39
27 Ps 57:8   28 Phil 4:4   29 1 Cor 2:9   30 Jn 14:2-3
31 Jn 16:22

EASTER V

O Lord, from whom all good things do come; grant to us thy humble servants, that by thy holy inspiration we may think those things that be good, and by thy merciful guiding may perform the same; through our Lord Jesus Christ. Amen.

This Sunday is called Rogation Sunday. The Rogation Days are days of special prayer, to be kept with fasting, for God's blessing on the growing crops. They are of early origin, and used in medieval times to be divided into two separate festivals, the Major Rogation on April 25, and the Minor Rogation on the Monday, Tuesday and Wednesday before Ascension Day. This Sunday was not originally part of Rogationtide, becoming so only in 1662.

On Rogation Days processional prayers were said or sung around the fields, and it was from these prayers, as set out in the Sarum Sacramentary, that Cranmer in 1545 formed our Prayer Book Litany, which was his first work of liturgical reform. Outdoor processional prayers used to be extremely popular in the medieval Church, and were used for many reasons. They were regularly said on Wednesdays and Fridays as Parish devotions, and Church leaders and monarchs would call for them to meet special needs. The Minor Rogations began as the result of such a call by the Bishop of Vienne in Southern France, when his diocese was troubled by volcanic eruptions, and King Henry VIII called for them to gain divine help (and popular support?) for his wars against Scotland and France in the early years of his reign.

However, one of the changes brought about by the quickening pace of the Reformation in the reign of his son, Edward VI, was the suppression of all such outdoor processions. The reason may have been the undoubted fact that some of these processions, for instance the Major Rogation, were associated with earlier pagan festivals, and this would have been particularly objectionable to the rising Puritan party in the English Church. Just as likely, however, is the fact that these popular outdoor processions were potentially subversive at a time of great religious upheaval. With the B.C.P. of 1549 went the first Act of Uniformity, which sought to change the Church in England into the Church of England, and to move the Church here in a Protestant direction. There were naturally opponents to these changes, and these largely unstructured religious processions gave much latitude to disaffected clergy to rally their flocks in opposition to what was being imposed on them from above.

However, as these processions were extremely popular, when times were more peaceful and the Anglican Reformation more established, they were reintroduced by Queen Elizabeth in 1559, but only under the strict control of the Royal Injunctions of that date. In the further revision of the B.C.P. and the final Act of Uniformity in 1662, the Major Rogation disappeared, and this Sunday was attached to the three days of the Minor Rogation to form the Rogationtide of four days that we now know. On the Monday, Tuesday and Wednesday, which were designated days of fasting, the Litany was to be used, and outdoor processions allowed. Later the processions became associated with the custom of 'beating the bounds'. Parish life in earlier centuries was a very important aspect of rural life for welfare reasons, and it was a matter of real concern that everyone should be aware of their Parish's boundaries. This annual reminder of them performed a necessary local service in a popular religious manner.

This Collect is Gelasian. It was altered in translation; 'good' was exchanged for 'right' in the invocation, and the adjectives 'holy' and 'merciful' were added in the petition.

Although this Sunday did not in medieval times have any direct connection with the Rogation Days that followed it, the opening invocation of this Collect is nonetheless appropriate for the agricultural theme of Rogation, for food and drink are certainly among the 'good things' of life. Men of faith have always seen food and drink as coming 'from God', and eating and drinking, therefore, as sacred activities. Even now, when we buy our food from shops and take our drinking water from the tap, it is not impossible to perceive the mystery of nature and the wonder of creation behind what is for us so easily obtained. Certainly it is harder now for us to acknowledge that these 'good things' come from God; our sophistication and affluence do mask this truth. Primitive people, who still eat only what they can gather from the land around them and drink only the water that is near at hand, will have a wiser perspective than ours. But we can still surely appreciate the truth of what the Psalmist wrote so beautifully about 2500 years ago. Both man and beast, he said, must turn to God in their search for food. Unless his generous hand provides, we are lost. 'These wait all upon thee', he writes, 'that thou mayest give them meat in due season. When thou givest it them they gather it; and when thou openest thy hand they are filled with good'.[1] It gives a charming picture of God, providing us personally with what we all need, and it also gives an ideal picture of man, ready to wait patiently in humble acknowledgement of his dependence upon him.

In medieval times there were a series of agricultural festivals, of which in the B.C.P. only Rogationtide and Lammas were kept. Plough Sunday on Epiphany I was not officially recognised and Lammas, although retained in the Calendar, was generally ignored. Lammas was an early or first harvest thanksgiving, the offering of the first fruits. (The word derives from Loaf-Mass). There would have been a final harvest thanksgiving, when all the work was done and the harvest 'safely gathered in.' These agricultural festivals, however, which were such a recognised part of medieval Church life, were not encouraged in the post-reformation Church. Perhaps this was because of the associations they undoubtedly had with paganism, which still hovered beneath the surface, as has been mentioned already. Perhaps, also, it had to do with the influence of Calvinism in our Reformation. Calvin taught that a basic moral corruption infected all

1 Ps 104:27-28

natural human life, with its desires and passions. To live naturally was to live sinfully. Not even the natural craving of a baby for his mother's milk was innocent; how much less the desire for food and drink in adults. Moreover, how could God bless the work we do to obtain our food when it is imposed on us as a punishment for sin?[2] How different was the insight of the Psalmist already referred to. He saw God giving us all we need, generously and joyfully, so that we may be happy, 'wine that maketh glad the heart of man, oil to make him a cheerful countenance, and bread to strengthen man's heart.'[3] The medieval Church understood this, and the Catholic revival in the last century rediscovered these popular agricultural festivals for our Church.

Behind the agricultural festivals of the medieval Church, however, did not just lie pagan practices which were Christianised. There was also the example of the Jewish religion. The greatest Jewish festivals were all agricultural festivals, as well as commemorations of historic events. Passover was the celebration of Spring, in which crops were growing and lambs were in abundance, Pentecost was the celebration in high Summer of the first fruits of the harvest, and Tabernacles was the Jewish harvest thanksgiving festival. In all these major festivals there was a conscious remembrance of all God's natural blessings, as well as his special mercies and promises to the Jews. The God of both the Old and the New Testaments is very definitely the God 'from whom all good things do come'. There is an important place, therefore, in Christian devotion for an appreciation of the natural, as well as the supernatural. Is this not what we mean when we describe Christianity as an incarnational religion, in which the ordinary side of life is 'hallowed and directed aright' by God who 'knows how to give good gifts to his children'[4]?

The petition in this Collect is for the grace (thy holy inspiration) to think and do what is right and good. In this it is exactly similar to the Collect for

2 Gen 3:17-19   3 Ps 104:15   4 Matt 7:11

Trinity IX and broadly similar to several others. This, however, can cause us no surprise, seeing that this is such a basic human need, and yet, although so much, indeed everything, depends upon us doing God's will, we cannot either 'think those things that be good or perform the same' without God's 'holy inspiration'. It is because of our failure to do God's will that so many 'good things' are withheld from us. 'Except the Lord build the house, their labour is but lost that build it'.[5] Nothing will succeed unless God approves of what we do.

The Rogationtide theme especially points us towards our need to obtain God's blessing upon the growing corn and fruit and vegetables in our fields and gardens at this time of early summer. In Deuteronomy, we may notice, Moses tells the children of Israel of the 'good things' that await them in Canaan, 'a land flowing with milk and honey', but, he says, everything depends on their keeping God's commandments. If they fail to do so, a curse will fall upon them, so that the good ground will withhold its blessings. If they are faithful and obedient, they can look for bountiful harvests. 'Blessed shall be the fruit of your ground and the fruit of your beasts, the increase of your cattle and the young of your flock.'[6] This was a warning often remembered by the prophets when hard times arrived, and they were quick to make the point, believing, as they did, that there were no such things as natural forces, only supernatural ones. God was in their eyes wholly in charge of sunshine and rain, warmth and cold. Their failure revealed his displeasure, their regular and sufficient arrival evidence of his continuing favour.

No doubt we are not required to think exactly as they thought about such things, but part of 'thinking those things that be good' (or right, for the Latin here is recta, not bona, which is used for good earlier in this Collect) with regard to agriculture is to make sure that our methods of farming are morally acceptable to our consciences. The emphasis given by Calvin to our natural tendency to sin may have been extreme, but nonetheless it is true

5 Ps 127:1   6 Deut 28: 3-6

that we can, and so often do, pollute and vitiate 'the good things' God gives us with serious consequences. By our greed we can poison fertile ground; by our short-sightedness we can destroy long term benefits; that some modern farming methods are cruel to live-stock has become fully apparent. The consequences, therefore, of some modern farming methods are being revalued, for it is recognised that factory farming and intensive farming are not bringing the blessings that had been expected, but rather the opposite. 'Thus you will know them by their fruits', said Jesus.[7]

In his comments on this prayer Canon Masterman makes a striking observation, 'God gives us his thoughts that we may turn them into deeds'. This truth helps us both to understand God's creation and to judge what is genuinely creative. Behind all creative activity is thought, decision and command. So the Bible starts with the vision of God deciding, and then declaring, and thus creating. 'And God said 'Let there be light', and there was light'.[8] St. John was being faithful to Genesis when he said, 'In the beginning was the Word'.[9] But it is the special contribution of the New Testament to show that behind God's creation there was something else as well, love. 'The Word became flesh' and revealed that truth. If, therefore, we are to be creative after the manner of God, that is in such a way as to bring blessings upon ourselves, we must let love direct both our thinking and doing. This is essential. 'This is my commandment, that you love...', [10] and in his Epistle St. John teaches how this has always been the real truth. 'Beloved, I am writing you no new commandment (in stressing the primacy of love), but the old commandment which you had from the beginning'.[11] But how unloving and unlovely is so much modern agriculture! This is, therefore, a real indictment. It may be statistically successful, but it is not a loving or lovely business. Can it, therefore, in our eyes merit the description creative? Although the Collect for this Sunday was not written with the needs of agriculture in mind, it is, nonetheless, most suitable for intercession on behalf of those needs today.

---

7   Matt 7:20   8   Gen 1:3   9   Jn 1:1   10 Jn 15:12
11 1 Jn 2:7

ASCENSION DAY
and
THE SUNDAY AFTER ASCENSION DAY

Grant, we beseech thee, Almighty God, that like as we do believe thy only-begotten Son our Lord Jesus Christ to have ascended into the heavens; so we may also in heart and mind thither ascend, and with him continually dwell, who liveth and reigneth with thee and the Holy Ghost, one God, world without end. Amen.

O God, the King of glory, who hast exalted thine only Son Jesus Christ with great triumph unto thy kingdom in heaven; we beseech thee, leave us not comfortless; but send to us thine Holy Ghost to comfort us, and exalt us unto the same place whither our Saviour Christ is gone before, who liveth and reigneth with thee and the Holy Ghost, one God, world without end. Amen.

The Collect for Ascension Day is basically the Gregorian Collect in the Sarum Missal. However, in translation Cranmer added the phrase 'with him continually dwell', which probably was suggested to him by an earlier Ascension Day Collect in the Gelasian Sacramentary. In 1662 the words 'Jesus Christ' were added to the invocation.

Ascension Day, as one of the great festivals of the Christian year, is given a Proper Preface and octave in the B.C.P. It falls on the fortieth day after Easter, following the teaching of Acts 1:3 in which the Ascension is seen as the final resurrection appearance. Ascension Day closes the Easter season and the short Ascension season of ten days is a time of joyful preparation for Whitsunday, as the Collect for the Sunday after the Ascension makes plain.

The Collect for the Sunday after Ascension Day was composed in 1549. It was inspired by the antiphon for the Magnificat sung at Vespers on Ascension Day according to the medieval Sacramentaries, but Cranmer in composing the Collect made a significant alteration. The antiphon spoke of Jesus as 'the King of glory' who ascended to heaven in triumph. The Collect, however, describes the Father as 'the King of glory', who exalted Jesus 'with great triumph' to his heavenly kingdom.

In the New Testament we find the Resurrection and the Ascension spoken of in both these ways. In St. Peter's first great sermon we hear of Jesus being raised by God the Father and exalted to 'his right hand on high'.[1] In St. John's Gospel, however, the initiative in both his Resurrection and his Ascension remains with Jesus.[2] St. Paul taught both doctrines! In Philippians it is the Father who exalted Jesus to heaven,[3] whereas in Ephesians Jesus ascended through his own power.[4] In the Collect for Ascension Day the manner of our Lord's Ascension is not mentioned, and we may notice that in Hebrews, where the role of the ascended Jesus is the main consideration of the Epistle, this particular matter is nowhere discussed. Consequently we can perhaps describe it as a distinction without a difference, although we should notice that the Creeds give preference to the former view.

The Ascension of Jesus is something in which we are to share, not only in the life beyond death, but in this life also. In this the Ascension is like the Crucifixion and the Resurrection. Just as we are through the grace of God at work in us to die to sin and rise again to eternal life, even while we live here on earth, so, as the Collect says, 'we may also in heart and mind thither ascend and with him continually dwell'. Our life in Christ is therefore, to include a spiritual experience of all these events in the life of Christ. We are to die in Christ, rise again in Christ, and also ascend in him, and thereby share in his glory. Although all this is to find its fulfilment hereafter, it is

1 Acts 2:24-33   2 Jn 10:18, 20:17   3 Phil 2:9   4 Eph 4:8-10

to begin here, as St. Paul makes clear to the Colossians. Our 'ascension' in Christ now is to transform our whole attitude towards life here, and to guarantee our eternal 'ascension' in Christ hereafter. 'If then you have been raised with Christ, seek the things that are above, where Christ is seated at the right hand of God. Set your minds on things that are above, not on things that are on earth. For you have died and your life is hid with Christ in God. When Christ, who is your life, appears, then you also will appear with him in glory'. [5] (This important theme is especially linked with God's promises, and further discussion on it is to be found in the commentary for Trinity XIV.)

The Resurrection and the Ascension are intimately connected, and there is a sense, already referred to, in which the Ascension can be described as the last of the resurrection appearances. The manner in which Jesus ascended was emphasising visually teaching that he had given verbally. He was going to heaven, not to return in his resurrection body. He would return, however, to be with them permanently, in his mystical Body, the Church, through the person of the Holy Spirit, who was to come upon them on the day of Pentecost. The Ascension, therefore, can be seen as a bridge event, linking the events of Easter and the events of Whitsun, as already mentioned. This thought is central to the theme of the Collect for the Sunday after Ascension. Easter is over; now we must move on to live out the crucified and risen life in the new Body of Christ, the Church. In this Collect the Church looks back to Easter and forward to Whitsun. The Ascension season is a short one, as befits a bridge season. We cannot linger here. We await the coming of the Holy Spirit.

However, the Ascension of Jesus is very much a festival in its own right. It stands for a special truth that is importantly different from that of his Resurrection. It declares categorically and unmistakably that we are

5   Col 3:1-3

welcome in highest heaven, a truth that the Resurrection of Jesus may have implied, but did not make crystal clear. St. Mary Magdalene sought to keep the risen Jesus with her on earth. But she was told that this could not be, although that did not mean that she would never see him again.[6] For that joy she must wait. Jesus ascended bodily, according to St. Luke's account of the event both in his Gospel and Acts.[7] The bodily resurrection and bodily ascension of Jesus are important because they teach that we ordinary human beings are really to be allowed into heaven. Certainly our bodies there will not be identical to our bodies here, but we will live there as our individual selves, conscious of our 'bodies' and capable of fellowship with others. We will truly be in that 'same place whither our Saviour Christ is gone before', and 'with him (and each other) continually dwell.'

But can we say anything with certainty about the nature of this heavenly life that the Ascension Collects bid us hope for, and prepare ourselves, even while we are here, to enter? St. Paul claims to have seen into this life, but either he could not, or he believed he should not describe it. All he says is this: 'I know a man in Christ who fourteen years ago was caught up into the third heaven – whether in the body or out of the body I do not know, God knows. And I know this man was caught up into Paradise – whether in the body or out of the body I do not know, God knows – and he heard things that cannot be told, which man may not utter'.[8] No doubt we wish that he had said much more, but we must take his silence as divinely meant and accept the wisdom of it. Did not the angel also say that we should not spend our time here 'looking into heaven'?[9]

Nonetheless what St. Paul says is full of significance and value for us. First, he confirms this Christian hope of a life for us beyond death. And how valuable that is! But secondly he describes himself in this context as 'a man in Christ', rather than simply as himself. Indeed later in the same passage he emphasises this description in such a way as to make a distinction between himself as 'a man in Christ' and himself as an ordinary man. It is

---

6   Jn 20:17   7   Lk 24:50-51, Acts 1:9   8   2 Cor 12:2-4
9   Acts 1:11

as if he looked at himself and saw two people. 'On behalf of this man (in Christ) I will boast, but on my own behalf I will not boast, except in my weaknesses'.[10]

We recognise the point that he is making here as that which he makes repeatedly in all his letters, that being 'in Christ' (his most characteristic phrase) is what matters, and all that matters. Therein, he declares, lies salvation from sin and newness of life, and this has the most important consequences for us both in this world and beyond it. Being 'in Christ' means both sharing in his mission in this world, and sharing in his life beyond it. Those who live 'in him' here will 'continually dwell' with him hereafter. There is nothing more that we need to know about the nature of this heavenly life, but this, he says, we may most certainly know. It is this truth that is as clearly central to the teaching contained in these Collects as it is to that of St. Paul, and indeed of the whole New Testament.[11] (But see also the commentary on Trinity VI.)

The Collect for the Sunday after Ascension Day talks of the Ascension as a 'great triumph.' This great triumph is the theme of Revelation Chapter 5. There the seer sees a vision of heaven. The book of life is brought out, but it is sealed and none can open it, even in heaven. How dreadful, it seems, that it will be permanently shut! But then Jesus appears upon the scene. He is the Lamb of God, the one who has been sacrificed and risen again, the victor over sin and death, and he is worthy and able to open that book, so that his fellow men may live. The seer sees him making his triumphal entry into heaven, and taking his rightful place at the right hand of the throne of God. He opens the book, and judgement begins. Moreover, to complete his joy, it is a judgement of salvation, for 'by his blood he did ransom men for God from every tribe and tongue and people and nation, and has made them a kingdom and priests to our God.'[12]

10 2 Cor 12:5   11 Rom 8:1, 2 Cor 5:17, 1 Jn 3:2   12 Rev 5:9-10

In the Epistle to the Hebrews Jesus is equally triumphant, and in heaven he reigns over and ministers to all mankind as our great High Priest. 'He reflects the glory of God and bears the very stamp of his nature, upholding the universe by the word of his power.' [13] He rules, seated 'at the right hand of the Majesty on high', 'till he makes his enemies a footstool for his feet.'[14] Yet he also ministers as well as rules, since he has opened up the sanctuary of heaven to us, and 'we (now) may draw near in full assurance of faith'.[15] There now he always lives to make intercession for us.[16] He is still our Jesus, 'who tasted death for everyone'. 'He is not ashamed to call us brethren'[17]. The incarnation is for ever, therefore his triumph is our salvation. No wonder there was rejoicing in heaven! It is unfortunate that Ascension Day is always on a Thursday, and sad that it is not a public holiday. It is a glorious festival and should be for Christians a day of special praise and thanksgiving, and how regrettable it is that the circumstances of modern life make this very hard for more than a fortunate minority.

13 Heb 1:3   14 Heb 1:3, 13   15 Heb 10:20-21
16 Heb 7:25   17 Heb 2:9-11

WHITSUNDAY

God, who as at this time didst teach the hearts of thy faithful people, by the sending to them the light of thy Holy Spirit; grant us by the same Spirit to have a right judgement in all things, and evermore to rejoice in his holy comfort; through the merits of Christ Jesus our Saviour, who liveth and reigneth with thee, in the unity of the same Spirit, one God, world without end. Amen.

This day, the birthday of the Church, is also the Jewish festival of Pentecost, so called because it comes on the fiftieth day after Passover. (Pentecoste is the Greek for fifty). In the Church world-wide it is still generally know as Pentecost, and is now so called in the A.S. B. The title Whitsunday, which was officially adopted by the Reformers, is, however, a popular title of early origin, and derives from this day being, with Easter, a special day for baptisms. Traditionally it has ranked second only to Easter in the Church's calendar, although in popular estimation, at least in our Church, Christmas is now considered a far more important festival. Indeed since the ending of the Whitsun Bank Holiday, Whitsunday is in danger of becoming like Good Friday and the Ascension a forgotten Major Festival.

This is the Gregorian Collect for this Sunday, with the addition of 'in all things' and the adjective 'holy' in the petition.

The first thought in the Collect is of the Holy Spirit as the teacher of the faithful. This is in agreement with Jesus's teaching. 'The Holy Spirit... will teach you all things and bring to your remembrance all that I have said to you.'[1] His manner of teaching is particularly described as reminding us of what Jesus taught. This is added justification for believing that the

1   Jn 14:26

teaching of Jesus in the Gospels is particularly binding upon us. In New Testament times the early Christians accepted the Jewish Scriptures, as Jesus himself did, as divinely inspired and sufficient. St. Paul writing to Timothy said, 'All Scripture is inspired by God and profitable for teaching, for reproof, for correction, and for training in righteousness, that a man of God may be complete, equipped for every good work.'[2] With that we can heartily agree, only including in our understanding of Scripture the New Testament, which did not then exist. And for us pre-eminent within Scripture are the teachings of Jesus, which include not only what he said, but also what he taught us by his life. It is the work of the Holy Spirit to take the words of Scripture and reveal God's will for us from them, that we might have 'a right judgement in all things.'

One of the main causes of the Reformation was the realisation that the Papacy had grossly exaggerated its teaching authority. The Church's teaching authority ought to be that of a humble and dependent mouthpiece of the Holy Spirit, basing all its doctrine on the teaching of Christ and the word of God in Scripture. While the Scriptures remained unavailable to the ordinary Christian it was all too easy for the Papacy to act with an authority unchecked by Scripture. It was the invention of printing as much as anything else that guaranteed that the Reformation was irreversible. It placed Christ again back on his chair as teacher supreme, for all could be reminded of 'all that he has said to us.' The appeal to Scripture became the hallmark of both the Reformation, and also the Counter-Reformation. So it has continued until this century.

In our time, however, a new reformation is under way, as many have observed. A major feature of it is the claim that the Holy Spirit may be heard speaking through other religions and many aspects of modern life and current affairs, as well as through Jesus in particular and the Scriptures generally. This is a decided departure from earlier tradition, and in consequence there is a crisis of authority. As scriptural judgements and prohibitions are challenged and altered to suit modern wisdom and manners, there arises an inevitable sense of uncertainty about what is right and wrong, and what true or false. Who has authority to declare 'right judgement'? Whose voice is of the Holy Spirit? Ours has been the era of ecumenism between Churches, but it has also been a time of disunity within Churches. It has been a period in which the charismatic movement has influenced all Churches, but it has also been a time that has seen the growth of a multiplicity of Churches within an increasingly fragmented Church, and even, sadly, a time of schism within our Anglican Communion. The threat, moreover, of further schism remains, though, most mercifully, it seems to have receded now within the Church of England.

This Collect points us to the truth that the Holy Spirit does not speak to us independently. 'He will not speak on his own authority', said Jesus, 'but whatever he hears he will speak... He will glorify me for he will take what is mine and declare it to you.' Then to stress how the Father and he speak with one voice, he added, 'All that the Father has is mine; therefore I said that he will take what is mine and declare it to you,' [3] for 'the Holy Spirit proceedeth from the Father and the Son.' This is the Spirit that speaks to the Churches.[4]

Consequently the Holy Spirit, although he is operating throughout God's creation, is not the voice of the world, for 'the world cannot receive him or know him'.[5] Rather he is the voice that convinces us of the sin of the world and of God's judgement upon it.[6] He also convinces us that in essence sin is failing to recognise Christ and to acknowledge his unique authority.[7] Those who do acknowledge his authority are God's 'faithful people', whom the Holy Spirit can teach. It is the belief of the New Testament that Christ alone can claim to 'have a right judgement in all things', and in order that we may also have 'a right judgement' the Holy Spirit points us to him. It is

3   Jn 16:13-15   4   Rev 2:7   5   Jn 14:17   6   Jn 16:11
7   Jn 16:9

to this supremely important end that the Holy Spirit formed and uses the Church, as is exemplified by St. Peter's sermon on the first Whitsunday in particular, and by the writings of the New Testament in general.[8] It is Jesus who is 'the light of the world', and 'the light of the Holy Spirit' that God sends is the same light.[9]

The Collect also bids us pray that through the operation of the Holy Spirit we may 'evermore rejoice in his holy comfort.' The special word that St. John uses for the Holy Spirit is' parakletos'. It is a word only found in St. John's Gospel, and particularly hard to translate. The A.V. has Comforter, the R.S.V. has Counsellor, the N.E.B. has Advocate, and some modern versions have simply Helper. The sense of the word is of someone who is helpful and intimate, but also of someone who is authoritative and strong. The word has connections with the law courts, and so the implication is that he has come to help us in our troubles. He is the one, then, who will guide and encourage and strengthen us through all life's trials and tribulations. He is therefore our most real friend, whose coming is essential to us. By going away from them in his Ascension Jesus told his disciples he was making room for the Paraclete to come and that, he said, was very much in their best interests.[10] His coming would bring new and permanent 'comfort and joy', such as the world could never take away.

We then, like the first disciples, are to know this help and comfort of the Holy Spirit. He is a strengthening (comfortare in Latin means to strengthen) and a joyful spirit, and he is to be with us 'evermore.' St. Paul described the Holy Spirit as the giver of 'love, joy, peace, patience, kindness, goodness, faithfulness, gentleness, and self control,'[11] or rather these virtues are 'the fruits of the Spirit.' This implies that they come slowly into our lives, as we are able to find room for them. To this end it is also the work of the Holy Spirit to 'cleanse the thoughts of our hearts,' a slow process, so that we may

8   Acts 2:14-36   9   Jn 8:12   10   Jn 16:17   11   Gal 5:22

'worthily love God.' Certainly when the Holy Spirit came upon the Apostles on the first Whitsunday he acted precipitately to change their lives, but even so it is clear from Acts and the Epistles that the process of their 'having a right judgement in all things' was distinctly slow. So the work of the Holy Spirit in our lives and upon our characters is also not going to be the work of a moment, not even of a life time, but of eternity. And how encouraging this thought is! We are, as the Collect says, 'to evermore rejoice in his holy comfort.'

The Collect speaks of the Holy Spirit coming 'at this time'. This does not, of course, mean that he has come only at the time of Pentecost in Jerusalem, as we read in the Acts of the Apostles, or that that was the first occasion of his coming. The Holy Spirit has been in the world from the beginning of creation. 'In the beginning God created... and the Spirit of God was moving...'[12]. Throughout history the Spirit of God has been moving, inspiring the hearts of men and women, opening their spirits to love and serve God and their fellow men. Through Israel's prophets, as especially mentioned in the Creeds, the Spirit of God has 'taught the hearts of (his) faithful people'. What happened on the first Whitsunday was therefore in some ways typical, rather than peculiar. Through the Holy Spirit God was speaking through chosen men. It was, nonetheless, a special and unique event, just as the Incarnation, the Crucifixion, the Resurrection and Ascension were all special and unique events. It was a special and unique event in the divine activity that we call the Gospel.

So what was happening? What was so special? In a word the Holy Spirit was creating the mystical Body of Christ on earth, the Church. Christ had ascended to heaven in his risen body, and there he ever-lives, our royal High Priest. In a sense his saving work was finished. Through what he had done the kingdom of God now and for ever lies open. Through faith and repentance, even while we live here, we may now enter that spiritual place

12 Gen 1:1

of obedience and freedom, of peace and joy, where love reigns. And this privilege of entering that kingdom, we do believe, will never be taken away from us. He has set before us 'an open door'.[13] But our Lord in heaven does not remain a distant figure, one who lived long ago on earth and now lives far away in heaven. Not at all. He comes to be with us still in his mystical Body, as he said, 'Lo, I am with you always to the close of the age'.[14]

So through the Holy Spirit Christ lives on earth, and not only in heaven. Through the Holy Spirit he has became incarnate again in the Church. There he lives to 'teach the hearts of (his) faithful people' through the words of Scripture and the Holy Spirit. Through his words in Scripture and the power of the Holy Spirit Jesus becomes every man and woman's contemporary. There we meet him, if we believe, and hear his voice. As it was for Moses, faith will give us the power to 'see him who is invisible',[15] and there we hear him too. He lives on also in his sacramental Body in the Eucharist, the celebration of which is so vital an aspect of the life of his mystical Body. There 'his faithful people' meet Jesus 'to the close of the age'. And more than that, they take him into their hearts so that he may indwell their lives.

Therefore he also lives on in the Church's many sided ministry. This, too, is all part of the work of the Holy Spirit, which continues to flow through the Church, giving it power and energy. 'Now you are the body of Christ and individually members of it. And God has appointed in the Church first apostles, second prophets, third teachers, then workers of miracles, then healers, helpers, administrators, speakers in various kinds of tongues'.[16] But all this variety of ministry is united through the Holy Spirit, who inspires all aspects of it, and also inspires the devotion of all to the one Lord. 'There are varieties of gifts, but the same Spirit, and there are varieties of service but the same Lord'.[17] 'All are inspired by one and the same Spirit, who apportions to each one individually as he wills'.[18] So the Bishop and the magazine distributor, the nun and the Church Commissioner, the missionary and the religious broadcaster are all united through the Holy Spirit,

13 Rev 3:8   14 Matt 28:20   15 Heb 11:27   16 1 Cor 12:27-28
17 1 Cor 12:4-5   18 1 Cor 12:11

and through him they are given power to have 'a right judgement' in all they have to do, and through him they are able to rejoice and be comforted as they make their contribution to the whole. None can say of another 'I have no need of you'.[19] But rather all are to have proper care for each other, recognising that 'if one member suffers, all suffer together, and if one member is honoured, all rejoice together'.[20] So we are, through the Holy Spirit, 'to build up the body of Christ... and, speaking the truth in love, to grow up in every way into him who is the Head, into Christ'.[21] That is our glorious hope, and because the Holy Spirit lives on in the Church, which he has created to be Christ's mystical Body, it is a hope that will be ultimately fulfilled, according to the Collect's ending, 'through the merits of Christ Jesus our Saviour, who liveth and reigneth with (the Father) in the unity of the same Spirit'.

19 1 Cor 12:21   20 1 Cor:12:25-26   21 Eph 4:12-15

TRINITY SUNDAY

Almighty and everlasting God, who hast given unto us thy servants grace, by the confession of a true faith, to acknowledge the glory of the eternal Trinity, and in the power of the Divine Majesty to worship the Unity: We beseech thee, that thou wouldest keep us stedfast in this faith, and evermore defend us from all adversities, who livest and reignest, one God, world without end. Amen.

Trinity Sunday only became an established festival in the Christian year in the 14th century. Previously this Sunday was kept simply as the final day of the octave of Whitsun or Pentecost, and as one of the four special days for ordinations. In 1334, however, Pope John XXII decreed that it should be kept as Trinity Sunday, in what was a general revision of the Calendar. It was seen as a fitting end to the first half of the Christian Year, in which through the season of Advent to Whitsun the Church remembers the main events of our Lord's life to the founding of the Church, and the ideal introduction to the second half of the year, in which our thoughts are directed more towards what Jesus said than what he did. The doctrine of the Holy Trinity therefore sums up what the early Church called the kerygma (Greek for the proclamation) and points to what is called the didache (the teaching). Therefore, as well as being a major festival in its own right, Trinity Sunday is a bridge festival linking the two halves of the Christian Year.

When Trinity Sunday was first introduced as a separate festival it was embraced with particular enthusiasm in England. The Sarum Missal, for instance, reckoned the Sundays that followed it as Sundays after Trinity, whereas in Rome they continued to be called Sundays after Pentecost. The Reformers, therefore, were continuing what had become standard usage in England when they gave the B.C.P. its Trinity season. This later became a distinguishing feature of Anglican usage as opposed to Roman Catholic usage, until the arrival of the A.S.B. and other Anglican Prayer Book revisions, which now follow the Roman terminology.

In the B.C.P. Trinity Sunday is given no octave, although it is designated a major festival by being given a Proper Preface. The use of its Proper Preface is expressly restricted to use on the Sunday only. This, however, is also in line with the mediaeval usage; the purpose for this unusual ruling was to emphasis the unity of the three Persons of the Godhead.

In the B.C.P. Trinity Sunday remains one of the four traditional days for ordination, following the Whit-week Ember Days.

The Collect is a translation of the Gregorian Collect, but one most unfortunate change was made by the compilers of the Book of 1662. The medieval Collect (correctly translated, as it happens, in 1549 but altered in 1662) made it clear that we were praying for protection from 'all adversities' through believing steadfastly in the vital doctrine of the Holy Trinity. Now the Collect reads as if we are asking of God two quite separate petitions, which are not necessarily connected. First we pray for 'steadfast faith' in the keeping of the doctrine of the Holy Trinity, and secondly for protection from 'all adversities'. It is clearly important that we interpret the B.C.P. Collect in the spirit of the medieval Collect, recognising the connection between these two petitions.

The doctrine of the Holy Trinity declares that we should understand God's inner being, his Godhead, as being Unity rather than One. This is in accord with the revelation of God in the New Testament, which reveals him to be a God who is to be loved and addressed as our Father, who has come amongst us as the Son, and who lives within us and between us as Holy Spirit, and yet he is one, whose essential unity is revealed most surely in his nature of perfect love.[1] Within the Godhead we are therefore to believe

1   1 Jn 4:8

that there is, and ever has been, and ever will be, from and to all eternity, loving fellowship between the Persons of the Holy Trinity. We are not to conceive of a God who ever existed in his 'divine majesty' in a state of divine loneliness. So in this Collect we affirm that 'in the power of the divine majesty we worship the Unity', not the oneness of God. Within the Godhead, therefore, from all eternity there is a perfect and complete giving and receiving of love, and this is what is meant by the phrase 'eternal life' in the New Testament.[2] The adjectives 'full, perfect, and sufficient', which the Prayer Book uses to describe the sacrifice of Christ, spring to mind, and are equally appropriate to describe the inner life of the Holy Trinity. It is this eternal and sufficient life of perfect love within the Godhead that is described in the Collect as 'the glory of the eternal Trinity'.

In the early centuries of the Church theological debate flourished and great theologians were born. It was then that the Creeds were composed, the most important of which is the so-called Nicene Creed. How to describe God in words that do justice to the mystery and glory of his life and being, that can be accepted by all as a sufficient sign of orthodoxy, and that can be used as a central part of worship, is clearly a matter of the greatest importance, and also difficulty. It should not surprise us that the search for such a Creed was the cause of fierce argument over a long period of time, and that in the end it failed in its purpose and became the main cause of the first great schism in the Church. In the Councils of Nicaea (325), Constantinople (381) and Chalcedon (451) the Nicene Creed was worked out, amended and finalised and at that time was agreed upon by the whole Church, both East and West. However, following largely the influential teaching of St. Augustine, the Church in the West became dissatisfied with the section in the Creed relating to the Holy Spirit, and in the third Council of Toledo (589) a fateful change was made that was to become, and still remains, the main cause of the split between the East and West, the Orthodox and the

2   Jn 17:1-3

Catholic Churches, that took place in 1054. This change is called the Filioque clause.

Filioque means 'and from the Son'. In the western version of the Nicene Creed, which is the version found in the B.C.P., for at the Reformation we remained faithful to our western roots in this matter, we declare that the Holy Spirit 'proceeds from the Father and the Son', the double procession, as it is called. This is not, however, the wording of the original Creed, which is that still used in the Orthodox Churches. The wording there is simply that the Holy Spirit 'proceeds from the Father'. This phrase has the merit of being precisely scriptural[3]. But it was argued in the West, again from Scripture, that the Holy Spirit proceeds equally from the Son. John 16.7 and 20.22 particularly support this view, and it was noticed also that St. Paul constantly stressed that the Holy Spirit was the Spirit of Jesus[4]. In the ensuing controversy, which rumbled on for six centuries, the eastern Church, while refusing to countenance any addition to the agreed text of the Creed, and also stressing that there must be a single source of Divinity, acknowledged that the Holy Spirit may indeed proceed 'through' the Son.

The difference between the two positions is clearly very small. It is a matter of emphasis. It has been suggested that the differing emphases give to the Holy Trinity, devotionally speaking, two different shapes. On the one hand by emphasising the supremacy of the Father a lineal shape emerges, as in the analogy of the sun, the rays of the sun, and the sunlight that illumines the earth, or the more scriptural analogy of the speaker, the word he speaks, and the sense that is conveyed to the hearer of the word. On the other hand, by stressing the truth that the Holy Spirit proceeds from both the Father and the Son one is projecting a triangular image of the Holy Trinity, and Holy Spirit being shown primarily as he who unites the Godhead rather than as he who reveals God, be it his nature or his will. Both versions use the same scriptural words for the Persons of the Holy Trinity. Both recognise the supremacy of the Father, and both are consis-

3   Jn 15:26   4   2 Cor 3:17-18

tent with the scriptural revelation of the divine nature as perfect love. However the eastern version of the Creed seems to lay the emphasis on the Father's supremacy within the Godhead, whereas the western version seems to lay the emphasis on the loving unity of the Persons within the Godhead.

In the Collect we hear of a 'true faith' that we are to 'confess'. But the wording of the Collect also makes it plain that we are considering in the doctrine of the Holy Trinity a truth that is not only to be 'acknowledged', and confessed, but also to be 'worshipped'. This insight reminds us of the stirring phrase in the Athanasian Creed, which is also part of the B.C.P. (This is a later Creed which was composed especially to support the western understanding of the relationship between the Persons of the Holy Trinity, and is not, therefore, used in the eastern Church.) There it states that 'the Catholic Faith is this, that we worship one God in Trinity and the Trinity in Unity'. Such language stresses the fact that, when we are considering theological truth, we are not considering the kind of truth which we may loosely call scientific truth, that can be proved by reason and understood solely in the mind. We are considering the higher kind of truth that can only be truly apprehended by the spirit; to grasp it our reason must work with our deeper insights, for such truth must be worshipped in the spirit, as well as acknowledged in the mind, if it is to be recognised as true and so able to be sincerely confessed. The Collect, therefore, does not depict the doctrine of the Holy Trinity as a theory that throws light on a puzzling problem, but as a truth that leads us on to worship God in all his 'glory' and all his 'power'.

The petition clause in the Collect was, as earlier described, changed in 1662, and consequently its original meaning has been altered. It needs, however, to be interpreted in its original sense, which recognised that true doctrine is a real protection against great dangers. The truth is that being 'steadfast in this faith' is a mighty defence against all adversities. Equally heresies are serious matters and very dangerous. St. John calls them 'lies', and his Epistles were written specifically to warn us of this truth. 'Who is the liar but he who denies that Jesus is the Christ', and then, to emphasise the seriousness of what he is saying, he declares such heresy to be the work of the Devil himself; 'This is the Anti-Christ, he who denies the Father and the Son'.[5] It is easy to take heresy lightly, and to suggest that sincerity and kindness are more important than truth. But wrong beliefs about God have the power to separate us from him; this is the measure of the harm they do. Because beliefs about God are inevitably expressed in worship, heresy amounts to idolatry.[6] We should, therefore, understand that in this Collect we are praying that we may be kept 'steadfast in our faith' in the doctrine of the Holy Trinity, because it is a defence against 'all adversities'. However many and varied our 'adversities' may be, they all stem from the power of evil in the world, and it is really from this power that we need 'evermore to be defended'. This permanent protection is our eternal salvation and, as the Athanasian Creed makes clear, salvation and truth are inextricably linked. 'He, therefore, that would be saved, let him thus think of the Trinity'. Right belief is not a peripheral concern. So the defence and confirmation of orthodoxy, and the patient search by scholars for theological agreement, is work of the highest spiritual importance, and this Collect may be seen as a prayer for those engaged in this work. Among the categories of sanctity recognised by the Church is that of Doctor, and the 1928 Prayer Book provides a Collect for Doctors in its Common of Saints. In it we pray that God will 'raise up faithful witnesses, who by their life and doctrine will set forth to all men the truth of thy salvation'. First among these saving truths is the truth of God as Holy Trinity.

5   1 Jn 2:22   6   1 Jn 5:21

TRINITY I

O God, the strength of all them that put their trust in thee, mercifully accept our prayers; and because through the weakness of our mortal nature we can do no good thing without thee, grant us the help of thy grace, that in keeping of thy commandments we may please thee, both in will and deed, through Jesus Christ our Lord. Amen.

This Collect comes from the Gelasian Sacramentary and is the Collect set for this Sunday in the Sarum Missal. In the former, however, this Sunday is called the second Sunday after Pentecost, whereas in the latter it is the first after Trinity. All our Trinity Collects are translations of the Proper Collects in the Sarum Missal, and the Sundays take their titles for the same source.

The opening of this Collect reminds us of many Psalms. 'I will lift up mine eyes unto the hills from whence cometh my help'.[1] 'God is my hope and strength, a very present help in trouble'.[2] 'The Lord is my light and my salvation, whom then shall I fear; the Lord is the strength of my life, of whom then shall I be afraid'.[3] These are just the opening verses of three of the best loved Psalms, but repeatedly the Psalms declare that God will protect us, and therefore we may trust him. It is not a matter of God protecting us only if we trust him, however much our trust in God helps him to look after us. Our trust does not earn us God's protection. He loves us. 'His mercy endureth for ever'.[4] This is the great truth about God in which we are to trust. Faith is our proper response to God's love and mercy. We must not doubt him. Yet however important a virtue faith is and however much our faith helps God to protect us, our faith is not the primary factor in God's protection of us, whether it be protection from material or spiritual

1 Ps 121:1   2 Ps 46:1   3 Ps 27:1   4 Ps 136:1 et al

danger. If this were not the case, we could really look after ourselves, and the grace of God would not be so vitally important. St. Paul puts the truth of the matter like this, 'For by grace you have been saved through faith; and this is not your own doing, it is the gift of God - not because of works, lest any man should boast'.[5] That's it. He alone is 'the strength of our salvation'.[6] So we should understand the opening invocation and petition in this Collect, therefore, not as a cri de coeur, but as a declaration of our sure confidence in God, in his 'strength' and 'mercy'. If this point is not taken we can turn this Collect into an anxious prayer, rather than one prayed out of an unanxious confidence in God's readiness to help us and his ability to do so. Certainly our needs are implied and our weakness is admitted, but such is our confidence in God that we are able to turn to him with our needs and in our weakness in sure faith and certain hope.

These virtues are the essential prerequisites of genuine prayer. We must always approach God with confidence born of faith and hope in him, and not, of course, with false confidence in ourselves. Indeed our confidence in God must be of the kind that drives out as utterly irrelevant and useless any conceited confidence in ourselves.

This is the truth that lies at the heart of the first beatitude, in which Jesus spoke of the 'poor in spirit' who possess 'the kingdom of God'.[7] There is a paradox here. The poor in spirit are not, as the phrase may suggest, people who have little. The opposite is true. They are those who are 'poor, yet making many rich, as having nothing, yet possessing everything'.[8] This is not because they are different to other people. The 'weakness of their mortal nature' is no less than anyone else's. But they fully admit and accept this truth about themselves, and they have put their whole trust and confidence in God. It does not matter therefore to them that 'they have no power of themselves to help themselves'. (Lent II) God has plenty of power, and in this power they put their trust. Because of this self-knowledge, and this confidence in God, which is the height of wisdom, they are uninhibited

5 Eph 2:8-9   6   Ps 95:1   7   Matt 5:3   8   2 Cor 6:10

in their faith. Having truly 'put their trust in God' and not in any other, least of all themselves, God has become for them a source of 'strength' that knows no limits.

But some may ask, 'How can we acquire such faith in God? Is there some dynamic source from which such confidence in God may enter our lives too?' Without doubt in the New Testament the main reason for having this total confidence in God is the Resurrection of Jesus. It was then preeminently that God revealed his power to protect us. It is as we look at Jesus, acknowledge what happened to him, and then through faith and hope find fellowship with the risen Christ, that we begin to grow in this necessary confidence in God. 'Through him you have confidence in God, who raised him from the dead and gave him glory', wrote St. Peter, 'so that our faith and hope are (now) in God'.[9] St. Peter was himself one to learn this lesson. How great was his confidence in himself! How false it proved to be![10] But it was St. Peter who witnessed to a new strength born of a new confidence, this time in God, when he spoke so boldly before the Sanhedrin. Then he made it plain that it was the Resurrection of Jesus, which he had experienced, that had enabled him to discover the full power of God, in whom he now entirely put his trust.[11] In the power of this confidence St. Peter and his fellow Apostles established the Church, for there is no limit to what is possible to those whose 'faith and hope are in God'. Their way to true faith can be our way too. It comes from a knowledge of the risen Christ.

The second petition in this Collect is for grace to obey God, and to obey fully, 'both in will and deed', that is gladly and willingly. We recognise in this prayer our fellowship with the Psalmist, 'O that my ways were made so direct that I might keep thy statues . . . Make me to go in the path of thy commandments, for therein is my desire . . . I have sworn and am steadfastly purposed to keep thy righteous judgements.[12] The heart of all

9   1 Pet 1:21   10 Mk 14:29-31, 66-72   11 Acts 4:5-22
12 Ps 119:5, 35, 106

truly Christian prayer is 'Thy will be done'. But this is not a prayer that we need pray only out of a selfless love of God, for our own best interests are always served by God's will being done. To love God is not to cease to love ourselves, and we know that God loves us far better and more wisely than ever we can love ourselves. In the doing of his will is our peace,[13] as well as his pleasure.

Obedience, of course, can be given willingly or reluctantly. Presumably it is better to obey reluctantly than not at all, as Jesus teaches in the parable of the two brothers, who were told to go and work in their father's vineyard.[14] However, our prayer here is that we may have 'grace' to obey. The quality of obedience we are praying for in this Collect, therefore, is such as we will give gladly and willingly 'both in will and deed'. How hard this is for us! Perhaps it may encourage us to recall that in the years of his ministry Jesus' disciples were often reluctant followers. On the road to Jerusalem St. Mark tells how Jesus went ahead of them, and they followed at a distance, puzzled and afraid.[15] Even at the very end, after his Resurrection, we read, 'when they saw him they worshipped him, but some doubted'.[16] St. Mary, however, is the pattern of all who are 'full of grace'[17] because her obedience was so perfect. 'Mary said, 'Behold I am the handmaid of the Lord; let it be to me according to your word'.[18] And it was she who told the servants at the wedding at Cana, 'Do whatever he tells you'.[19]

However, as his Crucifixion drew very near, we hear of Jesus talking to his Apostles in the garden of Gethsemane. He told them the time would soon come when he would not call them servants, but rather friends. The Holy Spirit would bring about such a change in them that he would no longer have to order them to do things, but rather he would be able to confide in them and share his longings with them. These they would carry out gladly and willingly, for a new relationship would unite them. 'If you love me, you will keep my commandments', he had said. But now he said, 'Because you love me, you will keep my commandments just as I have kept my Father's

13 Lk 19:42   14 Matt 21:28-30   15 Mk 10:32   16 Matt 28:17
17 The Hail Mary Prayer: Lk 1:28   18 Lk 1:38   19 Jn 2:5

commandments, because I abide in his love'. And the result of this love, that leads to this willing obedience, is the experience of joy that is known only by his Saints.[20] It is the service that is perfect freedom.

Willing obedience is the most obvious element in sanctity. Through it we 'please' God, for it is obedience 'both in will and deed'. Such obedience is not a matter of fits and starts, but a permanent and ever deepening characteristic of our lives. St. Paul reminded the Thessalonians of this, urging them to continue 'to live and please God' and to do so 'more and more'.[21] In the Confirmation service the Bishop's prayer is that we may 'increase in the Holy Spirit more and more'. So too in the prayer of Absolution in Morning and Evening Prayer we pray that God will grant us his Holy Spirit that 'those things may please him which we do at this present.' Undoubtedly we may count on the Holy Spirit to assist us, if our resolve is honest. It will not be easy, but it will be possible, as St. Paul assures us. 'Therefore, my beloved, as you have always obeyed, so now ... work out your own salvation with fear and trembling, for God is at work in you, both to will and to work for his good pleasure.'[22] His pleasure and our joy are inseparable. Just as we can do 'no good thing' without God's grace, we can feel no real joy unless we please him.

20 Jn 15:9-11   21 1 Thess 4:1   22 Phil 2:12-13

TRINITY II

O Lord, who never failest to help and govern them whom thou dost bring up in thy steadfast fear and love; keep us, we beseech thee, under the protection of thy good providence, and make us to have a perpetual fear and love of thy holy Name, through Jesus Christ our Lord. Amen.

Basically this is the Sarum Collect for this Sunday, which had been the Collect for the Sunday after the Ascension in the Gelasian Sacramentary. In 1549 what was a short simple prayer was literally translated, but in 1662 it was both changed and lengthened, and in particular the important but difficult concept of our protection by divine providence was introduced.

The Collect seems to visualise a loving yet disciplined home, in which children are being brought up. We are to see ourselves as these children and God as our parent, who 'dost bring (us) up in his steadfast fear and love.' All children need 'help' and 'protection', for they cannot in all things fend for themselves. They are dependent creatures. There is no fault in this, because it is their nature to be so. But they must not rebel against those who provide their necessary protection. They must let themselves be 'governed.' To this end they should show 'fear and love' towards those who bring them up. Only then will they be brought up in safety and happiness. One recalls the third Collect for Morning Prayer, in which we pray that 'all our doings may be ordered by thy governance' lest we fall into 'sin and danger.'

Sadly it is also natural for children to rebel. This is the consequence of 'the sin of the world' that infects our world and all in it, and what theologians have termed 'original sin.' To 'fear and love', and especially to do it 'steadfastly', that is gladly and willingly and without reluctance, is, on the other hand, the consequence of grace. Such an attitude towards all our governors, and especially towards God, is supernatural rather than natural. We see it, of course, exemplified in Jesus. He from the first was filled with supernatural grace, for he was conceived of the Holy Spirit. Therein lies his only difference from us, but is it not a huge difference?[1] In childhood 'he was obedient' to his parents. They were consequently utterly 'amazed' when he got lost, going off to the Temple alone, but so, too, was he amazed that they should not have known where he would be. It was no act of disobedience that took him there, but rather one of obedience to his heavenly Father, that his earthly parents did not at the time understand. In Jesus, therefore, this 'steadfast fear and love' from the beginning to the end of his life enabled him to be brought up perfectly, both by his earthly parents and his heavenly Father. So 'he increased in stature, and in favour with God and man.'[2]

Upbringing is not a matter of all things being done for us, but rather a means of bringing out our potentialities and developing our characters. Good parents should be, therefore, like St. Mary, who 'pondered' such things 'in her heart', which means that she prayed constantly about them. Her child was God's Son; there was an uniqueness about her vocation and task. But do not all parents have a similar vocation and task? Their children are also of God and not just of them. Their duties in bringing up their children likewise require prayerful pondering, if they are not to fail. Towards God they too need 'steadfast fear and love', no less than their children, if they are to bring them up well. If it is sought, God 'never faileth' to give this help, for their children are both theirs and his. Moreover, what duty is more sacred than the upbringing of children? But how will parents bring up their children properly, if they themselves have not been well brought up? So the problem is circular, rather as this Collect is, and in the original it was even more so. We must let Christ break into the circle, starting a new one that leads on to real success. The original Collect started, 'Lord, make us to have a perpetual fear and love of thy holy name,'

1 Heb 4:15   2 Lk 2:41-52

which the Reformers made its ending. He needs to start the process, and by his grace keep us in the right way. We must let him, gladly and willingly and without reluctance, knowing our need. Then all will be well.

Fear and love, which are linked in this Collect, may appear opposites rather than complements. (See Epiphany III). It is godly fear or 'fear of the Lord' that is envisaged here, not worldly or craven fear. 'The fear of the Lord is the beginning of wisdom', but it is also something that 'endureth for ever.'[3] Only craven fear is incompatible with love.[4] Christ came indeed to save us from such fear, so that we 'might serve him without fear.'[5] In our divine upbringing, however, in which God 'never faileth', godly fear as well as love will for ever play a part, so the Collect speaks of 'perpetual fear and love.'

'Fear and love' find their true harmony in worship, and worship is the true purpose of our lives and of our upbringing. The Book of Revelation gives us an insight into what 'perpetual fear and love of God's holy name' means in its vision of life in heaven. It is shown as being essentially a life of worship. There we shall fully realise the supreme worth of God and of our Lord. In Chapters 4 and 5 the recurring word is 'worthy.' 'Worthy art thou, our Lord and our God'... 'Worthy art thou to take the scroll'... 'Worthy is the Lamb'... They are worthy to receive our fullest worship. 'And the living creatures said 'Amen', and the elders fell down and worshipped.'[6] The fulfilment of our upbringing here in 'steadfast fear and love' is that we may experience 'perpetual fear and love of his holy name' hereafter. Here we know these virtues in this life within time, there we are to know them in the life beyond time, but these essential virtues, and all other such signs of grace, constitute what is common ground between these two existences. 'The steadfast fear and love' that we must learn to have here is a preparation for 'the perpetual fear and love' that we shall know hereafter.

---

3   Prov 1:7, Ps 19:9   4   1 Jn 4:18   5   Lk 1:74   6   Rev 5:9-14

The additional thought introduced into this Collect by the Reformers concerns the working of divine providence. Providence speaks of the mysterious manner of God's provision for us. While we are little children the things we most need are provided by our parents, as if by magic. We cannot understand how it all happens. We take it all (or nearly all) for granted, for it is an unusual child that is truly thankful, and a foolish parent that expects too much gratitude. So with us and God. We take his providence for granted every day, and if in our prayers we consider the matter, we shall come surely to agree that 'e'en eternity's too short to extol thee.'[7] If we go on our way believing that God will provide for all our real needs, we will not be disappointed. 'Abraham called the name of that place "The Lord will provide."'[8] He spoke much more than he realised, for on that spot centuries later the Lamb of God was provided as 'a sacrifice for the sins of the whole world.' In consequence we too are saved, not just to live longer like Isaac, but even to enjoy eternal life. Such is the true measure of his provision for us. He gave his Son, and 'he who has the Son has life.'[9]

The Collect speaks of our divine protection as well as upbringing, and the mysterious part providence plays in that also. As we look back on our lives we can see something of its benign activity, and recognise some of its agents. Clearly they are sometimes our friends. 'Then Jonathan said to David, Go.'[10] Sometimes, mysteriously, they are those we might consider our enemies. 'When she opened the basket she saw the child, and lo, the babe was crying. She took pity on him and said, "It is one of the Hebrew children."'[11] Sometimes we notice how suffering or illness has intervened to our advantage, and a temporary evil has turned out to be a permanent blessing. 'He said to me, "... my power is made perfect in weakness". I will all the more gladly boast of my weaknesses that the power of Christ may rest upon me.'[12] More mysteriously still we can sometimes even experience the agency of angels, or of messages through dreams. 'An angel of the Lord appeared to Joseph in a dream and said, "Rise and take the child and his mother and flee."'[13]

---

7   George Herbert – Hymn 'King of glory, King of peace'   8   Gen 22:14
9   1 Jn 5:12   10 1 Sam 20:42   11 Ex 2:6   12 2 Cor 12:9
13 Matt 2:13

But above all we will be conscious of prayer as the agent of God's protecting providence, both our own prayers and the prayers of others. Through prayer God's word speaks to us and his Spirit is allowed to guide us. 'I know that through your prayers, and the help of the Spirit of Christ, this will turn out for my deliverance', says St. Paul.[14] Prayer assists God in his providential care of us. In his famous passage in Ephesians 6 St. Paul mentions many things that assist God's protection of us, but he ends his list by stressing that above all else we should 'pray at all times in the Spirit, with all prayer and supplication.'[15] We can and should do this both for ourselves and for others. Jesus said, 'Whatever you will ask in my name I will do it.'[16] And to emphasise the point he repeated it. So we may be sure that our prayers are both heard and needed. 'This is the confidence which we have in him,' said St. John, 'that, if we ask anything according to his will, he hears us.' And then he added, 'and we know that we have obtained the requests made of him.'[17] But St. Paul goes further and teaches that we may hope for even more than we ask for. He speaks of 'him who by the power at work within us is able to do far more abundantly than all that we ask or think.'[18] The power of intercessory prayer, then, is dynamic and explosive, affecting all and sundry for good. It is, as St. James said, something that 'has great power in its effect.'[19] 'The protection of God's good providence,' which is so important in our upbringing, waits, to some extent at least, upon our prayers. Just as regular prayer is the main means to 'make us to have a perpetual fear and love' towards God, so it is also the main means to assure us of 'the protection of his good providence.'

14 Phil 1:19   15 Eph 6:18   16 Jn 14:13   17 1 Jn 5:14-15
18 Eph 3:20   19 Jas 5:16

TRINITY III

O Lord, we beseech thee mercifully to hear us; and grant that we, to whom thou hast given an hearty desire to pray, may by thy mighty aid be defended and comforted in all dangers and adversities; through Jesus Christ our Lord. Amen.

The Collect is Gregorian. The ending of the 1549 translation was expanded in 1662 by the mention of 'all (the) dangers and adversities', in which we need to be both 'comforted' as well as 'defended'. This addition, however, makes the prayer much closer in spirit to the medieval Collect. The point is this. The opening phrase in the Latin is far stronger than our English translation. There it started, 'Deprecationem nostram, quaesumus, Domine, benignus exaudi', which means, 'Lord, we pray thee, mercifully hear our prayer for deliverance'. 'Deprecatio' is specifically a prayer for deliverance, as in the Lord's Prayer. Cranmer's opening fails entirely to give the sense of fear in the face of danger that is an essential part of the Latin original. Bishop Cosin's new ending, therefore, may be seen as compensating for the prayer's inadequate beginning.

The Collect's opening words are very simply a prayer to be heard, for we are in earnest. Then, as if to reassure ourselves of God's willingness to hear our prayer, we remind ourselves that it is he himself that has initiated our prayer in the first place! Sometimes it may seem that we are praying to a God whose attention must be caught. So the Psalmist protests, 'Up, Lord, why sleepest thou; awake and be not absent from us for ever. Wherefore hidest thou thy face and forgettest our misery and trouble?'[1] But of course it is never so with God; 'his ears are open to our prayers.'[2] Elijah had great fun mocking the prophets of Baal, who thought like that. 'O Baal, answer us', they cried. 'Cry louder', taunted Elijah, 'either he is musing, or he has

1   Ps 44:23-24   2   1 Pet 3:12

gone aside, or he is on a journey, or perhaps he is asleep and must be wakened!'[3] Jesus repeatedly urges us to pray, for God was one that answers prayer, and, moreover, he assures us that, if we pray in his Name, our prayers will most certainly always be heard and answered.[4]

The Collect stresses 'our hearty desire to pray.' It is natural enough to pray, but not all prayers are heartfelt. When they are it is usually because we are in dire need! Indeed this Collect is concerned with our 'dangers and adversities.' It has therefore a familiar ring about it. 'Hear my prayer, O God, and hide not thyself from my petition,' pleads the Psalmist with obvious 'hearty desire.' 'The enemy crieth so and the ungodly cometh on so fast, for they are minded to do me some mischief, so maliciously are they set against me. My heart is disquieted within me, and the fear of death is fallen upon me.'[5] The cause of our 'hearty desire to pray' is so often the fear of suffering and death. In extremis most people pray, some perhaps for the first time with 'hearty desire.'

But it is not just outward 'danger and adversity' that calls forth a 'hearty desire to pray.' We are just as likely to be moved to heartfelt prayer by our sins and the spiritual suffering they cause us. Who does not recognise the truth of the Psalmist's lament, 'I am ... sore smitten; I have roared for the very disquietness of my heart'?[6] Who has not felt with him, 'My sins have taken such hold upon me that I am not able to look up... and my heart hath failed me,' even if we have not been moved by a similar honesty to confess as much to God.[7] But we are wise to allow our 'hearty desires' to be fully expressed. We should not be too ashamed to admit that it is pain and fear that usually prompt our most heartfelt prayers. The way to freedom is via the truth,[8] and it is simply the truth about us that we are physically weak and spiritually sinful. Jesus himself encourages us to pray in our weakness, trusting the love and power of God to come to our aid, and to give to us all that we most need.[9]

But we can be moved to pray from our hearts for other reasons too. We

| 3 | 1 Kgs 18:27 | 4 | Jn 14:14 | 5 | Ps 55:1-4 | 6 | Ps 38:8 |
| 7 | Ps 40:15 | 8 | Jn 8:31-32 | 9 | Lk 11:9-13 | | |

should not say for better reasons, for to pray in our times of need is so right and proper. But perhaps we can acknowledge there are worthier reasons for prayer. 'Like as the hart desireth the water brooks, so longeth my soul after thee, O God. My soul is athirst for God, yea, even for the living God. When shall I come to appear before the presence of God?'[10] Do not such words express the worthiest desires of our heart? And the Psalmist beautifully suggests that the desire of our heart for fellowship with God is indeed the voice of God within us drawing us to himself. 'My heart hath talked of thee, 'Seek ye my face.' And how blest we are if we can from our heart then reply, 'Thy face, Lord, will I seek.'[11]

St. Paul confirms this teaching in Romans 8. Our prayers, he says, are indeed the activity of God within our hearts. Although we are surrounded without by pain and confusion, and within ourselves there is all the folly and weakness so natural to us, yet, because the Holy Spirit has come into our lives we are enabled from our hearts to cry out in faith and love, 'Abba Father', just as Jesus did. Moreover, 'the Spirit helps us in our weakness, for we do not know how to pray as we ought, but the Spirit himself intercedes for us with sighs too deep for words'. Often our 'hearty desires' are so deep that we hardly understand them, let alone are able to express them coherently. We need not be distressed at this experience, says St. Paul, because 'he who searches the hearts of men knows what is the mind of the Spirit, because the Spirit intercedes for (us) according to the will of God.'[12] In our prayer, therefore, the devotional proverb holds good, 'Let go and let God.' In all aspects of the spiritual life we can rely in faith and hope and love on his active help. 'He who calls you is faithful, and he will do it.'[13]

Our 'hearty desire' in this Collect is that we are 'defended and comforted in all dangers and adversities.' The last words of this phrase were added in 1662, but they help considerably to bring out the true meaning of the

10 Ps 42:1-2   11 Ps 27:9   12 Rom 8:26-27   13 1 Thess 5:24

prayer. It should be noticed, however, that we are not asking to be defended 'from' danger and adversity, but 'in' these adverse circumstances. We may indeed pray, as we do every Evensong, to be 'defended from the fear of our enemies', and as a consequence of such divine protection to experience 'rest and quietness.' But it is a rest and quietness of the spirit rather than the body that we should seek. Although we are certainly instructed to pray for deliverance from the power of the Evil One by Jesus, to pray for protection 'from' all ordinary danger and adversity would be the soft prayer of the spiritually uncommitted, and not one we could properly pray 'through Jesus Christ our Lord.' We are called by him, we know, 'to take up our cross daily.'[14] The New Testament on almost every page confirms that to be a Christian is a physically dangerous business, but spiritually an infinitely safe calling. It is as the Psalmist says, 'Because he hath set his love upon me, therefore will I deliver him... He shall call upon me and I will hear him., yea, I will be with him in trouble. I will deliver him and bring him to honour.'[15] We may be sure that he will be with us 'in all dangers and adversities', if we set our love upon him.

And the introduction of the word 'comforted' to go alongside 'defended' in this context surely confirms this interpretation of the Collect. The proper meaning of comfort is to make strong. We are praying here that we may be spiritually strengthened as well as defended 'in all dangers and adversities.' This makes sense and gives a proper unity to the petition. Our prayer is exactly that of St. Paul for his fellow Christians in Ephesus, that God will 'grant (us) to be strengthened with might through his Spirit in the inner man.'[16] Then 'all will be well, all manner of thing will be well,' as St. Julian perceived. 'Yea, though I walk through the valley of the shadow of death I will fear no evil, for thou art with me, thy rod and thy staff comfort me.'[17]

14 Lk 9:23   15 Ps 91:14-15   16 Eph 3:16   17 Ps 23:4

TRINITY IV

O God, the protector of all that trust in thee, without whom nothing is strong, nothing is holy; increase and multiply upon us thy mercy; that, thou being our ruler and guide, we may so pass through things temporal, that we finally lose not the things eternal: Grant this, O heavenly Father, for Jesus Christ's sake our Lord. Amen

This is the Gregorian Collect to which three changes were made. The word 'all' was added to the invocation, and two other more significant changes made to the petition. Between them they have given the prayer both a more general sense and a greater sharpness of meaning, a combination of factors that is not the contradiction in terms that it may seem ! The Latin Collect referred only to the good things that happen to us in a way that suggested that they alone are of eternal value. It ran, 'that we may so pass through the good temporal things (per bona temporalia) that we do not lose the eternal things (ut amittamus aeterna)'. By omitting the word 'good' in his translation Cranmer, in a very proper and helpful way, has made the prayer more general in character, for all aspects of our lives are important and have significance for our eternal destiny. Then, by the addition of the word 'finally', a greater sharpness was added to the prayer, for the sense of warning in it is now more clearly emphasised.

In the finely worded opening to this Collect God is declared to be the source of all real safety and all real strength, as well as the source of all holiness. However, although the last concept is surely uncontroversial, the first two equally surely are. Do we believe this? This Collect poses very hard questions and tests our faith to the uttermost. The addition of the little word 'all' to the medieval Collect only adds to our problem.

Repeatedly the Collects begin with an ascription of trust in God's power and an acknowledgement of our weakness. (Sexagesima, Lent II, et al). At first sight this seems the most natural starting point for our prayers, but it is nonetheless open to criticism from without and doubt within. The Psalmist speaks for many as he turns to God in his troubles. 'Lord, how are they increased that trouble me. Many are they that rise up against me'. (And, worse still). 'Many are there that say to my soul, there is no help for him in his God.'[1] We have the example and teaching of Jesus to encourage us to turn simply to God in all our troubles, whatever form they may take, and that should perhaps be the end of the matter. But, though we do so most faithfully, we certainly do not always receive all the safety and strength that we seek.

Jesus may encourage us to turn to God in every time of need, but as we look at the Cross, we may well wonder what kind of answer we can expect! In asking for safety and strength, are we asking for what God is not going to give us? Such a question is surely almost impossible to keep out. Certainly we know it was one repeatedly asked by faithful Jews all down the centuries, and felt too by the earliest Christians. David may have been saved from and given strength to defeat the giant Goliath, but as a nation the Jews had been successively overcome by their giant neighbours, from the Assyrians to the Romans. To this the prophetic answer was that, even though the Jews deserved their suffering, God in his mercy would send a Messiah, who would redeem his people, saving them from their enemies and 'from the hands of all that hated them.'[2] But when the Messiah came, he was crucified. For Jesus certainly there seemed to be 'no help for him in his God'. In the face of so much innocent suffering in the world, surely this truth can worry us still. Cleopas still speaks, as it were, for many Christians when he said in perplexity, 'We had hoped that he was the one to redeem Israel.'[3]

It is not until we link our ideas of safety and strength to holiness, as is done in this Collect, and as Jesus did in his answer to Cleopas, that we shall get a truthful answer to this problem of suffering, and especially innocent suffering, in a divinely created world, or be able to accept that answer with

1 Ps 3:1-2   2 Lk 1:68-71 A.V.   3 Lk 24:21

thanksgiving. But it is hard to perceive how 'it was necessary for Christ to suffer these things, and so enter into his glory.'[4] The rational response to our natural desire for safety in a dangerous world is the ugly one of creating all manner of defences behind which we can shelter. But the sword is a two-edged weapon, and whether we think in personal or national terms, the truth is that such protection is always in the end a source of further danger, however dangerous life may appear without it. 'All who take the sword will perish by the sword.'[5] The real truth that Jesus teaches, and which we find so hard to accept, is that our true enemy is not human at all, and therefore nothing of human origin can be the source of our real safety and strength. 'I tell you, my friends, do not fear those who kill the body, and after that have no more that they can do. But I warn you whom to fear: fear him who after he has killed can cast into hell; yes, I tell you, fear him.'[6]

So the Gospel challenges us to believe that real safety and strength lie in holiness. In another context we hear that 'many said to Jesus, "This is a hard saying; who can listen to it."'[7] Surely this is another. But we separate our hopes of safety and our understanding of strength from holiness at our ultimate peril and confusion. If we can hold them together, however, we will then be able to face life as St. Paul bids us, and say, 'If God is with us, who is against us?... Shall tribulation or distress or persecution or famine or nakedness or peril or sword (overcome us)? No, in all these things we are more than conquerors through him who loved us.'[8] The New Testament leaves us in no doubt that we are called to such an heroic faith in God, and that this quality of trust in him is the brave heart of holiness.

God's protection, we should notice, is called in this Collect his 'mercy', which we pray he may 'increase and multiply upon us.' As we have already noticed it is called this too in the Benedictus, where Zachariah sang of how God's mercy would enable us to enjoy both safety and holiness. 'We, being delivered out of the hands of our enemies, might serve him without fear, in holiness and righteousness before him all the days of our life.'[9] This merciful protection, however, like all God's gifts is not such as the world can

4   Lk 24:26   5   Matt 26:52   6   Lk 12:4-5   7   Jn 6:60
8   Rom 8:35-37   9   Lk 1:74-75 A.V.

give. It is, of course, of far greater value. Just how much greater the Collect goes on to make plain.

The main petition is that our minds should not be set upon earthly things.[10] We are pilgrims that 'pass through things temporal.' 'Here we have no lasting city, but we seek the city which is to come.'[11] Repeatedly in the New Testament we are urged to take this unworldly view of our lives. For us to be earth-bound in mind and heart is real tragedy. That many are so minded was for St. Paul a matter for tears.[12] We are citizens of heaven, he says,[13] and so we may be filled with hope, as we move towards the fulfilment of that extraordinary privilege.

Although St. Paul speaks of this frequently, particularly in his last, or prison, Epistles, 2 Corinthians is the place one especially turns to to hear his teaching on this matter. He is quite ready to admit the difficulties that face us. 'We are afflicted in every way... perplexed... persecuted... struck down... Here indeed we groan... and sigh with anxiety.' But because of faith 'we do not lose heart'... and 'are always of good courage.' This is because we are conscious of great things happening within us, an inner spiritual clothing taking place, preparing us for what is in store for us through Christ. 'Though our outer nature is wasting away, our inner nature is being renewed every day.' For the trials and tribulations of this life are 'preparing for us an eternal weight of glory beyond all comparison, because we look not to the things that are seen, but to the things that are unseen; for the things that are seen are transient, but the things that are unseen are eternal.'[14] It is a tremendous declaration of faith in the reality of the life that awaits us, and a stirring call to us to live as hopeful pilgrims in the light of that faith in this dangerous world.

The Collect, however, also warns us of the tragic possibility that we may 'finally lose the things eternal' by the way in which we 'pass through things temporal'. The word 'finally' was added in the translation of this Collect. It

10 Phil 3:19   11 Heb 13:14   12 Phil 3:18   13 Phil 3:20
14 2 Cor 4:7-5:10

adds force to the warning, and also earnestness to the petition. But, praise be, God himself is to be our 'ruler and guide' as we 'pass through things temporal'. It is his loving desire, probably far more than our own, that we do not 'finally' fail to attain to 'the things eternal'. One of the most encouraging texts in the Gospels is 'Fear not, little flock, it is your Father's good pleasure to give you the kingdom'.[15] We must certainly not take our sins lightly. They are what separate us from God and, therefore, what may make us 'finally lose the things eternal'. But not only must we repent of our sins with all due seriousness, but also we must 'unfeignedly believe' in the readiness of God to forgive and his power to save, as the prayer of Absolution in Morning and Evening Prayer reminds us. No one has ever been more strict in his teaching about sin than St. Paul, but he also urges us to be totally confident in the saving power of God. The truth is that God is 'for us', so what does it matter 'who is against us? He who did not spare his own Son but gave him up for us all, will he not also give us all things with him'.[16] Of course he will! So we are to go forward confidently, but not complacently. That is the implicit teaching of this Collect.

As noticed earlier (see commentary on Easter 1) this is one of four Collects in which God the Father is mentioned as well as Jesus in its ending. Perhaps because of this we are supposed to see a distinction of role in our salvation for the Father and the Son in the two words 'ruler and guide'. The Father is always our ruler, who commands our obedience. He sent, however, his Son to be our guide. He is 'the way' that we are to follow, as we pass through things temporal on our way to things eternal. It was loving obedience to the Father's will that guided and protected Jesus on his pilgrimage, as it will us. His was the strength of true holiness, a holiness that we may share through the Holy Spirit that he gives us. It is as we allow God, Father, Son and Holy Spirit, to rule in our hearts and guide us in our actions, that we may in safety 'pass through things temporal (so) that finally we lose not the things eternal.' 'Lead me, Lord, lead me in thy righteousness'; 'for it is thou, Lord, only that makest me dwell in safety'.[17]

15 Lk 12:32   16 Rom 8:31-32   17 Ps 5:8, 4:9

TRINITY V

Grant, O Lord, we beseech thee, that the course of this world may be so peaceably ordered by thy governance, that thy Church may joyfully serve thee in all godly quietness; through Jesus Christ our Lord. Amen.

This is one of the Collects that come originally from the Leonine Sacramentary, the earliest Sacramentary, circa 440.

The western half of the Roman Empire in the early years of the fifth century was being overrun by Goths and Huns, and this Collect reflects those troubled times. The Dark Ages had begun. It is a prayer, however, that in time was wonderfully answered, as the Dark Ages receded and the Church became the creative force that renewed Europe, from whence it later went out to evangelise the world.

In relation to this thought it is interesting to notice that in translation Cranmer made a distinct change in this Collect's petition. He makes us now pray that the Church might 'serve' God, whereas the original prayed only that she might be free to worship him. Does the change reflect the very different times in which Cranmer lived as compared to St. Leo? It may be claimed, however, that the faithful worship of believers in those earlier dangerous years kept open the door for the active service that particularly concerned the evangelically minded Reformers a thousand years later, and that we can see in this new wording evidence of the way God answered this Collect's older wording.

––––––––––––––––––

Surely we are living in better times. For over forty years the world at large, and Europe in particular, was overshadowed by the threat of nuclear war. Quite suddenly this threat has been lifted. The mushroom cloud that darkened our lives has moved away. It is almost as if a modern dark age is making way for a more enlightened one, as we know has happened before. For this present mercy we should thank God. We have prayed that peace between the nuclear powers might be maintained, and it has been. We have prayed, also, that new attitudes in international affairs might arise that will banish the threat of global nuclear war for ever, and it seems that this too may be happening. The horrendous nuclear weapons of modern warfare are being withdrawn on all sides from offensive to defensive positions, and reduced in number. Sadly costly minor wars are still occurring, and violence still raises it ugly and dangerous head all over the world. Civil war, terrorism and military adventurism, fed by oppression, greed and fanaticism are constant reminders that the evils that lead to war are not dead anywhere in the world. But there is no denying that a change has taken place 'in the course of this world', which is being more 'peaceably ordered', and for this we should surely thank God.

We discussed the difficult problem of God's sovereignty particularly in the commentary for Epiphany II, and we have noticed how the problem is a consideration in other Collects. We shall meet it again in future Collects. But that is as one would expect, since belief in God's sovereignty is basic to all prayer. The Collects confirm the truth that we pray most often out of a sense of need, and in the belief that God can help us in our need. After all, if we have come to believe that God cannot help us, why pray to him? This is what happened when the Israelites reached the promised land. They were faced with many new problems, and they doubted God's ability to assist them in their new home. Certainly God had rescued them from Egypt, and by his 'governance' had most marvellously ordered the course of events for them in the desert. But could he produce crops and make cattle fertile? Could he send rain when it was needed? So the Israelites broke the first and great commandment, and turned to worship local fertility gods. Moreover, as they became settled, they became increasingly like any other people, making alliances with neighbours, which included allowing the worship of their various gods.

In these ways they ceased to believe truly in the power of God to 'order the course of this world'. They became just like any other worldly-minded nation.

To the prophets, however, this sensible behaviour was the unforgivable sin of apostasy, which was so particularly terrible for the Israelites, because God had chosen them to be different, giving them the privilege of receiving his commandments and the promise of his special protection. The Deuteronomic Moses spells it out. 'What great nation . . . has a god so near to it as the Lord our God is to us? What great nation . . . has statutes and ordinances so righteous as all this law?'[1] Let them be loyal and obedient, he said, and God would surely 'so peaceably order the course of this world' for them that 'they might joyfully serve him' in the land he was giving them. The words of the Collect echo the words of the prophets.

But it was not to be. 'They rebelled and grieved his holy Spirit, therefore he turned to be their enemy'.[2] 'Your iniquities have made a separation between you and your God, so that he does not hear,' said Isaiah.[3] Nevertheless although the history of Israel was tragic in the extreme, and they were overrun constantly by their enemies, their alliances in no way protecting them, the prophets were still able to preach a message of hope, as well as of judgement. Such is God's mercy and power, they said, that he can always forgive and renew, even to the creation of new heavens and a new earth, in which 'the wolf and the lamb shall feed together and the lion shall eat straw like the ox . . . for they shall not hurt or destroy in all my holy mountain, says the Lord.'[4] Such hopes point to the Gospel.

However, this longed-for peace and security can never be separated from the honouring of God and the life of righteousness. The first commandment can never be broken with impunity; 'there is no peace for the wicked'.[5] Man must never seek to dominate, and claim centre stage. True life can only

---

1 Deut 4:7-8   2 Is 63:10   3 Is 59:2   4 Is 65:25
5 Is 48:22

revolve around God and his will. Man-made things will perish, as must man himself, unless God saves him. Without God 'we are dust and to dust we shall return'.[6] We cannot for long 'order the course of this world' to our own liking. We may try. We may defeat some enemies. But only God creates what we long for, lasting peace.

It is, however, just this that we believe that God in Christ has given to us. This gift is part of what is called in the Gospels the kingdom of God.[7] In and through Jesus God has come to establish his reign on earth, as it is in heaven. His is a kingdom of peace and order, fulfilling the dearest hopes of the prophets. But, as they foretold, his ways are not exactly our ways[8] and his kingdom is different from the kingdoms of this world. The poor in spirit possess it, as do those who suffer for righteousness' sake.[9] The parables of Jesus teach us about this divine kingdom; the way it grows and the way it should be valued;[10] the way it must be waited for, and the way it must be worked for;[11] the way it is like so many things we see all around us, and the way it operates so differently to the way ordinary life is conducted.[12] But central to all this varied teaching is the affirmation that this kingdom is definitely coming, and is indeed already establishing itself.[13] We are to seek it above all things,[14] full of hope of experiencing it, for 'it is your Father's good pleasure to give you the kingdom'.[15] In spite of all dangers and difficulties, we are therefore to remain confident that 'the course of this world is being ordered by God's governance' and in the end 'all the earth shall be filled with his majesty. Amen. Amen.'[16]

The true purpose for which we should seek peace and security is that we may serve God joyfully, with devotion and in tranquillity.

Joy is a small word for a great blessing. We have discussed it particularly in connection with the Collect for Easter IV. It is much more than happiness, being independent of outward circumstances. It is something

6   Gen 3:19   7   Mk 1:15   8   Is 55:8   9   Matt 5:3, 10
10 Matt 13:33, 44   11 Matt 13:1-9   12 Lk 15:3-7, 18:24-30   13 Matt 10:7
14 Matt 6:33   15 Lk 12:32   16 Ps 72:19

that the Saints all experience, and evidence that they are filled with joy is one of the essential qualifications for their canonisation. It is always 'joy in the Lord',[17] for it is the joy that comes from being always in his company, and that is why no-one can take it from us.[18] We may be called upon to experience it within much suffering, and so it is that we may even come to rejoice in our sufferings,[19] even though we can never for that reason be content to witness suffering in others. Indeed, joy is particularly experienced in the service of others and in the sharing of, and alleviation of, suffering of every kind.[20] Perhaps, above all, joy is experienced in forgiveness and the renewal of life.[21] However, the basis of joy is the assurance that God reigns 'in the course of this world', and that in the end it will 'be so peaceably ordered by his governance' that his children may for ever 'joyfully serve' him, both here and hereafter.

The Collect also prays that this service may be 'in godly quietness'. 'Be still then, and know that I am God. I will be exalted among the heathen. The Lord of hosts is with us; the God of Jacob is our refuge.'[22] The inner love, joy and peace which the Saints know comes preeminently from their ability amid the clamour of the world to be quiet with God. This 'godly quietness' is something which we must seek until we find it. Its foundation is faith, and the means of acquiring it is prayer. 'Why art thou so heavy, O my soul, and why art thou so disquieted within me? O put thy trust in God, for I will yet give him thanks, which is the help of my countenance, and my God.'[23] This is part of the traditional vesting prayer of the priest as he prepares himself for Holy Communion, and said in order that he may celebrate the holy mysteries 'in godly quietness'. All around the Church 'the winds blow and beat upon her'. But she is founded upon the rock, who is Christ.[24] So we may conduct our worship 'in godly quietness', even though sin continues, the Church herself is disunited, and the outside world is not at peace.

---

17 Phil 4:4   18 Jn 16:22   19 Matt 5:11-12   20 2 Cor 1:3-7
21 Lk 15   22 Ps 46:10-11 23 Ps 43:5-6   24 Matt 7:24-25

The prayer of this Collect is especially for the Church, which is God's special instrument for the bringing in of his kingdom. It is not, however, outside the kingdom. It too, no less than the world, waits for its coming to experience the fullness of joy and 'godly quietness'. Christ's Resurrection, says St. Paul, guarantees that it will all be as the Gospel bids us hope. Christ has conquered our real enemy to peace, the Evil One, and in the end will 'deliver the kingdom to God the Father after destroying every rule and every authority and power. For he must reign until he has put all his enemies under his feet . . . When all things are subjected to him, then the Son himself will be subjected . . . that God may be everything to everyone'.[25] His body on earth, the Church, is included in this final perfect subjecting of the Son to the Father. Then this prayer will be fully answered.

25 1 Cor 15:24-28

TRINITY VI

O God, who hast prepared for them that love thee such good things as pass man's understanding; pour into our hearts such love toward thee, that we, loving thee above all things, may obtain thy promises, which exceed all that we can desire; through Jesus Christ our Lord. Amen.

This is the Gelasian Collect, and surely one of the most lovely in the B.C.P. In 1662, however, a significant change was made to the 1549 translation, which had been faithful to the Latin. Instead of 'loving thee in all things', we now pray 'loving thee above all things.'

The beautiful opening to this Collect, full of spiritual excitement, reminds us of various texts. The most obvious is 1. Cor. 2 : 9, which is largely a quotation of Isaiah 64 : 4. St. Paul is talking there about the Holy Spirit. He declares that it is he who reveals to those, whom St. Paul describes as 'mature' Christians, the hidden things of God. "What no eye has seen, nor ear heard, nor the heart of man conceived, what God has prepared for them that love him", God has revealed to us through the Spirit.' There are, however, numerous other texts, one might indeed say the whole New Testament, which confirm what the Collect says. God has prepared for us most wonderful things in heaven, to which we are to look in hope as our 'inheritance.' After all, says St. Paul, is not this the natural thing for parents to do for their children, to provide an inheritance for them.[1] Our heavenly Father, therefore, has prepared, as we should expect, 'good things' for us, and they are 'such good things', 'far more than we can ask or think'[2], and 'exceed all that we can desire.' Like his peace, they 'pass all understanding'.[3] It is 'an inheritance that is imperishable, undefiled and unfading,' which God has 'kept' for us, prepared and 'ready to be revealed' when the time is ripe.[4]

---

1   2 Cor 12:14   2   Eph 3:20   3   Phil 4:7   4   1 Pet 1:4-5

Is this not a thrilling prospect? It is the truth that makes the Saints, who are so aware of these things, await death, not only without fear, but even with an eager expectation. St. Paul spoke with total confidence of what awaited him, but in a manner that is free from any suspicion that he thought he was going to be specially treated. He spoke of a future for himself in heaven as just part of what every Christian could look forward to. Such a conviction was simply 'keeping the faith.' To Timothy, as he considered his approaching death, he said quite naturally, 'There is laid up for me a crown of righteousness' and then continued, 'and not only for me, but also for all who have loved his appearing.'[5] So it is, as this Collect declares, that for all those who love God there is an inheritance, a 'crown of righteousness,' 'such good things as pass man's understanding,' prepared for them in heaven. Why should we ever doubt it? Is this not simply all part of what the Creed describes as 'the life of the world to come?'

In the case of St. Paul, of course, he had been granted some special experience of what awaited him. He says that he had been 'caught up into Paradise and heard things that cannot be told.'[6] And others, too, have been similarly privileged, and what they say is to encourage the faith of us more ordinary Christians. We should listen to their witness. Nor are they all people who have lived long ago. Let me quote Dorothy Kerin, who founded the Home of Healing at Burrswood, near Tunbridge Wells in 1948, and who chose this Collect as her special prayer for use at all her Healing Services. After many years of acute illness, when still a young woman, she died physically and entered heaven. This is her witness in her book 'The Living Touch': 'I seemed to drift into space, no longer conscious of my body, but my spirit was overflowing with joy and love and a transcendent feeling of supreme happiness impossible to describe... I passed on... and saw coming from every direction white robed figures... their movements making lovely music; they all looked as though they were coming and going with some definite purpose. No words of mine can express or exaggerate the exquisite

5   2 Tim 4:8   6   2 Cor 12:3-4

beauty of the scene.' She called this experience her 'beautiful day.' Then she met our Lord, who asked her to return, for he had work on earth still for her to do, work which later was described to her by him as a mission 'to bring faith to the faithless, comfort to the comfortless, and healing to the sick.' She did return to life, for by an act of God she was miraculously and instantly healed of all the various diseases, for they had been many, that had caused her 'death'. Dorothy Kerin died a second time over fifty years later in 1963 at Burrswood at the age of 73, after a ministry blessed by innumerable acts of healing, which faithfully fulfilled our Lord's commission to her. It is such events and such witness that confirm that there is indeed a world 'prepared for them that love God.' The wonders of the physical universe are almost unimaginably marvellous; so why should not the wonders of the heavenly world be such as 'pass man's understanding?' The Saints, to whom a tiny part of these wonders have been revealed, witness to the fact that they are.

The main petition is that we may so love God that we enter into our 'promised' inheritance, 'which exceeds all that we can desire.' But, as in the Collect for Quinquagesima, we recognise that we are not going to love God as we should, or even as we would wish to, without his grace. Our prayer here, therefore, is essentially the same as for Quinquagesima, that God would 'pour' his Spirit of love (agape) 'into our hearts.' We discussed in that earlier commentary the meaning of agape, and what was said then holds good for this prayer also. Nevertheless, let us remind ourselves of the assurance that this blessed experience which may happen to us and in us is indeed God's gracious will for us. 'Hope does not disappoint us, because God's love has been poured into our hearts through the Holy Spirit, which has been given to us.' [7]

How are we to use this divine gift of love? As we have noticed, the 17th century Reformers altered their 16th century predecessor's literal transla-

7   Rom 5:5

tion of the medieval Collect. Perhaps we have another case here of Calvinist influence. To those who so greatly stressed the power of evil in the world, it would seem misleading, if not thoroughly unchristian, to suggest we can love God 'in all things', since so much in this world had to be avoided. Did not St. John stress this truth? 'Do not love the world or the things in the world. If anyone loves the world, love for the Father is not in him.'[8] And did not Jesus confirm the inherent danger in the possession of many 'things', for they can become gods we love and serve? 'No one can serve two masters; for either he will hate the one and love the other, or he will be devoted to the one and despise the other. You cannot serve God and mammon.'[9] So, for whatever reason, in this Collect the preposition 'in' was replaced by 'above.' Certainly its meaning could not now be criticised. As the Collect is undoubtedly seeking to lift our eyes towards the heavenly vision of eternal things, as opposed to earthly things, 'above' may have also seemed a more appropriate word, as well as a safer one.

The use of 'in', however, can easily be defended. In spite of what St. John said in his Epistles, Jesus in his Gospel says that 'God so loved the world'[10], and that Christians should serve the world, even as he came to serve it and save it from the power of evil.[11] The Incarnation implies God's love for the world and his willingness to bless the ordinary affairs of men, since in Jesus he entered personally into them. Jesus has sanctified ordinary life and all the ordinary 'things' that we must do and possess in order to live. We do not live by bread alone, but we need it and Jesus provided it. As he said, God knows we have need 'of all these things', and if we love and serve him in righteousness 'all these things' will indeed be ours.[12]

The truth is, then, that both are equally acceptable words to use. And if we interpret their meaning with simplicity, are we not praying that we may love God in all circumstances and more than anything else? Both must be acceptable to all opinions. Is there then any reason why we should not use both together? That is indeed what the Burrswood Fellowship has decided

8   1 Jn 2:15   9   Matt 6:24   10   Jn 3:16   11   Jn 17:15-18
12   Matt 6:32-33

to do, so that now their prayer is that 'we, loving thee in all things and above all things, may obtain thy promises.' A beautiful prayer has thereby been strengthened, especially for those committed to the cause of healing. The combination of the two prepositions balance each other admirably. They encourage worldly involvement while at the same time establishing the primacy of eternal things. Together they exactly bring out the force of our Lord's injunction that we 'seek first' God's kingdom and righteousness, and then worldly blessing will follow naturally.

This Collect, however, may be open to criticism from another angle. When we pray 'that we may attain thy promises', are we being encouraged to love God simply for what we may get? Is that why we want love, because it brings such wonderful rewards? Surely it is not so, although, if it was so, it would not avail us anything. 'God is not mocked.'[13] If we seek to love selfishly, we will soon experience disillusionment. 'We gain nothing.'[14]

Canon Masterman, however, makes the attractive point that we must not disappoint God! He longs for us to share his life of perfect love. He invites us to do so. He knows what joy it will bring us. Two of our Lord's parables involve weddings. Are we not being guided in them to recognise how much God loves us, how much he desires us to share his life? But we must respond. Is the reason why the guest was thrown out because he lacked the required wedding garment of a responding love for God?[15] The promises of God may indeed 'exceed all that we can desire', but they are what God so much desires to give us. He longs 'to give us all things'[16], and for us to love him is above all things what he desires. Three times the risen Jesus asked Peter, 'Do you love me'[17]. And should not we recognise those words as being addressed to us also? So we may believe that it is to this most desired end that God gives us his grace, that we and he may rejoice together in eternal life. For us there can be no 'such good thing' better than this. [But see also Trinity XIV.]

13 Gal 6:7   14 1 Cor 13:1-3   15 Lk 22:11-14   16 Rom 8:32
17 Jn 21:15-17

TRINITY VII

Lord of all power and might, who art the author and giver of all good things; graft in our hearts the love of thy Name, increase in us true religion, nourish us with all goodness, and of thy great mercy keep us in the same; through Jesus Christ our Lord. Amen.

This Collect, though clearly based on the Gelasian Collect for this Sunday, has been so much altered in translation that it constitutes virtually a new prayer, and surely a particularly lovely one.

This Collect opens in a familiar manner. Several Collects invoke God as the source of all power and the giver of all that is good. They are, after all, the twin foundations on which all Christian prayer rests. Because God is both powerful and generous, we can pray to him with confidence. 'Have no anxiety about anything, but in everything by prayer and supplication with thanksgiving let your requests be made known to God.'[1] 'If you then, who are evil, know how to give good gifts to your children, how much more will your heavenly Father give the Holy Spirit to those who ask him.'[2] He will indeed give us 'far more abundantly than we ask or think'[3], even the best, his very self.

'Is anything too hard for the Lord?'[4] 'What is impossible with men is possible with God' said Jesus.[5] But what is possible is not always expedient, so like Jesus we must always pray ready to accept the answer "No". For God is not only the 'giver of all good things', he is also the withholder of all that may harm us. And he knows what that may be better than we do ourselves. So our Lord received the answer "No" in the garden of Gethsemane, and St. Paul received the same answer in Asia Minor. Both prayed three times for what the Father refused three times. So there could be no doubt in their

1   Phil 4:6   2   Lk 11:13   3   Eph 3:20   4   Gen 18:14   5   Lk 18:27

minds concerning his will for them. They accepted it, and could do so because they knew that they had prayed to him who was 'the Lord of all power and might' and 'the author and giver of all good things.' Similarly, just because our Father is such a God, we too are able to accept his will when it is not as we might wish it to be. He may refuse our requests, but 'he has said, "I will never fail you nor forsake you."'[6] Even 'if we are faithless, he remains faithful, for he cannot deny himself.'[7] Whatever happens to us, therefore, we are to remain confident that the final outcome of events will bring to us and others a blessing, for we know that 'his grace is sufficient for us'[8] and that 'with Christ he will give us all (good) things.'[9]

The Collect's petition follows the sequence of events that we find in horticulture or husbandry. God is prayed to as one that will look after our souls as the husbandman looks after his fruit trees. Jesus often takes the same theme for his parables, as does St. Paul in Romans. He is addressing Gentile Christians when he writes, 'If some of the branches were broken off and you, a wild olive shoot, were grafted in their place to share the richness of the olive tree, do not boast over the branches.' All Christians, he teaches, whatever their background, are dependent on the 'root'. That is what matters. 'If the root is holy, so are the branches.'[10] The passage is a bit tortuous, but the meaning is simple enough to understand.

Here, however, we have a rather different request, that 'the love of thy Name' may be grafted into 'our hearts.' The analogy seems to have been turned upside down! We are not the root; we are the branches. It is we, surely, who must be grafted into the divine, not the divine grafted into us. Is not this the force of our Lord's parable of the vine. 'I am the vine, you are the branches. He who abides in me, and I in him, he it is that bears much fruit, for apart from me you can do nothing.'[11] Does this Collect, then, in any way suggest something false or mistaken?

6 Heb 13:5   7 2 Tim 2:13   8 2 Cor 12:9   9 Rom 8:32
10 Rom 11:17-24   11 Jn 15:5

The point being made, however, is clearly different to that made by our Lord in John 15. The image conveyed is very simply of God looking after us. It is the same as that made in Isaiah's beautiful parable of the vineyard. God there is likened to a husbandman, who created a vineyard and loved it very much. 'Let me sing for my beloved a love song concerning his vineyard,' says the prophet. The vineyard is Israel, whom God created as his special people and whom he has cared for so assiduously; but to no avail. 'He looked for it to yield grapes, but it yielded wild grapes.'[12] We, too, are the object of God's love, and he hopes great things for us. He cares for us and protects us that we may 'yield fruits of increase',[13] the fruits of his Spirit. The force of our prayer here is that we should not disappoint God, as the Israelites did. Our desire is that we should be like 'the tree planted by the waterside that brings forth its fruit in due season.'[14] To this end we pray that God's grace may enable us to really love God, and that we may grow in the ways of 'true religion,' and that we may both do good and become good, and that all this may be a reality throughout our lives. This is, therefore, surely not in any way at all a mistaken prayer.

The title Name is a synonym for God, with particular reference to his character. 'You shalt not take the Name of the Lord your God in vain'[15] means essentially the same as 'hallowed be thy Name'[16], the one putting negatively what the other puts positively. The Name of God was considered so holy that it could not be uttered, and in the Old Testament it was concealed under the mystery of four consonants J H W H, which amounted to the sound of a breath (In the A.V. this is transliterated Jehovah and in other versions Jahweh). At the burning bush, however, we are told that God answered Moses' request to know his Name with the mysterious declaration, 'I am who I am'.[17]

It is central to Christian faith, however, that Jesus has finally and fully

12 Is 5:1-2   13 Ps 107:37   14 Ps 1:3   15 Ex 20:7
16 Matt 6:9   17 Ex 3:14

revealed the character of God. 'No one has ever seen God; the only Son, who is in the bosom of the Father, he has made him known.'[18] Therefore at the end of his life Jesus could say, 'I have made known to them thy Name, and I will make it known.'[19] So we now know God's Name, which is Father and love.[20] Our prayer here is that a true appreciation of this revelation may be 'grafted' into 'our hearts.' Perhaps, therefore, we should complete the text from the High Priestly Prayer in John 17. Jesus makes known the Father's Name 'that the love with which thou hast loved me may be in them, and I in them.' This is a true grafting, a spiritual indwelling such as we pray for at each Holy Communion service, that through the power of the indwelling Spirit 'we may perfectly love thee, and worthily magnify thy holy Name.'

Next comes the prayer that we may increase in 'true religion.' In the Collect for Easter III we considered how through Baptism we were 'admitted into the fellowship of Christ's religion.' It is especially through the Holy Communion, to which the idea of 'grafting' has already led us, that we shall continue to increase in 'true religion.' The Sacraments are our essential means of grace, together with the Scriptures and our own prayers. In our consideration of the Collect for Easter III, we had occasion to quote that key text, Acts 2 : 42. The early Christians 'devoted themselves to the Apostles' teaching and fellowship, to the breaking of bread and the prayers.' In this way the early Church certainly 'increased', for 'the Lord then added to their number day by day.'[21] The 'increase' involved in this prayer, however, need not refer to numbers at Church, though it may. Rather it seems that we are praying here for an' increase' in the quality of our Christian lives. Inevitably that word reminds us of our Confirmation, when it was prayed that we would 'daily increase' in the spiritual life. St. Paul's prayer for the Colossian Church includes the same thought; 'We have not ceased to pray for you, asking that you may... lead a life worthy of the Lord... bearing fruit in every good work and increasing in the knowledge of God.'[22]

18 Jn 1:18   19 Jn 17:26   20 Rom 8:15, 1 Jn 4:8
21 Acts 2:47   22 Col 1:9-10

Mention of good work brings us to the third strand of our petition, which is that we may do and become and remain good, 'nourished with all goodness'. Jesus was quite sharp with the man that 'ran up and knelt before him and asked, "Good Teacher, what must I do to inherit eternal life", and Jesus said to him, "Why do you call me good. No one is good but God alone."'[23] The goodness we seek, then, is a divine characteristic, part indeed of God's holy Name. When talking about behaviour, Jesus demanded that his disciples should not be satisfied with merely keeping the letter of the Law. They were to keep the spirit of it, and so be 'perfect as your heavenly Father is perfect.'[24] St. Peter confirms this extreme requirement when he says, 'As he who called you is holy, be holy yourselves in all your conduct; since it is written, 'You shall be holy, for I am holy'.[25] So there are no limits to the meaning of 'goodness' and, therefore, we cannot give it limits here.

To aspire to such heights, however, may seem so utterly beyond what is reasonable as to make this Collect extreme, even ridiculous. And so it would be, if God were not 'the Lord of all power and might, and the author and giver of all good things.' Moreover, the prayer is that we are to be 'nourished with all goodness', which implies that this is not something to be acquired in a moment. We are to grow in goodness, for goodness is to be our regular food. And as there is no limit to the meaning of goodness, so there is no time limit set for our nourishing and growing. The means for this necessary nourishment have been given us 'through Jesus Christ our Lord.' They are the traditional means of Word and Sacrament. 'Truly, truly, I say to you,...those who hear the voice of the Son of God shall live.'[26] 'Truly, truly, I say to you, unless you eat the flesh of the Son of man and drink his blood, you have no life in you.'[27] There is no getting round that 'truly, truly.' They are equally the means of our 'grafting' and our 'increasing' and our 'nourishing.' They also 'keep us in the same.' They 'keep our hearts and minds in Christ Jesus', [28] which means 'unto everlasting life'.

It may be noticed that the fourfold petition in this Collect, for grafting,

---

23 Mk 10:17-18   24 Matt 5:48   25 1 Pet 1:16   26 Jn 5:25
27 Jn 6:53   28 Phil 4:7

increasing, nourishing and keeping, is essentially similar to the main petitions in the Lord's Prayer. We pray first here that God may graft in our hearts the love of his Name, and we pray first in the Lord's Prayer that we may hallow his Name. We pray next here that we may increase in true religion, and in the Lord's Prayer that we may always do his will, which is the true heart of true religion. The third petition here is that we may be spiritually nourished, and the third petition in the Lord's Prayer is also for nourishment with the food that God alone can give. Finally we pray here that through the 'great mercy' of God we may be ever kept both faithful and true, which implies that we well recognise the danger that we may fall away; in the Lord's Prayer we pray that, being forgiven ourselves and forgiving others, we may be preserved in temptation and delivered from all evil. Is not this therefore in essence the same prayer? And is not this the prayer that our Father both desires to answer, for he is 'the author and giver of all good things', and is able to answer, for he is 'the lord of all power and might'? And is not this a great comfort?

TRINITY VIII

O God, whose never-failing providence ordereth all things both in heaven and earth; we humbly beseech thee to put away from us all hurtful things, and to give us those things which be profitable for us; through Jesus Christ our Lord. Amen.

This Collect, which is Gelasian, was given a new opening in 1662. The 1549 translation had started, 'God, whose providence is never deceived'. This was not only a negative clause of uncertain meaning but it was also unfaithful to the original, for it ignored the important phrase 'in ordering the things that are his' that followed it in the Latin. It was no doubt to recapture for this prayer the essential meaning of that omitted phrase that Bishop Cosin altered its beginning, and his positive invocation is a great improvement on Cranmer's.

We have already several times been required by the Collects to consider the concept of God's sovereignty (e.g. Epiphany II and Easter IV). In this Collect we find the related concept of God's 'providence', which is also referred to in the Collect for Trinity II. There the Collect speaks of God's 'good providence', here of his 'never-failing providence.' There God's providence is seen as something that 'protects us', here as something that 'orders all things, both in heaven and earth.' The literal meaning of providence is foresight (providentia), but since the word relates to God, whose power is almighty, as well as his knowledge complete, providence has the additional meaning of a force predestining events according to the divine will. Therein lies our difficulty in understanding the concept of divine providence, for if our freedom of will is genuine, how can our lives be predestined? God's knowledge may be such as he can foresee the outcome of all things, even our behaviour over which he allows us the freedom 'to refuse the evil and to choose the good,'[1] but how can he 'order' our behaviour, so that it obeys a predestined pattern, and still respect our freedom?

The way that we can, as it were, square this circle is to perceive again that God is love. We saw how this truth was the key to understanding the mystery of God's sovereignty (see Epiphany II), and we can see how it is the same with respect to the mystery of God's providence. What is 'never-failing' and 'ordereth all things' everywhere is love.[2] We are indeed made free, because we are made in the image of God. But our freedom is limited to freedom to love whom or what we will. Love we must, and the mystery of our being lies in the truth that only when we love God do we experience 'perfect freedom.' So it is God's own Spirit, the Spirit of love, that brings us 'into the glorious liberty of the children of God[3], for 'where the Spirit of the Lord is, there is freedom.'[4] Consequently, strange, even illogical, as it may appear, we are not really free when we are simply doing our own will, unless in our will we are freely seeking to do God's will. We are only free when God 'ordereth all things' in our lives, and his providence is operating to control us. So it is that the two apparently irreconcilable truths combine harmoniously in God's sovereign love. On the one hand he creates us out of love to be able to freely do his will, and so experience 'perfect freedom.' On the other hand we discover, by the working of love within us, the wonderful privilege of being God's children, who are predestined to love him freely out of our own free will, according to his 'never failing providence.' In spite of the cost in suffering that this involves, both for God and for us, is this not Good News?

The petition that follows is a double one, but so necessary are both parts that the prayer is like a coin with two sides. Its value is wholly dependent on both being given equal emphasis. We pray first that we may be protected from evil, and secondly that we may be blessed with good. We cannot

1   Is 7:15   2   1 Cor 13:7-10   3   Rom 8:21   4   2 Cor 3:17

worthily ask for an easy, trouble-free life in Christ's name. Equally, it would be unrealistic and unprincipled in a world in which 'our adversary, the Devil', is always around eager to harm us[5] to ignore the danger and reality of evil. We must not deceive ourselves[6]. Held together, however, they make a wise and proper Christian prayer.

To pray this Collect, moreover, we must most definitely be in earnest, for its wording clearly tests our sincerity. First, we pray that God will 'put away from us all hurtful things', but how can he do this, if we welcome them and enjoy them? This prayer, as we have seen, makes us consider our free-will and the proper part it must play in our spiritual and physical safety. Does not this prayer, however, imply that we must also ask for God's grace to give us wisdom and strength to discern what these hurtful things are, and to put them from us for ourselves? This is, therefore, essentially the same prayer as the Collect for Advent Sunday, where the request for grace is explicit. Without doubt the world is full of 'hurtful things', especially things that are hurtful to our spirits. How distressing this can be! 'My soul hath long dwelt among them that are enemies unto peace' bewailed the Psalmist.[7] But we must cope with this fact of life. Jesus prayed for his disciples, and therefore for us, 'I do not pray that thou shouldest take them out of the world, but that thou shouldest keep them from the Evil One.'[8] By the grace of God directing us, obeyed from within our hearts, gladly and willingly, God's 'never-failing providence' may be experienced as a force 'ordering all things' that happen to us, and protecting us from 'all hurtful things.'

We have already mentioned the part God's grace must play in educating us in what are the things that hurt us. (Advent I et al.) We do not necessarily know what they are. Just as the forbidden fruit in the Garden of Eden was attractive to Eve[9], so many things that can hurt us seem attractive to our worldly spirits. We are told that even 'Jesus grew in wisdom'[10], and so we should expect to grow in the perception of right and wrong, especially as it

5   1 Pet 5:8   6   1 Jn 1:8   7   Ps 120:5   8   Jn 17:15
9   Gen 3:6   10 Lk 2:52

relates to ourselves. We are not all called to experience everything! In the realm of physical activity, clearly what is safe for one person to do may not be safe for another[11]. And is this not equally true in spiritual things? To enjoy the best we often have to put away good things, which would be, or have become for us, 'hurtful'. So some are called to celibacy, some to poverty, and others to peculiar service. There will be sacrifices required in all true vocations, in which some good things will have to be put away as 'hurtful things.' To assist in the working out of God's 'never-failing providence' requires of us an unnatural wisdom born of God's grace, for which we must pray, for it is hard for even the most learned to understand 'heavenly things.'[12]

Not all hurtful things, however, are harmful. Indeed, as we know well, some things that hurt us, especially if they hurt such as our pride, can be most 'profitable for us'; which thought introduces us to the second half of this petition. It is no shallow prayer, that we may enjoy always what is pleasant. Such a prayer would be unavailing as well as unworthy, for, as the writer of Hebrews warns us, 'The Father disciplines us for our good, that we may share his holiness. For the moment all discipline seems painful rather than pleasant; later it yields the peaceful fruit of righteousness to those who have been trained by it.'[13]

However, whatever we may think about the worthiness of being guided by the profit motive in business life, Jesus certainly encourages us to pursue that motive wholeheartedly in our spiritual lives! Is this not the clear teaching of the parable of the talents? We must seek to make a good profit for our Master, for he is going to require that of us, and no excuses will be readily accepted for failure. Even if we are careful to keep the commandments and live good lives, we are still to perceive that 'we are unprofitable servants, who have only done what was our duty.'[14] We are to become

11 Rom 14:13-23   12 Jn 3:12   13 Heb 12:10-11   14 Lk 17:10

'profitable servants', and so please God. In the parable, we notice, he did not object to being called 'a hard man'.[15]

The Collect, however, on the surface hardly includes this thought of giving pleasure to God, since we pray only for what is 'profitable for us.' But is not our holiness above all else what is both 'profitable for us', and also what above all else pleases God? And is not this most desired of all ends only achieved through the mysterious operation of God's 'never-failing providence' ordering all things in our lives? We do not become holy by 'taking thought' in a worldly manner, in order to bring about this unworldly end,[16] but rather by accepting and using all that God gives us, and responding in a spirit of praise and thanksgiving and, if need be, courageous self-surrender, to all his gifts and to his providential guidance. Then 'all things will work together for good' for us, for we, 'whom he foreknew, he also predestined to be conformed to the image of his Son.'[17] This is the way his providence works, which is so 'profitable for us.' Everything becomes grist for the divine mill. All the loose ends of our lives can be 'gathered up, that nothing be lost.'[18] It is the work of God's providence to make our lives whole as well as holy, for indeed the two words are related.

We have interpreted the 'us' in the Collect as referring to ourselves only. But we should perhaps extend it to include everyone, and especially those with whom we live, for this is a prayer of the universal Church. Then it becomes a prayer of intercession, and also a challenge to us to see that we do not contribute to what is 'hurtful' to others, and that we do contribute to what is 'profitable' to them. We are called to work and to witness for God and to assist his saving work in Christ. 'Let us then pursue what makes for peace and for mutual upbuilding.'[19]

This is no easy assignment. 'Behold I send you out as sheep in the midst of wolves, so be wise as serpents and innocent as doves.'[20] But in spite of the

15 Matt 25:24   16 Matt 6:25   17 Rom 8:28-30   18 Jn 6:12
19 Rom 14:19   20 Matt 10:16

difficulties we shall be up against, we are to believe that behind us is the whole force of God's 'never-failing providence'. It may seem that we battle against the in-built ways of the world, but the divine power of love has broken in in Christ and the tide of events is moving in the way God wills, for he in Christ and through Christ 'ordereth all things,' not only in heaven, but also on earth. This is not something that we shall necessarily see with our outward eyes, but only through the eyes of faith and hope. 'In the world you have tribulation, but be of good cheer, I have overcome the world.'[21] The 'hurtful' will be put away and the 'profitable' given, and 'we shall see the salvation that the Lord will work for us.'[22] So we have no need to be afraid of what the future has in store for us and our loved ones. Rather we should be full of confidence.[23]

A further truth, moreover, is involved here. Beneath the somewhat impersonal concept of God's 'never-failing providence' lies the much more attractive and personal truth of his never-failing presence. 'Lo I am with you always' was Christ's parting promise to his Apostles.[24] So God in his 'never-failing providence' is not ordering the affairs of our lives from a distance, but rather is active within them, within the very activities of our minds and spirits. It is in this mysterious, intimate way that he can control our lives from within as well as from without, protecting us from the 'hurtful' and providing us with the 'profitable'. It is 'Christ in us' that allows even us to have 'the hope of glory'.[25]

21 Jn 16:33   22 Ex 14:13 (A.V.)   23 Ps 23:4   24 Matt 28:20
25 Col 1:27

TRINITY IX

Grant to us, Lord, we beseech thee, the spirit to think and do always such things as be rightful; that we, who cannot do anything that is good without thee, may by thee be enabled to live according to thy will; through Jesus Christ our Lord. Amen.

A beautiful Collect, in which most of the words are of one syllable, and in this Cranmer's translation faithfully reflects the simplicity of the Latin original. However, a significant change was made in 1662. This Collect is from St. Leo's Sacramentary, and in 1549 it was correctly translated in its petition 'who cannot be without thee'. Bishop Cosin changed this to 'who cannot do anything good without thee', a more practical and active consideration altogether. What was said about the Collect for Trinity V, another Leonine prayer, therefore, which was also changed in translation in the same direction, is probably relevant here as well.

————————————

Although the original wording of the Collect implied that we need divine help both 'to think and do always such things as be rightful', the change in 1662 makes that absolutely clear. The word translated rightful is rectus, which can have the same theological meaning as the Greek word dikaios, and means right or righteous in the eyes of God. Dikaios, dikaioo (I make righteous) and dikaiosune (righteousness, of which God is the source) are extremely important New Testament words, and central to Pauline theology in particular. We are not by nature 'righteous', said St. Paul, nor can we make ourselves 'righteous'. But God can do this for us, and indeed he has done so through Jesus Christ. This is the heart of the Gospel, and St. Paul in Romans uses this quasi-legal language to explain it. This theology is echoed in this Collect. We cannot naturally even think, let alone do, what is rightful, that is right in God's eyes. We are recognising the situation that

St. Paul described: 'I know that nothing good dwells within me, that is, my flesh... I do not (even) do what I want... (because) of 'sin which dwells within me'.[1] It is from this perverse spirit that indwells our 'flesh' that we need redemption, and that is something that God must do for us. And the Gospel proclaims that that is indeed what God in Christ has done.

However, we must respond to this divine redemption of us with faith and repentance. Of all the things that are 'rightful', this necessary response is the most rightful. So St. Paul speaks of us being 'made righteous' or 'justified' by faith.[2] Yet even so we have not the power to do even this unaided by God's grace[3], and so among the good things we are praying for in this Collect the first is for the grace to take this initial 'rightful' step. True life consists of seeking after righteousness, and, finding we cannot attain what we long for of ourselves, of turning to God in repentance and faith, and then of discovering that he can enable us to live, not necessarily as we first envisaged, but as he wills for us. For this to become true for us we need, as the Collect says, as a gift from God, 'the spirit to think and to do always such things as be rightful'. That spirit is nothing less than himself, the Holy Spirit. It should, surely, be printed with a capital S, although in the B.C.P. it is not.

The Collect underlines the truth that thought precedes action (we 'think' and then we 'do'). However, as we have been already led to remember, the really crucial thoughts in our lives are the thoughts of our hearts, rather than the thoughts of our minds (e.g. Lent III). The thoughts of our minds lead only to specific actions and activities, but the thoughts of our hearts form our characters, and so control the whole direction of our lives. [4] If our characters should be evil, our plight is really serious. 'If then the light in you is darkness, how great is the darkness ?'[5] So we pray as we prepare to receive Communion, that the Holy Spirit will 'cleanse the thoughts of our

1 Rom 7:18-20   2   Rom 5:1   3   Eph 2:8-9   4   Lk 6:45
5   Matt 6:23

hearts'. And this is what will happen if the Holy Spirit will 'direct and rule our hearts', and not merely our minds. (Trinity XIX). And then, as we should expect, if our thinking is 'rightful' through the inspiration of the Holy Spirit, we will know peace with God as our great reward. 'Whatever is true', says St. Paul, 'whatever is honourable, whatever is just, whatever is pure, whatever is lovely, whatever is gracious, if there is any excellence, if there is any praise, think about these things…and the God of peace will be with you'.[6] It is a subject worthy of the stirring language used.

However such wise guidance is not easily followed by us, being the kind of people that we are, muddled, uncertain and anxious, as well as sinful. And even when we perceive clearly what is 'rightful' for us to do, we are still so often unable to do it. Although thought precedes action, action all too often does not follow thought. With God, of course, it is different. His thought expressed in his word does not fail or 'return to (him), but it shall accomplish that which (he) purposes, and prosper in the things for which (he) sent it'.[7] Jesus is God's word active in human flesh, accomplishing that which he purposes. It is, therefore, only when we are in Christ, that we are sure similarly to 'prosper', both thinking and doing what is 'rightful', being really able to match the one to the other, and thereby being 'enabled to live according to (God's) will'.

In this context another point arises. The word 'think' in this prayer may seem to imply that the intelligent and educated have an advantage in this matter of living 'rightfully'. Without doubt intelligence and education do give advantages in some areas of life. But do they give them in the highest and most important? This clearly was a real issue in Corinth, as 1 Corinthians makes plain.[8] After all many of the earliest Christians were slaves with no education whatever. Such were deemed 'the low and despised in the world'. But St. Paul is at pains to contradict any such teaching. Indeed he says that in fact the intelligent and educated are, if anything, at a disadvantage when it comes to understanding 'the word of

6   Phil 4:8-9   7   Is 55:11   8   1 Cor 1:18-31

the cross', which is at the heart of the Gospel. The call to take up 'our cross' is not at all a sensible vocation, and he quotes Isaiah to show that it has always been the case that the intelligent and educated have been particularly reluctant to obey God. We will not act in a 'rightful' manner, unless we 'think' in a 'rightful' spirit. And such thinking is not by any means always taught in the schools in which our minds are trained. To think 'rightfully' we need to possess 'the mind of Christ'.[9] 'Have this mind among yourselves, which is yours in Christ Jesus', taught St. Paul. That is the answer; but then he goes on. Though he was God he 'humbled himself' to live the life of total obedience.[10] That is the true wisdom, the 'wisdom of God', which even little children can possess, and which alone leads on to 'righteousness and sanctification and redemption'. So at the heart of this prayer for 'rightful' thinking lies an implied emphasis on the vital virtue of humility, without which the truths of the Gospel will always be too deep for us to understand, no matter how intelligent or educated we may be.

The purpose of our prayer is the great purpose of the Christian life, 'to live according to God's will.' 'Thy will be done.' Those four words sum up what should be our whole ambition. It is all as simple as that, and as difficult. One of the main benefits of using these prayers of our Prayer Book is that they recall us to the real essentials of true religion. They do not allow us to become dominated by some passing political problem or some special social concern. Doing God's will will have a political dimension and require social action, but we must not change the order in which God has revealed his commandments. We go astray if we do. This is because we do not actually have 'the spirit to think and do always such things as are rightful.' We cannot 'live according to God's will' in a worldly manner and from a worldly spirit, so we should notice how the prayer 'Thy will be done' comes after 'Hallowed be thy Name.' We cannot accomplish the one before we have sincerely set our hearts to do the other. This truth is implied in this Collect,

9   1 Cor 2:16   10   Phil 2:5-8

and indeed in all the Collects.

We are dependent creatures, and it is the height of wisdom to acknowledge this. Our freedom of will does not make us independent of God. This is emphasised in this Collect. We have no power of ourselves to serve God truly, or to do good to others, or even to help ourselves properly. The Christian life is not, therefore, a natural kind of life, but rather a super-naturally oriented life, in which we freely seek of our own will to live in accordance with God's will. Nature is of God, but it, like us, is infected with evil. Just to live naturally is going to mean living below the level of God's true will for us. But God has entered the natural world, in which 'we live and move and have our being'[11], in order that we may live on earth according to attitudes and customs that apply in heaven. If we do this, we, like Jesus, become instrumental in creating the kingdom of God on earth, as it is in heaven, something that happens whenever, by God's grace, 'we are enabled to live according to God's will.' This may seem extravagant language to use, but St. Paul was apparently in no doubt of what was involved in being a Christian; he saw it as 'the immeasurable greatness of God's power in us who believe' working out the divine will to bring its blessings on all both within time and beyond time, till God 'fills all in all'.[12] How truly amazing the truth of the Gospel is! 'O the depth of the riches and wisdom and knowledge of God! How unsearchable are his judgements and how inscrutable his ways!'[13] The challenge is too great for us, we may be tempted to say; the call too frightening in its grandeur. But 'he who calls (us) is faithful, and he will do it'.[14] So if we pray this prayer with faith and humility we may yet pray it with confidence and hope.

11 Acts 17:28   12 Eph 1:15-23   13 Rom 11:33   14 1 Thess 5:24

TRINITY X

Let thy merciful ears, O Lord, be open to the prayers of thy humble servants; and that they may obtain their petitions make them to ask such things as shall please thee; through Jesus Christ our Lord. Amen.

This Collect derives from the Leonine Sacramentary. Cranmer, however, took his opening from the Gelasian version of this Collect, which was a rewriting of the earlier Collect, and only the main petition from the original.

It should not surprise us that the Collects repeat themselves, and that the opening of this Collect reminds us of many others. (Epiphany I and II, Septuagesima, Trinity I and III et al.) We are praying here, as we were in all those other Collects, with importunity, which in prayer is a virtue specially praised by Jesus. There are difficulties in understanding this virtue, which are not lessened by the fact that his main teaching on it is set in the context of a parable and a healing story that are both among the more puzzling of their kind in the Gospels. In the parable of the Unjust Judge Jesus ends by saying, 'Hear what the unrighteous judge says. And will not God (also) vindicate his elect who cry to him day and night?'[1] To the Syrophoenician woman, who so annoyed his disciples by her persistence, Jesus said, 'O woman, great is your faith! Be it done for you as you desire.'[2] We see, then, that to pray with importunity in no way implies a proud or untrusting spirit. Rather, as the parable and the healing story make plain, it implies real sincerity and genuine faith. We have to make a effort if we are to succeed in anything, and prayer is no exception. The parable of the Unjust Judge is prefaced, 'He told them a parable to the effect that they ought always to pray and not lose heart.'[3] We must beware above all things lest our prayers become dispirited, and we relapse into mere formalism.

1 Lk 18:6-8   2   Matt 15:21-28   3   Lk 18:1

God does hear our prayers, but we pray here not only that God may hear our prayers, but that we may be able to make them more worthy of his attention.

The Bible teaches us plainly that God loves us all[4], but it also leaves us in no doubt that there is a difference between the wicked and the righteous in God's eyes. It does make a difference what sort of people we are, even in the realm of prayer. 'The eyes of the Lord are over the righteous and his ears are open unto their prayers.'[5] 'The prayer of a righteous man has great power in its effect.'[6] Surely there is no real problem here. It would be far harder to understand the way of prayer, if it was otherwise. 'You ask and do not receive, because you ask wrongly, to spend it on your own passions.'[7] Is not this just as one would expect, that God will refuse to give us what is not in our best interests to receive? We know that Jesus taught that everything we ask for 'in his Name' would be granted us.[8] But we also fully realise that this is not a mere formula for successful prayer, but rather an encouragement to holiness. The key text is John 15 : 7: 'If you abide in me and my words abide in you, ask whatever you will, and it shall be done for you.' It is the prayers of the Saints that have power, because they are Saints. And the prayers of Saints are not petitions offered by rote, or merely as occasion may require. Rather they are the constant turning of the heart and mind towards God, ever seeking his will for themselves and others, for they 'abide in' Christ.

We speak here of 'the prayers of thy humble servants.' Importunity goes with humility rather in the same way as zeal goes with meekness. The humble person is able to be bold in prayer, because he is so confident of God's love, and so sure in his dependence on that love. He knows that he is not disturbing God by approaching him in prayer! Nor is he frightened of being misunderstood; and if he is being silly or wrong, he knows his prayer will be refused or forgiven. So he is childlike in his trust, but also in his passion and his persistence.

---

4   Jn 3:16   5   Ps 34:15   6   Jas 5:16   7   Jas 4:3
8   Jn 16:23

We can, however, be very silly and very wrong in the nature of our prayers. We can be guilty of vain repetition, such as is childish rather than childlike. 'In praying do not heap up empty phrases as the Gentiles do, for they think they will be heard for their many words. Do not be like them, for your Father knows what you need before you ask him.'[9] Then Jesus gave his disciples his prayer. In it we have all the essentials of prayer, and all that is essential for us to pray for. As the last Collect reminded us, we do not know what 'to think or do' in any situation without God's Spirit as guide. 'We do not know how to pray as we ought,' but St. Paul assures us that the Holy Spirit will 'help us in our weakness'.[10] This does not mean we should not make every effort to pray intelligently. 'I will pray with the spirit and I will pray with the mind also,'[11] says St. Paul in another context. But often our desires are perverse, and certainly none can foresee fully the consequences of any action we or others may take. So we are conscious of deepseated uncertainty, and we can often only lift up situations in faith and hope, trusting in the love and the power of God. St. Paul teaches that such a method of prayer will not go unrewarded. 'The Spirit himself (then) intercedes for us with sighs too deep for words. And he who searches the hearts of men knows what is in the mind of the Spirit, because the Spirit intercedes for the saints according to the will of God.'[12] To pray in this manner, we may believe, is pleasing to God. The Spirit himself' will 'ask such things as shall please him.'

St. Paul ends his first letter to the Thessalonians, 'Finally, brethren, we beseech and exhort you in the Lord Jesus that as you learned from us how you ought to live and to please God, you do so more and more.'[13] It is naturally the desire of every Christian to please God, and we all know the first requirement. 'Without faith it is impossible to please God.'[14] And after faith comes hope and love, 'and the greatest of these is love.'[15] These are the foundation virtues, or theological virtues, for they create and cement our

9   Matt 6:7-8   10 Rom 8:26   11 1 Cor 14:15   12 Rom 8:26b-27
13 1 Thess 4:1   14 Heb 11:6   15 1 Cor 13:13

relationship with God. Only through them can we hope to 'please God both in will and deed', as we learnt in our study of the Collect for Trinity I.

There is also absolute need, on what might be called the negative side of the spiritual life, for repentance and forgiveness. These are really very positive virtues, and they only have the appearance of being negative, since they are all about 'casting out' and 'putting away from us' evil and sin. To repent and forgive, however, we know pleases God greatly, for 'there is more joy in heaven over one sinner that repents' than there is even over the sight of many good lives,[16] and 'if (we) forgive men their trespasses, our heavenly Father also will forgive (us)', so that our fellowship may be unbroken.[17]

These, then, are the really necessary things. We can imagine other things are more vital, but 'these shall please the Lord better than a bullock that hath horns and hoofs (the expensive offerings of the religiously minded). The humble shall consider this and be glad.'[18] Such things are in the reach of us all. So we believe that the greatest of Saints is the Blessed Virgin Mary, who sang of God 'exalting the humble and meek.'[19] We pray here that we may 'ask such things as shall please God.' Solomon's prayer is said to have pleased God, because he sought only the spirit necessary to do his duty according to God's will.[20] So with us; we are to ask only for what is necessary for us to fulfil our duty in the circumstances in which God's providence has placed us, or as the Catechism puts it, 'in that state of life unto which it shall please God to call us.' We please God by being content with what is his good pleasure, and allowing ourselves to be guided by him in all things, after the example of our Lord, who could say, 'He has not left me alone, for I always do what is pleasing to him.'[21] But to experience such a blessing upon us, we must pray with importunity after the example of the Saints, and in the spirit of this simply worded Collect.

---

16 Lk 15:7   17 Matt 6:14   18 Ps 69:32-33   19 Lk 1:52 (A.V.)
20 1 Kgs 3:9-10 21 Jn 8:29

TRINITY XI

O God, who declarest thy almighty power most chiefly in showing mercy and pity; mercifully grant unto us such a measure of thy grace that we, running the way of thy commandments, may obtain thy gracious promises, and be made partakers of thy heavenly treasure; through Jesus Christ our Lord. Amen.

This is the Gelasian Collect expanded in 1662. The 1549 Collect was a literal translation of the original, in which we were said to be 'running to thy promises', rather than in 'the way of thy commandments.' And the prayer that we 'may obtain thy gracious promises' is an addition to 'being made partakers of thy heavenly treasure', which in the original stood alone. The prayer for grace is also differently expressed. Originally it was for abundant grace, but now only for 'such a measure of thy grace'.

The opening is a particularly attractive one. The Collects often call upon God to show us 'mercy and pity' (Advent IV, Epiphany IV, Sexagesima et al). We are weak and God is strong. Our prayers so often naturally arise out of our need, and our knowledge that God can help us. But will he? Yes, he will, for he is full of 'mercy and pity.' 'He is gracious and merciful, slow to anger and of great kindness.'[1] 'To the Lord our God belong mercies and forgivenesses,' and this is true 'though we have rebelled against him.'[2] These texts, which are particularly familiar from frequent use at Morning and Evening Prayer, are among a huge number that might be quoted from Scripture to assure us of this truth. 'Mercy and pity' are constant and certain attributes of God's character or Name: they 'endure for ever,'[3] and 'will follow us all the days of our life.'[4]

This divine 'mercy and pity' is described here as a sign of God's 'almighty

---

1   Joel 2:13   2   Dan 9:9   3   Ps 107:1 et al   4   Ps 23:6

power.' This is not how the world sees things, for there 'mercy and pity' are often seen as signs of weakness rather than strength. Power is measured there by the ability to punish and destroy. But in the kingdom of God it is not so. This is because God is love, and in his invincible love his sovereignty is revealed. He has the power to redeem, a power that the world lacks. To forgive mankind and to redeem the world are indeed the ultimate signs of God's omnipotence. We are told how Moses saw a vision of God on Mount Sinai and angelic voices proclaimed to him, 'The Lord, the Lord, a God merciful and gracious, slow to anger and abounding in steadfast love and faithfulness, keeping steadfast love for thousands, forgiving iniquity and transgression and sin.'[5] And Jesus confirms this vision in all that he taught and did. It is central to the Gospel, in which we are to put our trust, and out of which we are to say our prayers.[6]

Our first petition is appropriately for grace. 'Give us grace.' (Advent I). These words are the central petition of the first Collect. They reappear in various forms in so many that follow. Here we ask for 'such a measure of thy grace,' implying that we seek only such as we may need in the present circumstances of our lives. This is what we shall receive, according to the assurance given to St. Paul in his time of special need; 'My grace is sufficient for you.'[7] Our main concern, therefore, is not "Will God provide", but, "Can we and will we receive and use his grace?" In St. Paul's case he was told that God's 'power (was) made perfect in (his) weakness', and this revelation relates interestingly to the point we are considering in this Collect. Divine 'mercy and pity' cannot become the all-powerful agents for good that they may be for us where they are up against pride and self-confidence. They must be received, so we shall only experience their power when we are humble and meek. Only then shall we be of a mind to receive God's grace gladly and willingly, and 'in such measure' as God may give it to us.

The gift of God's grace, however, does not take away our free will and our need to use it in a spirit of ready obedience. The phrase 'running the way of thy commandments' implies very ready obedience. 'I made haste and prolonged not the time to keep thy commandments'.[8] However, our readiness to obey may have to take the form of readiness to wait, patiently seeking the grace and guidance needed to know and do God's will. 'Let us run with perseverance (or patience) the race that is set before us, looking to Jesus, the pioneer and perfecter of our faith.'[9] It is those who 'wait upon the Lord' that renew their strength, so that they can 'run and not be weary, and walk and not faint.'[10] So God's grace is given 'in such measure' as suits the tempo, as well as the circumstances, of our lives.

The second petition is a two-fold one, that 'we may obtain thy gracious promises, and be made partakers of thy heavenly treasure.' But the two are one, viewed as it were from different sides, ours and God's. We seek to obtain what God gives; he wants to give what we desire. Canon Masterman puts it very simply, 'We want to obtain his gracious promises.' The sense of urgency portrayed here relates this time to our seeking rather than to our obeying. Both attitudes, however, are worthy, so let us ask ourselves how much we really want and seek after what God has promised to give us. In Hebrews this thought is a major feature of the faith of the great men and women of faith in the Old Testament. They are shown as people who looked hopefully forward, deeply conscious of God's promises, in which they passionately believed. According to the Old Testament these promises were often repeated. First they were made through Noah to all mankind.[11] Then they were made again to Abraham, to whom God revealed his intention of using his descendants as his special instrument.[12] They were renewed through Moses to these descendants, now rescued from slavery in Egypt[13], and through David, God's specially chosen King, under whom they had become established in the promised land.[14] The 'gracious promises' of

8 Ps 119:60   9 Heb 12:1   10 Is 40:31   11 Gen 8:21-22
12 Gen 17:1-8   13 Deut 5   14 1 Chron 17

God, therefore, have the character of a divine covenant with us, because they place those to whom they are made under a sacred obligation. They must be responded to, therefore, and co-operated with, if they are to be obtained. Failure to do this does not nullify them, but it does delay them. We respond to them and obtain them through faith; without faith they cannot be obtained. But this faith must be active and characterised by obedience to God's revealed will for us, because 'faith without works is dead'.[15]

Now it is our belief that all these divine promises were fulfilled in Jesus, and in their fulfilment a new covenant with new promises has been inaugurated with all mankind. His death and resurrection and the coming of the Holy Spirit have both fulfilled the old and established the new. Hebrews says, 'In speaking of a new covenant (God) treats the first as obsolete, and what is becoming obsolete and growing old is ready to vanish away'.[16] This new covenant is created by new promises of a 'new heaven and a new earth.'[17] This new covenant has, therefore, most wonderful consequences. 'Therefore, if anyone is in Christ, he is a new creation; the old has passed away, behold the new has come.'[18]

We, then, are the heirs of the promises made to mankind ages ago. Of the Old Testament heroes we are told, 'All these, though well attested by their faith, did not receive what was promised since God had foreseen something better for us, that apart from us they should not be made perfect.'[19] 'Running to thy promises', therefore, was a lovely and appropriate phrase, and perhaps it is a pity it was changed. It speaks of us entering eagerly into this new covenant, and embracing the promises that created it. They involve our salvation in eternal life. 'This is what he has promised us, eternal life.'[20] This is 'our treasure in heaven',[21] for which once we really know about it, we will gladly give up all manner of treasure on earth to possess.[22] After all, 'what will it profit a man if he gains the whole world and forfeits his life? Or what shall a man give in return for his life?'[23] Nothing

15 Jas 2:26 (A.V.)   16 Heb 8:13   17 Is 66:22, Rev 21:1   18 2 Cor 5:17
19 Heb 11:39   20 1 Jn 2:25   21 Matt 19:21   22 Matt 13:44
23 Matt 16:26

can really be more important for us than this, and that we shall partake of his life, which is in his Son,[24] is indeed God's gracious promise to us.

Besides faith the way that this promised gift of life in Christ becomes real for us, the way we 'obtain' it and 'partake' of it, is especially through the sacraments of Baptism and Holy Communion. Once for all we 'obtain' this 'gracious promise' in Baptism. Frequently we 'partake of this heavenly treasure' in Holy Communion. They are the main means of grace, through which God gives us grace 'in such measure' as we may need it to live according to his commandments, which also involves helping others as well as ourselves to' obtain' and 'partake' of it. On this thought Canon Masterman makes a lovely point. 'Heavenly treasure does not grow less as new claimants come to partake of it. For of all spiritual things it is true that they increase by giving.' Jesus said 'It is more blessed to give than to receive'.[25] Heavenly treasure is for spending, not for keeping. The more readily we spend it, the more certainly will it grow.[26] So our appreciation of all that God has so 'graciously promised' and of the true value of his 'heavenly treasure' increases as we take hold of the one (God's promise) by faith and spend the other (heavenly treasures) in love; this is how the new covenant works.

So this is a particularly lovely prayer that starts in a spirit of faith and humility, continues in a spirit of eager obedience and ends in a spirit of seeking, assurance and hope.

24 1 Jn 5:11   25 Acts 20:35   26 Lk 6:38

TRINITY XII

Almighty and everlasting God, who art always more ready to hear than we to pray, and art wont to give more than either we desire or deserve; pour down upon us the abundance of thy mercy; forgiving us those things whereof our conscience is afraid, and giving us those good things which we are not worthy to ask, but through the merits and mediation of Jesus Christ, thy Son, our Lord. Amen.

This is the Gelasian Collect, but changed and lengthened, both in 1549 and again for the Book of 1662. (See commentary)

We start the Collect by reminding ourselves that God is always ready to hear our prayers, and, what is more, to answer them with overwhelming generosity, giving us even more than we have asked for, and certainly much more than we deserve. In its redrafting, however, by the Reformers, the declaration that this is all due to 'the abundance of God's mercy' was omitted, and this phrase, which had been the main part of the invocation, was replaced at the start of the petition. Although the invocation in this Collect is still lovely, and describes so very well what we mean by 'the abundance of God's mercy', it is perhaps a pity that the phrase itself was moved from the Collect's opening; the point being that to dwell on the mercy of God makes the ideal spring-board for our prayers. It is what we may utterly rely upon, for 'his mercy endureth for ever'.[1] (There are few more common phrases in the Old Testament than that.) Mercy means 'steadfast love', and it is often translated as such in modern versions. God loves us, and always has, and always will. That is what we are declaring here, and we should try to let that truth possess our hearts and minds. To recall it certainly makes the perfect preparation for prayer.

1 Ps 136:1 et al

The words of the invocation, however, do very well describe God's steadfast love of us; and they also describe our wavering love of God. How reluctant we are to pray! How little we ask for! How undeserving we are of his many blessings! This Collect surely makes some valid points, which we should take to heart. Jesus taught how God knows and cares. We do not have to approach him with elaborate rituals or frenzied cries for help. 'Ask, and it will be given you'.[2] He knows our needs before we ask for anything, and can be guaranteed to give us always and only what is best for us.[3] We are to approach God without craven fear, confident in his steadfast love. 'He gives to all men generously and without reproaching', says St. James. All that is required of us is that we ask in faith and hope and love.[4] But is not this just where we fail so miserably?

The ultimate assurance to us, however, that God does hear and answer our prayers is the knowledge that we may pray to him 'through Jesus Christ'. This phrase ends all our Collects, and it should be prayed as a vital and integral part of them. In St. John's Gospel we hear Jesus teaching his disciples to pray 'in his Name'.[5] Hebrews tells us of how the glorified Jesus, as man's High Priest, 'always lives to make intercession for us'.[6] St. Paul describes the mystery of the Christian life as 'Christ in us, the hope of glory'.[7] Because we are all parts of Christ's mystical Body, the Church, we are always praying 'through him' and 'in his Name'. So we have 'sure and certain hope' that our prayers are heard, and answered according to God's will, though not, of course, necessarily according to our will. Glorious things, therefore, will come about through prayer because of this. And this surely is the greatest possible encouragement to us to pray. Because this is true, we should 'have no anxiety about anything, but in everything, by prayer and supplication with thanksgiving , let our requests be made known to God. (Then) the peace of God, which passes all understanding, will keep our hearts and minds in Christ Jesus.'[8]

---

2 Lk 11:9   3 Matt 6:8, Lk 11:11-13   4 Jas 1:5-7

5 Jn 14:13-14   6 Heb 7:25   7 Col 1:27   8 Phil 4:6-7

Our petition is, first, that through God's mercy we may be forgiven. The B.C.P. makes no bones about it, we are 'miserable sinners', and we are led to confess and repent and seek forgiveness in what some today consider too abject a manner. Certainly on occasions the Collects declare that we are sinners meriting punishment (Septuagesima, Lent IV); on others we declare that the frailty of our nature is such as it is certain to lead us into trouble and temptation. (Epiphany III, IV). In the prayer of Confession in the Holy Communion we tell God how 'grievous' and 'intolerable' a burden our sins are. However, although it is mentioned in the Homily before Communion and the Visitation of the Sick, and is everywhere implied, it is only here that our conscience is mentioned in these public prayers of the Church.

What is this mysterious spiritual organ? The Greek word translated conscience in the New Testament (suneidesis)means having the ability to know oneself. So the conscience is an inner light or wisdom, whereby we recognise spiritual truths about our actions and character. Our conscience, therefore, registers sin, and warns us against it. The voice of conscience is vividly and faithfully portrayed in Romans 7, as St. Paul tells of his internal struggles and frequent defeats. It plays a vital, though usually uncomfortable, and often unwelcome, part in our spiritual lives. For our conscience to become dead to sin, however, is an appalling disaster, and that is what can happen. We can become 'futile in our thinking' and 'our minds become darkened.'[9] Through consorting with false religious practices or indulging in evil activities of any kind our consciences can become 'seared'.[10] Few words of Jesus are more chilling than his observation, 'If your eye is not sound, your whole body will be full of darkness'.[11] Equally, how fortunate we are, if we can say in all sincerity, 'I always take pains to have a clear conscience toward God and toward men'.[12]

However, it is few who can say such a thing, and for most of us the best that we can hope for is that our consciences should not cease to make us 'afraid'.

9   Rom 1:21   10 1 Tim 4:2   11 Matt 6:23   12 Acts 24:16

The fear of the Lord is such a necessary spiritual virtue, and it is the inspiration of so much that is good. It is 'the beginning of wisdom', and those without it are declared 'abominable'![13] This holy fear, emanating from our consciences, is of God, guiding us to confess and repent and seek forgiveness. The third Collect at Evensong (Lighten our darkness, we beseech thee, O Lord) may be taken as a prayer that our consciences should never become inactive, and so cease to shed their light upon our lives and all that motivates them, as well as one for grace to see clearly amid the surrounding darkness of this sinful world. There is no need to be ashamed that our consciences make us ' afraid'. Rather we should feel relief that they are working for our soul's good.[14]

However, they often do not give us clear messages. They can be the means of us feeling guilty, but yet strangely unable to confess precisely what it is that is 'making our consciences afraid'. There is, we may notice, a sense of imprecision in the petition in this Collect, that is so typical of this experience. We ask here for forgiveness for that of which we are not quite sure, only our consciences warn us that sin exists within. St. Paul speaks revealingly of 'the things now hidden in darkness' that lie within our souls. We may look at ourselves with sincerity, but we can see ourselves only 'as in a mirror dimly'. The time will come, however, when God 'will disclose the purposes of our hearts', which puzzle and confuse us, and then 'we shall understand (ourselves) fully, even as we have been fully understood'. Then justice shall be done, and seen to be done, 'for every man will receive his commendation from God'.[15] Meanwhile we live in a twilight world, in which our consciences are often afraid.

Against this anxiety, however, we may put our confidence in 'the abundance of God's mercy'. We believe absolutely in this mercy, for we declare in the Creed that we believe 'in the forgiveness of sins', all sins whatsoever! Indeed we must believe this, for it is the very heart of the Gospel. But what if we do not know what we have done wrong, or where we are going wrong?

---

13 Ps 36:1-2   14 1 Jn 3:19-22   15 1 Cor 4:5, 1 Cor 13:12

The words of the Psalmist come to mind. 'Who can tell how oft he offendeth? O cleanse thou me from my secret faults'.[16] This should not surprise us, nor must we let it distress us too greatly, but the B.C.P. in its wisdom points us towards the comfort of Sacramental Confession and Absolution, when this becomes an intolerable problem for us. 'If any of you cannot quiet his conscience... let him come to some discreet and learned Minister of God's Word that he may receive the benefit of absolution, together with ghostly counsel and advice, to the quieting of his conscience, and the avoiding of all scruple and doubtfulness'. What a blessing it is, if we can 'hold the mystery of our faith with a clear conscience',[17] and we can, so long as 'we come to the light'[18] and believe firmly in 'the abundance of God's mercy', which assures us of his forgiveness of all our sins. It is as the Prayer Book declares; he forgives us, who are penitent, 'according to (his) promises declared unto mankind in Christ Jesus our Lord.' (See also commentary for Ash Wednesday and Trinity XXIV.)

The ending of this Collect was considerably changed in 1662. In 1549 Cranmer cannot be said to have succeeded very well. Then we prayed, 'giving unto us that that our prayer dare not presume to ask'! And also no mention was made of the necessary 'merits and mediation' of our Lord, if we are to obtain what we most need. What we have now, therefore, is a great improvement, making this not only a much more felicitously worded prayer, but also a much more devotional one.

Having asked for forgiveness for all ours sins, the known and the unknown, we ask now for all 'those good things', which we need and want, even those which for various reasons we cannot or do not ask. Specifically we mention 'those good things for which we are not worthy to ask'. But our minds are so confused by the bright lights of 'the world, the flesh and the Devil', that we also cannot see straight enough to know what we really do need or want.

16 Ps 19:12   17 1 Tim 3:9   18 Jn 3:21

We are bombarded on all sides by worldly advertisements. We are the prey of fashion, the great predator. On all sides our appetite for possessions is stimulated. We are educated incessantly to understand our rights and to insist upon them. Our upbringing can encourage false ambitions and prejudiced attitudes towards others. Perhaps above all we are encouraged to equate 'good things' with the merely temporal and transitory, food, sex, comfort, entertainment, holidays and such like. The fact is that we approach God, not only in a state of sin, but also in a state of folly, ignorance and confusion.

The prodigal son returned home hoping, one imagines, for 'good things, for which he was not worthy to ask', even though he asked only for what he believed it was reasonable to ask.[19] The Centurion came with a request, for which he knew, according to the conventions of the time, he had no right to expect Jesus to take any notice.[20] Indeed in the Lucan account the Centurion did not even feel himself entitled to approach Jesus personally.[21] How wrong they both were! The prodigal was certainly 'given more than either he desired or deserved', and the Centurion was most warmly praised, as well as having his request instantly fulfilled. Nonetheless we cannot but feel like both the prodigal and the Centurion, and no doubt it is right that we should. To some extent, at least, we are in their shoes. A sense of unworthiness becomes us. We often read how the great figures of the Bible came to recognise their presumption in their approach to God. 'I have uttered what I did not understand, things too wonderful for me, which I did not know'.[22] 'I am not worthy of the least of all the steadfast love and faithfulness, which thou hast shown to thy servant'.[23] 'And when Elijah heard (the still small voice of God speaking to him) he wrapped his face in his mantle'.[24]

So with us, but with us there is a great difference, such as makes all the difference. And here our thoughts are taken back to the affirmation contained in the invocation, and our comments on it. We can approach God

19 Lk 15:18   20 Matt 8:8   21 Lk 7:1-10   22 Job 42:3
23 Gen 32:10   24 1 Kgs 19:11-13

through Jesus Christ, and all that that implies. We do not need to know exactly what to ask for, any more than we need to fully know all our sins. We do not have to be worthy to pray to God, because Christ is worthy, and he is our great High Priest; and we may pray trusting in his 'merits and mediation'. Dorothy Kerin, the foundress of Burrswood, teaches what she called a 'little way of prayer', when we draw near to God in petition and intercession. By an act of the will, we are to put ourselves into God's presence, and by an act of faith recognise his love and power. And then, without any attempt to tell God what we need, or what another needs, 'without asking or beseeching', we are to simply rest in him, in his power and love revealed and mediated through Jesus Christ, and accept with thanksgiving and hope all that he gives, however much or however little. 'In this way' she says, 'God gives himself to his beloved in quietness.'[25] It is after all he himself whom we really need, even more than all 'the good things, for which we are not worthy to ask'. And this he gives us, through Jesus Christ and his Holy Spirit. It is in this way, 'on the just and the unjust', that he continually, like 'the sunshine and the rain',[26] 'pours down upon us the abundance of his mercy.'

25 Burrswood Healing Service   26 Matt 5:45

TRINITY XIII

Almighty and merciful God, of whose only gift it cometh that thy faithful people do unto thee true and laudable service; grant, we beseech thee, that we may so faithfully serve thee in this life, that we fail not finally to attain thy heavenly promises; through the merits of Jesus Christ our Lord. Amen.

This is the Leonine Collect, amended and lengthened. The medieval opening is unchanged, but the petition has been redrafted twice, and given a new direction. The Latin Collect read, 'that we may without stumbling run to thy promises'. This was changed first in 1549 to become, 'that we may so run to thy heavenly promises that we fail not finally to attain the same', and then again in 1662, when the concept of service in the invocation was repeated in the petition to replace the more ambiguous one of running. The idea of service now dominates the whole prayer. However, by using the adverb 'faithfully' it may be said that the 1662 Collect kept the eager spirit of the original, that was particularly attractive.

Perhaps a more significant change was made in the 1549 amendment, which was kept in 1662, when the adjective 'heavenly' was added to the promises mentioned. This appears to give the Collect a new and other-worldly direction, which was strengthened in 1662 by the introduction of the word 'finally'. So the theme of this Collect has been both expanded and simplified, and we now pray that, through serving God here, we may attain to his promises hereafter.

There are two main considerations in this Collect; on the one hand the service of God, that is to be fulfilled here, and on the other the promises of God, that are to be attained hereafter. The Collect suggests that our attaining the latter depends on our faithfulness in attending to the former. No-one reading the New Testament can doubt that Christians are supposed to be servants, both of God and of each other. This truth, moreover, is the one that has specially governed the thinking of the Church in this century. This is the age of the Social Gospel, Christian Aid, and the Servant Church. Nevertheless the New Testament does not give a clear picture of what is meant by Christian service and a Christian servant. There are two particular difficulties that make for possible confusion of mind on this matter. The first is that the idea of a servant in the New Testament is crucially influenced by Isaiah II's reference to a special Servant of God in four poems, usually called the Servant Songs. The special truth about this Servant is that he suffers innocently and willingly. The second is that the kind of service and the kind of servant most often referred to in the New Testament is slavery and a slave (douleia & doulos). Slavery is something that we have no first-hand knowledge of at all, and the idea of it is utterly abhorrent to us. In the 1st century, however, it was not only common-place, but also accepted as normal and legitimate. There is no protest made against slavery as an institution in the Bible, only against cruelty to slaves. The Christian slave-owner was not commanded to free his slaves, only to love them.[1] To us it seems amazing that this is so, and surely even more that slavery and a slave are set before us as the ideals of Christian service and a Christian servant, but it is so.

In the New Testament there are a number of other aspects of service and a variety of words generally translated servant in the New Testament. Most of these are incidental and unimportant. But two are important. The first of these is diakonos, with its verb diakonein. Here we are talking usually about willing, voluntary service, as in 'Martha served'.[2] The second is latreia, with its verb latreuein, which describes religious service of God, and the prophetess Anna, who 'served God with fastings and prayers night and day',[3] typifies this kind of service. So these are four different kinds of

---

1   Philemon, Eph 6:9   2   Jn 12:2   3   Lk 2:36-37

service, and they set before us different ideals of servants. But they fall into two groups, nonetheless. The first two speak of extraordinary aspects of service, such as will neither have any attraction for ordinary people, nor will arouse any general sympathetic understanding. The second two, however, speak of the kinds of service that are both recognised and applauded by the general public and widely expected of Christians and the Church.

When we talk today about Christian service, as we do so often, we usually mean the latter kinds of service. They are closely related, and even in New Testament times they began to overlap. Diakonos became very soon an ecclesiastical title, a deacon,[4] and diakonia became a word to describe the general ministry of the Church.[5] From the earliest times it was appreciated that the life of the Church was to do with feeding the hungry and healing the sick. Our Lord set an unavoidable example, and the story of the early Church in Acts and the directions of the writers of the Epistles show that the early Church sought 'faithfully to serve' each other and the general public in this way, and so it has continued down the ages to our own time. Such is what may be called the warm and attractive side of Christian service, but there is the other vision and ideal of service that is far more radical and much less congenial. Moreover it is the more prominent of the two in the New Testament.

It would be hard to exaggerate the importance of the four Servant Songs of Isaiah II.[6] They concern God's special Servant, who suffered innocently and vicariously, and whose fate was redemptive in its power. Originally they may have referred to the Israelites as a chosen people, but for us the point is that they were accepted both by Jesus and by the early Church as prophesying the role of the Messiah and the mission of the Church. In this matter Mk 10 : 45 and Acts 8 : 30-38 are especially important. The former text is a key one, and it shows clearly how Jesus recognised that this Servant of God, who suffered so much and whose sufferings were sacrificial

---

4   1 Tim 3:8, Phil 1:1   5   Rom 11:13   6   Is 42:1-4, 49:1-6, 50:4-9, 52:13 - 53:12

in a redemptive way, foreshadowed his fate and explained his mission. The last of the Songs, in particular, is an extraordinarily detailed prophecy of his Passion. The result of this is that the concept of a 'servant of God' in the New Testament is inextricably linked to innocent, vicarious and redemptive suffering.

This link with the Suffering Servant of Isaiah II has its own links with the 'slave theology', which is so marked a feature of St. Paul's Epistles, but which undoubtedly stems from our Lord's own teaching. Immediately before the text, Mk. 10:45, where Jesus speaks about himself as being the kind of servant that gives his life as a 'ransom for many', after the example and image of the Suffering Servant, we hear him teaching his disciples about the complete difference between greatness in the world and in God's kingdom. 'You know that those who are supposed to rule over the Gentiles, lord it over them, and their great men exercise authority over them. But it shall not be so among you; but whoever would be great among you must be your servant, and whoever would be first among you must be slave of all'.[7] Coming, as it does, just before such a special reference to himself, we can hardly doubt that this is a further reference to himself, who is undoubtedly 'first among us'. So we are seeing the link between the image of the Suffering Servant and the image of the slave, as the ideal of Christian service and the Christian servant, born out in the life and death of Jesus.

This 'slave theology' also comes very particularly in our Lord's teaching that we cannot be the slave of two masters.[8] We must, however, serve one or the other; we must be the slave of God or the slave of powers in rebellion against him. This is exactly as St. Paul saw the truth. But, as St. Paul stresses, this is not bad news, but good! In the world slavery was man's ultimate misfortune, and such misfortune mirrors the fate of those who are slaves to sin. But slavery in God's service, with him as our owner, is our ultimate blessing. Such slavery St. Paul describes as freedom and sonship, so freedom in this context is a relative word. Our freedom from 'slavery to

7   Mk 10:42-44   8   Matt 6:24

sin' only opens the way for us to become willing and eager slaves of God; this is the truly desirable slavery, for it is only God's slaves, who know 'the glorious liberty of the children of God',[9] 'whose service is perfect freedom'[10]. Such thinking is central to St. Paul's teaching on Baptism. Through Baptism we 'have been set free from sin and have become the slaves of God'. But this is marvellous; 'the return (we) get is sanctification and its end eternal life'.[11] So we are to live out our lives here 'serving the Lord' (douleuontes - as a slave)[12] and also as 'the slaves of one another'.[13] (See also the commentary on the Christmas Collect).

Nor is this teaching in disagreement with St. John. The classic description of Christian service is found in the story of Jesus washing the Apostles' feet.[14] The word for servant is again doulos, for Jesus then was acting the part of a household slave. Pointedly he asks, 'Do you know what I have done to you?' Then he answers his own question. 'I have given you an example'. Then again in Chapter 15 we hear how servants (douloi again) may be changed into friends, 'if you do (gladly and willingly) what I command you'.[15] We become the slaves of our friend, or the friend of our master, and such slavery is characterised by peace and joy. (See also John 8 : 31-36). The same teaching is found in St. Peter's first Epistle. There he speaks directly to slaves who have been baptised. He tells them that Jesus became in spirit one of them, 'leaving (them) an example'. They may be the lowest of the low in the eyes of the world, whereas in fact they are in the best of company and beloved and precious in the sight of God. (See also Phil. 2: 7 - taking the form of a slave). The title slave was, moreover, one that the Apostles fastened onto and used with pride, sometimes in conjunction with their special title of Apostle, in which case the title 'slave' was given precedence.[16] St. James and St. Jude, as well as St. Peter and St. Paul, all start their Epistles declaring that they are 'slaves of God', or 'slaves of Jesus Christ'.

'True and laudable service of God', then, is no easy service. It is inextricably linked, according to the New Testament, with innocent suffering and the

total commitment, without rights, holidays or qualifications that characterises the service of a slave. For this reason the New Testament vision of
a servant has a chilling, as well as a warm aspect to it. Even though heroic
is a truer description, Isaiah's words still apply, 'He had no beauty that we
should desire him'.[17] To aspire to such service is not something anyone does
in their own strength, and the Collect stresses that the desire and the
ability to serve like this is God's 'only gift'. Inspired by God's grace,
however, we can become 'faithful people' capable of such service, as St. Paul
experienced and explains. 'As servants of God we commend ourselves in
every way; through great endurance, in afflictions, hardships, calamities,
beatings, imprisonments, tumults, labours, watchings, hunger'.[18] Then he
goes on to speak of the benefits and blessings that also attain such service,
which brings us to a consideration of the second part of the Collect's
petition.

Our reward for faithful service is the attaining of 'heavenly promises'. The
phrase reminds us of the reward of the faithful servants in the parable of
the Talents. 'Well done, good and faithful servant (doule)... enter into the
joy of your master'.[19] Jesus also spoke to the Apostles about the joy that
awaited them, when their lives of obedient and faithful service were over,
lives in which sacrifice and suffering were to be so marked an ingredient.
It was such that none would be able to take from them.[20] As already
mentioned, this reward was also linked with a wonderful change in their
relationship, from that of servant (doulos again) to that of friend. 'You are
my friends, if you do what I command you. No longer do I call you slaves,
for a slave does not know what his master is doing; but I have called you
friends, for all that I have heard from my Father I have made known to
you'.[21] A major aspect of this reward, then, for 'faithful service' is the joy of
understanding and co-operating with the purposes of God for the world.

17 Is 53:2   18 2 Cor 6:4-5   19 Matt 25:21   20 Jn 16:22
21 Jn 15:12-15

But while we are here we are going to have to continue to live lives of obedience and faithfulness. Only hereafter will the full consequences of a life of 'true and laudable service' be attained.

Yet we know that to say this is not to describe all the New Testament's teaching on this matter. In the medieval Collect, as we have mentioned, there was a strong suggestion that the promises, to which we are to look as our reward for faithful service, are not confined to the hereafter, and we saw that it was only in the redrafting of the Collect by the Reformers that the idea of service became linked wholly with this life, and the fulfilment of God's promises linked wholly with the life of heaven. We must say, however, that this new emphasis is not borne out by Scripture.

Several Collects mention the promises of God. We have already had occasion to mention aspects of these promises in discussing the Collects for Easter IV, Trinity VI and XI, and the subject is central to next Sunday's Collect also, where the general theme is so very similar to this Collect. So we can safely leave further discussion on this important matter to next Sunday's commentary. Suffice to say here that, although God's promises are certainly 'heavenly promises', and are involved in all that is included in that word 'finally', which was added in 1662, that does not mean that they are not also fulfilled on earth and in time. This both/and aspect about the fulfilment of the promises of God is called by theologians 'realised eschatology', which important truth will particularly concern us in the next commentary.

TRINITY XIV

Almighty and everlasting God, give unto us the increase of faith, hope, and charity; and, that we may obtain that which thou dost promise, make us to love that which thou dost command; through Jesus Christ our Lord. Amen.

This Collect is also Leonine, with one revealing alteration in its translation. (See commentary)

There are two petitions in this Collect, which may not at first sight seem related to each other. The first is that we increase in the great virtues of faith, hope and love. The second is that, through a life of loving obedience, we may obtain all the blessings and benefits that God has promised us in Christ.

'Faith, hope and charity' (agape) are the so called theological virtues, for they are active in and essential for any direct, personal relationship with God. Without them how can we have a relationship with God? They are the basic virtues of a true religion. To be a true Christian we must have both an interior devotion and an exterior obedience. We must keep what is the kernel of the Law, loving God and loving our neighbour; but the second obedience must spring out of the first. To be a good fellow, an excellent neighbour, a philanthropic person and a supporter of charities, without having any devotional life, is not the New Testament understanding of a Christian. We have, of course, our Lord's warning that in the end 'not everyone who says to me, 'Lord, Lord', shall enter the kingdom of heaven, but he who does the will of my Father, who is in heaven',[1] to prevent us from getting over-pious. But we are not likely to do the will of our heavenly Father in our own strength. Indeed, the clear teaching of the New Testament is that we definitely will not. And if we really aspire to do that

1   Matt 7:21

will, the virtues of faith, hope and love toward God are absolutely necessary.

So it is that St. Paul writes to the Colossians, 'We always thank God, the Father of our Lord Jesus Christ, when we pray for you, because we have heard of your faith in Christ Jesus, and of the love which you have for all the saints, because of the hope laid up for you in heaven'.[2] To the Corinthians, in an even more famous passage, he concludes what he describes as 'a still more excellent way' by saying, 'so faith, hope, love abide, these three; but the greatest of these is love'.[3] These are the virtues in which we must increase, if we are to grow as Christians. Since they are theological virtues, however, they can only grow in us if we pray, and it is out of prayer in all its aspects that faith is increased, hope strengthened and love deepened. Only God can 'give unto us' this blessed increase, for which we pray in this Collect, and in our prayers we should often ask for it. And if we ask sincerely, why should we doubt that he will give it to us? He knows 'how to give good gifts'. He will even 'give the Holy Spirit to those who ask him',[4] and it is he, who brings to birth, and increases, these virtues within us. But in order that we 'obtain' such blessings he must give them.

The Collect's two petitions, therefore, are closely related, although their relationship as expressed in the original Collect has almost certainly been changed by Cranmer in a protestant direction. The second petition should probably be rendered 'that we may deserve that which thou dost promise,' and not just 'that we may obtain that which thou dost promise'. The Latin word in question is 'mereamur', with which our word merit is linked. Perhaps it can have the general meaning 'we may obtain', although the idea of deserving to obtain is then implied. However any idea that we might merit or deserve redemption by virtue of our good works, or even our holiness of character, was anathema to the Reformers and a major cause of controversy with the Church of Rome at the time. Cranmer's translation here, therefore, though acceptable to protestant ears almost certainly

2   Col 1:4-5   3   1 Cor 13:13   4   Lk 11:13

changes the sense of the original Collect. Very strangely, however, it would appear that in the Collect for Trinity XXV Cranmer seems to have altered the sense of that Collect in an opposite direction! (See relevant commentary.)

In the second petition we pray for the spirit of loving and willing obedience that will enable us to 'obtain that which God dost promise'. This is essentially the same prayer as last Sunday's Collect, and brings us to consider what God's promises consist of, and how, when and where they are obtained. This is a consideration that takes us to the very heart of the Gospel. The good news of the Gospel is that these promises of God have indeed been fulfilled in Christ,[5] but to explain the way in which this fulfilment has come about for us, theologians use the strange phrase 'realised eschatology'. What do they mean?

The word derives from eschatos, the Greek for last, and it means the study of the last things, that is the end of time and of all creation. There is much about this end in the Bible, and in the New Testament several phrases are used to describe this climactic event, such as 'the close of the age'[6], 'the end of all things'[7] and 'the last day'[8] or 'last hour'.[9] Now, as one studies these and other like passages, it becomes clear that they have a mysterious way of referring both to things that have taken place, and to things that have not yet taken place, as if they are the same things. So the end of all things has come about, and yet is still to be accomplished; but these are not two different ends that are being mentioned. Our salvation has been accomplished, and the judgement of the world has been declared, yet both await us in the future; and again these are not two different salvations or two different judgements, but the same. So, too, we are risen 'to newness of life', but we also await a resurrection on the last day; and yet these are not two resurrections.

This merging of the 'now' and the 'then' is a very important part of the

---

5   Mk 1:14-15   6   Matt 13:39   7   1 Pet 4:7   8   Jn 12:48
9   1 Jn 2:18

280

Gospel message. In Christ the future has arrived, but yet it does not cease to be the future. How are we to understand this? The answer lies in the fact that Christ is not just a man of history, as other men are. He is one with the eternal Father, whose life exists outside time and space. Christ, therefore, is not himself subject to the events of the absolute end, being like the Father immune from the laws that govern them. All ordinary things in this world have an end, and their life is subject to destruction and death. But it is the essence of the Gospel that, if we are in Christ, we too will share in his immunity from the ultimate, eschatological climax that awaits creation and all creatures. He has set up a kingdom that has no end,[10] and into this eternal kingdom we are called by him.

How do we, however, enter this kingdom with its amazing 'promises' of eternal life and protection 'in the last hour'? It is by faith and repentance and Baptism.[11] When Jesus began his ministry, what was involved in it was summarised by St. Mark: 'The time is fulfilled and the kingdom of God is at hand'.[12] The time referred to here is the time before the final judgement, when time comes to its end, and as 'the time is fulfilled', the reign of God in his kingdom takes over. With the arrival of God's Son, the promised Messiah, this is what has happened and is happening. This is the tension and excitement of the Gospel. In Christ we are to step out of the life that is destined to come to an end in death and destruction, and enter into a 'newness of life' that is destined to unite us eternally with God.[13] This is to 'realise' now what will be hereafter and for ever, and this is what is meant by 'realised eschatology'.

As we have said, several Collects mention the promises of God. In them, and especially in last Sunday's Collect, these promises appear to concern things that lie ahead of us, rather than things already to hand. This week's Collect, however, leaves room for the truth that we are stressing here that these promises may be 'obtained' even in this life, and not only hereafter.

10 Lk 1:33   11 Acts 2:38-39   12 Mk 1:15   13 Rom 6:4, 8:1

This 'obtaining' of God's promises, however, is to be experienced even as we 'love his commandments', indeed it cannot be experienced unless we do love them.

Our own spiritual experience surely confirms this both/and truth. We experience the reality of Jesus with us 'always', as he promised[14]; but we note and rejoice in the further promise that he will be with us also at 'the close of the age' to take us with him into eternity. Then we know that the promise of the Holy Spirit's coming has already been fulfilled[15]; but we note and rejoice in the further promise that the Holy Spirit 'will declare things that are to come'[16] and be within us 'the guarantee of our inheritance until we acquire possession of it.'[17] Then again God forgives us now, according to his promises declared unto mankind in Christ Jesus our Lord; but our forgiveness is an ongoing reality, something that is to shield us for ever against the power of evil, enabling us to escape the final destruction of all that is evil, as grimly described by John the Elder, 'then if anyone's name was not found written in the book of life he was thrown into the lake of fire'.[18] Through Christ the 'then' becomes merged with the 'now', although a distinction between them still exists. Christ and his kingdom has come, but we still pray, 'Come Lord Jesus'[19] and 'Thy kingdom come'. We can experience such paradoxical spiritual truths, and the reason is because 'Jesus Christ is the same yesterday and today and for ever.'[20]

So we have obtained, and yet we must continue to await the fulfilment of all that we have obtained, according to God's promises. In a sense God has already fulfilled all his promises; and yet in a sense they await their fulfilment. On the one hand we live within eternity, 'our lives hid with Christ in God'[21]; on the other we live as part of a world doomed to death and destruction and sharing in its fate,[22] but we are not to consider the sufferings of this present, temporal existence worthy of comparison with the glory that is to be revealed to us, when the promises of God to us are eternally 'obtained'.[23] Meanwhile we must 'love that which thou dost command', and we pray here that he may 'make us' do so.

14 Matt 28:18-20   15 Lk 24:49, Acts 2:16-18   16 Jn 16:13
17 Eph 1:14   18 Rev 20:15   19 Rev 22:20   20 Heb 13:8
21 Col 3:3   22 Rom 8:21-23   23 Rom 8:18

TRINITY XV

Keep, we beseech thee, O Lord, thy Church with thy perpetual mercy; and, because the frailty of man without thee cannot but fall, keep us ever by thy help from all things hurtful, and lead us to all things profitable to our salvation; through Jesus Christ our Lord. Amen.

This is the Gelasian Collect. It is very similar to that for Trinity VIII.

As we draw towards the end of the Christian Year the Collects mention the Church comparatively frequently, praying for its protection, guidance and sanctification. Hitherto the Church has only been mentioned specifically twice, (Epiphany V and Trinity V), although the spiritual fellowship that is the Church has been mentioned on several occasions in a variety of ways. In the Collects, however, the Church is always God's Church, not ours. So we always pray for 'thy Church', or 'thy family', or 'thy faithful people', or 'thy household'. These prayers of our Prayer Book are not just the prayers of a Church, but of 'the holy Catholic Church', in which the Apostles Creed teaches us to put our trust.

The word translated Church in the New Testament is ecclesia, which means something called out. Its meaning stems from the Hebrew word qahal, that had the same essential meaning. The Israelites believed themselves to be a people chosen, or called out, by God to become special for God, God's own people. 'We are called by thy Name' said Jeremiah.[1] They were a people created by God's Word, and also preserved by that Word.[2] Solomon in his prayer at the dedication of the Temple asked that he and his people might always remember their special calling and obey the special obligations inherent in it. But he also prayed that they might be

1 Jer 14:9   2 Ps 107:20

able to presume on God's special mercy towards them and his readiness to protect them.[3] As they were called out from the peoples who surrounded them, so they put their trust in this divine choice.

In the New Testament we see the belief, often expressed, that the Church was the true spiritual descendant of the Israelites of the Old Testament , but perhaps nowhere more clearly than in 1 Peter, where it is described as 'a holy nation, God's own people... called out of darkness into his marvellous light'.[4] In his High Priestly prayer (John 17) Jesus, who, like Solomon, is both King and Priest, describes God's people as those called 'out of the world' by him to be God's instrument 'in the world'. He, their Lord and their God, would continue to be 'in the midst of them' and would 'leave them not' for, like Israel of old, the Church is 'called by his Name'. Like Israel also the Church is created by God's Word, and is 'sanctified' by God's Word. Although such sanctification comes to us through obedience to and trust in that creative and protective Word, even in our disobedience and unfaithfulness we may yet rely upon the 'perpetual mercy' of God. And we recall here with special emphasis this mercy that always 'keeps us'. Even though we must surely emphasise, as Solomon did, the thought that we must always be obedient to and trustful of that Word that creates, protects and sanctifies, yet inevitably we will rely, knowing ourselves, much more on his mercy than on our own obedience for this needful protection. This deep truth dominates this most devotional Collect.

In the main petition that follows we pray for help and guidance, and we do so out of a strong sense of need and dependence. We often remember our weakness and dependence on God in the Collects. It is part of the necessary confession of the truth, that is to sanctify us. We confess here that 'the frailty of man without thee cannot but fall', but this is not the pessimistic declaration that at first sight it may appear to be. We have just declared our

3   1 Kgs 8:14 ff   4   1 Pet 2:9

faith in 'thy perpetual mercy', and since we are members of 'thy Church', we are therefore never 'without thee'. Certainly this Collect expresses the truth about us, but not, as it were, the whole truth. In spite of our essential weakness we may yet live victoriously. So with St. Paul we can also say, 'I can do all things through him who strengthens me'.[5]

Therefore we are to be 'strong and of good courage', neither frightened nor dismayed, 'for the Lord our God is with us wherever we go'.[6] We are not to lose our sense of holy fear, but we may lose all sense of craven fear, because we can hope for God's help in keeping us from 'all things hurtful'. We have had occasion to distinguish carefully the difference between the temporal and the eternal in painful things (Trinity VIII). We cannot expect to be spared the former, since our Lord accepted them and we are to follow him, but we may indeed be hopeful of escaping all that may eternally harm us. We may hear St. Paul's prayer for the Colossian Christians as applying to us today; 'May you be strengthened with all power according to his glorious might, for all endurance and patience with joy, giving thanks to the Father, who has qualified us to share in the inheritance of the Saints in light. He has delivered us from the dominion of darkness and transferred us to the kingdom of his beloved Son, in whom we have redemption, the forgiveness of sins'.[7] This is what God had done for us according to his 'perpetual mercy', and since we are never to be 'without' him, our 'frailty' need no longer worry us.

How paradoxical the truth about our relationship with God so often appears! So in this case, the truth is that our weakness and God's power are complementary to each other, rather than in opposition to each other. St. Paul in 2 Corinthians stresses this. Our 'frailty' does not hinder the working of God's power in and through us. What alone hinders that power to work for us is our claiming that it is ours rather than his. We do have God's power given to us through his 'perpetual mercy', but it is still all his, as St. Paul explains. 'We have this treasure in earthen vessels to show the transcendent power belongs to God and not to us'.[8] This is the mysterious way the power of God operates in and through us to bless, guide and redeem us. David Flagg, when Chaplain of Burrswood, expressed this paradoxical truth, which is so particularly relevant to those engaged in the Church's Ministry of Healing, like this; 'Only our frailty can become the resting place of God's power'. But operating from that base it can work wonders.

'Lead me, O Lord, in thy righteousness, because of mine enemies', said the Psalmist. 'Make thy way plain before my face'.[9] It is the same prayer here. 'Thy righteousness' and 'thy way' are the essential ingredients of 'all that is profitable to our salvation'. Among these profitable things may be some hurtful things, for God, like a wise Father, 'disciplines us for our good, that we may share his holiness. For the moment all discipline seems painful rather than pleasant; later it yields the peaceful fruit of righteousness to those who have been trained by it'.[10] Our pride must be hurt, our consciences must be 'sore smitten', and our lazy ways painfully disrupted before this 'discipline' is over, and we can enjoy the 'fruit of righteousness'. But we must believe that we are being led towards our eternal salvation by 'the Father of spirits', however hard the road.

That this road may be very hard indeed for some is undeniable. We are to believe, however, that no pain need be in vain, and that 'all things' may find a place in God's purposes at the last. Twice in the Collect we mention 'all things'. Some, however, of them are sure to be evil things and only some what we can describe as good. This must not dismay us, or upset our faith. We are called to endurance and patience and to be of a quiet mind, until our suffering is over, or till all is made plain to us of its meaning and purpose. We are to go on loving, believing and hoping, being utterly convinced that beneath us and around us are the everlasting arms. Sometimes the pain involved in our serving the afflicted is in its way as acute as that of being

8   2 Cor 4:7   9   Ps 5:8   10   Heb 12:10-11

afflicted ourselves. Dr. Leslie Weatherhead has this very helpful prayer in one of his books for those who care for the very ill: 'Give serenity and cheerfulness to those who watch over them. Let the atmosphere of every sick room be full of thy presence and peace and even joy: the joy of those who know how to fight, and how, for the time being, to accept, and how to do both without bitterness, knowing always that the everlasting arms are round them and that God's everlasting purposes will one day be fulfilled'.

Such brave prayers, however, and the prayer contained in this Collect, cannot be prayed except 'through Jesus Christ our Lord'. He it is that gives us hope that we may be ever 'kept', a word also used twice in this Collect. Because of God's 'perpetual mercy' which is able to 'keep' us, we may believe that 'all things work for good with those who love God, who are called according to his purposes'.[11] As members of the Church we have been so called. So we can always be full of hope in the face of adversity.[12] 'Blessed is the man whose strength is in thee, in whose heart are thy ways, who going through the vale of misery use it for a well, and the pools are filled with water. (He) will go from strength to strength'.[13] Moreover 'as the outcome of our faith we obtain the salvation of our souls'.[14] So we do not lose heart. Though our outer nature is wasting away, our inner nature is being renewed every day. For this slight momentary affliction is preparing for us an eternal weight of glory beyond all comparison, because we look not to the things that are seen, but to the things that are unseen; for the things that are seen are transient, but the things that are unseen are eternal'.[15] So it is that through the 'perpetual mercy' of God the 'hurtful' may be 'profitable to our salvation'.

11 Rom 8:28   12 Rom 8:24-25   13 Ps 84:5-7   14 1 Pet 1:9
15 2 Cor 4:16-18

TRINITY XVI

O Lord, we beseech thee, let thy continual pity cleanse and defend thy Church; and, because it cannot continue in safety without thy succour, preserve it evermore by thy help and goodness; through Jesus Christ our Lord. Amen.

This is the Gelasian Collect with a changed ending. We pray now that the Church may be 'preserved evermore' by God, whereas the original Collect prayed that it might be 'governed evermore' by him. It is therefore reminiscent of the Collect for Lent V, where these verbs are combined.

We pray first that the Church may be 'cleansed'. The Church is not a fellowship of particularly good people. We all know that! It is rather a fellowship of sinners, who recognise this truth about themselves, repent, and believe in their forgiveness. When St. Paul writes to 'the Church of God which is at Corinth', he says he is writing to those who are 'sanctified in Christ Jesus, called to be saints...',[1] but in what he writes he makes it clear that those early Christians were far from faultless. We are, then, to believe that we are forgiven our sins, 'sanctified in Christ Jesus' and by 'God's continual pity cleansed', but also that we remain sinners, in constant need of God's forgiveness and of his grace to enable us to 'cast away the works of darkness' and 'to cleanse our hearts and minds'. The mercy is that we may pray for these things in sure and certain confidence, knowing that God will exercise his pity continually. 'O Lamb of God that takes away the sins of the world', we pray, 'have mercy upon us'. The tense is the eternal present. Christ, who died 'once for all' 'for the sins of the whole world', continues to cleanse and defend us from sin through his 'continual pity' that is never withdrawn from us.

---

1   1 Cor 1:2

In Ephesians St. Paul likens the Church to a bride and Jesus to a bridegroom, and the relationship between the Church and Christ to that of marriage. The words used are both beautiful and exciting. 'Christ', he says, 'loves the Church and gave himself up for her, that he might sanctify her, having cleansed her by the washing of water with the word, that he might present the Church to himself in splendour, without spot or wrinkle or any such thing, that she might be holy and without blemish.'[2] As things are, however, we are not worthy of our heavenly lover, and our relationship with him is therefore still that of an engagement. But then in the Jewish custom of those times betrothal was so serious and firm a relationship that it was termed part of marriage. So we read that 'Mary had (only) been betrothed to Joseph, before they came together', and yet he is called her 'husband' and is 'resolved to divorce her'.[3] While we are 'the Church militant here on earth' our marriage to our Lord is not, as it were, fully consummated, for he has yet to 'present us to himself in splendour'. The Church is guilty of many a spot and many a wrinkle. It is divided, worldly and unloving. But because we are so beloved there is the hope of glory for us. In Revelation the seer foretells the final marriage ceremony in heaven, which is surrounded by angelic rejoicing. 'Let us rejoice and exult and give him glory', they cry, 'for the marriage of the Lamb has come, and his Bride has made herself ready'. This hopeful vision seems to be behind this prayer for the Church's cleansing, and for the time to come when she is worthy to be 'clothed with fine linen, bright and pure'.[4]

But as we know well, the time for such rejoicing and such splendour has not yet arrived. But this hope is set before us, and the Holy Communion is a kind of anticipation of the final marriage festival, and also a form of guarantee that it will take place. 'The angel said to me, "Write this: Blessed are those who are invited to the marriage supper of the Lamb".'[5] In Holy Communion we receive and accept such an invitation, becoming sacramentally 'one flesh' with our husband, even though the fullness of all that is

2 Eph 5:25-27   3 Matt 1:18-19   4 Rev 19:7-8   5 Rev 19:9

implied in Holy Communion has yet to be established. 'Cleanse our hearts and minds' we pray then. This cleansing by the Holy Spirit is also our surest form of defence against all that is evil, as well as the preparation that is needed for us to become eternally 'one flesh' with our Lord. In this sacrament he 'continually' cleanses and defends his Church, which even now may be called his Bride and his Body.

The second part of the petition in this Collect is that we might be 'preserved evermore by God's help and goodness'. As we pray for this protection, we again acknowledge, as we did last week , our weakness in the face of many dangers. But again we can pray in confidence. We know ourselves to be the objects of God's love. He pities our weakness. He is committed to our safety. We share his life, and he indwells ours. We are 'the Body of Christ' as well as his Bride. It is the Father's gracious purpose to bring us fully into his kingdom.[6] The Church is not like other societies , however much it may outwardly resemble them in its organisation, for it is under supernatural control. We here acknowledge our dependence on God. We 'cannot continue in safety without thy succour' , even though other societies can. We are not independent of God, but dependent on him. Such is the nature of the Church, and we should rejoice in this truth.

This Collect then is not to be interpreted as an anxious prayer. No doubt it behoves us not to be over-confident just because God is so good. 'Do not be proud, but stand in awe' says St Paul.[7] But he has 'made us his own'.[8] It is for us, as Isaiah said it was for Israel, 'You are my servant, in whom I will be glorified'.[9] He has set his love upon us and he will 'hide us in the shadow of his hand'.[10] Some of the Collects can be made to sound anxious if the emphasis is wrongly placed, and this is one such. Certainly it is in our weakness that we pray, but because we are his Church such weakness becomes a source of strength, and we can pray with confidence for cleansing, protection and guidance.

---

6   Lk 12:32   7   Rom 11:20   8   Phil 3:12   9   Is 49:3
10 Is 51:16

As has been mentioned, 'preserve' has taken the place of 'govern' in the original Collect. It is doubtful if it is a happy change of verb, certainly in the context of modern usage. We may be tempted to think we are praying that some kind of divine preservation order will be placed upon us! We should, however, particularly note that we are praying in this Collect for the Church's reformation, and not just for its preservation. Reformation and preservation are not incompatible concepts. Quite the contrary. To be preserved by God, we must constantly be reformed. Unless we are 'cleansed' by reformation we will not be worthy of being 'defended'. Moreover, as the word 'continually' implies this reformation will have to be a continuing process.

However, these concepts of reformation and preservation both have peculiar dangers attached to them, however necessary and beneficial they may be in themselves. Both must be of God, but both can be of the world. What the Church needs is the kind of reformation that preserves and the kind of preservation that ensures reform. This is not easily obtained as the history of the Church makes plain. It is vital that God in his 'continual pity' controls any reformation of it, for the Church cannot 'continue in safety' unless he does so. So this is a very deep and subtle prayer. It stresses that the Church's preservation must include not only God's guidance and control, but also its willingness to be reformed wherever and whenever necessary. But these two concepts are not easily held together. In these days of internal confusion within our Anglican Communion it would seem to have a special relevance.

It is, however, surely helpful, as we pray for our Church today, to stress that the Church is a pilgrim body. Like Israel of old it is moving towards a promised inheritance. It is the future, therefore, rather than the present that we want 'preserved evermore'. Here we have no lasting city, but we seek the city that is to come'.[11] That is the city which the Patriarchs foresaw by faith, while they 'lived in tents'. That is the city which has unshakeable

11 Heb 13:14

foundations, that will be 'preserved evermore', and 'whose builder and maker is God'.[12] When it is finally established, however, it will be found to be one with the insecure and divided pilgrim Church of the present which, although always in need of reformation, will in some mysterious way be found to have essentially helped God both in its building and making and in its ultimate preservation. Consequently this is not only a most relevant prayer but also one to be prayed with assurance and hope, as the Church seeks today amid passionate debate that divinely guided kind of reformation that both preserves and unites it, and the kind of preservation that enables it to cope with changing circumstances and new challenges both now and in the future.

12 Heb 11:10

TRINITY XVII

Lord, we pray thee that thy grace may always prevent and follow us, and make us continually to be given to all good works; through Jesus Christ our Lord. Amen.

This is the Gregorian Collect with the one addition of the word 'all' in the final petition.

––––––––––––––

This is one of the shortest and simplest of the Collects, but it contains considerations of the greatest importance. It starts, as so many other Collects have, (Advent, Easter, et al) by asking for God's grace. Is there a more important request, or one that should be more regularly 'on our lips and in our hearts'? In Ephesians St Paul talks of 'the immeasurable riches of (God's) grace', and says that our salvation is dependent on it. Faith and repentance, as our response , play their part, but it is essentially 'by grace (we) have been saved'.[1]

The Collect speaks of the grace of God that both 'prevents and follows' us. Ascetic theologians divide grace into two categories, habitual grace and actual grace. Sometimes the first category is also called prevenient or sanctifying grace, since it is a prevenient gift of God that alone makes it possible for us to have a truly spiritual life. This gift of grace is in fact God himself coming into our lives. He brings with him true life, and the power to love and know him. This grace is described by St Paul as 'the love of God (that) has been poured into our hearts through the Holy Spirit, which has been given to us.'[2] It is called habitual because it inhabits us, so that we may be even described as 'temples of the living God'.[3]

We are accustomed to associate the word grace with Jesus, and very often, especially in St. Paul's Epistles, it is linked with him.[4] However, grace is

1   Eph 2:7-8   2   Rom 5:5   3   2 Cor 6:16
4   1 Thess 5:28 et al

also linked with the Father as well as our Lord.[5] But we should not divide the Persons of the Godhead in such a way as to create three Gods. And we should notice how St John also speaks of both the Father and the Son 'making their home' with us,[6] as well as the Holy Spirit indwelling us. So when we speak of habitual, sanctifying or prevenient grace we mean God himself, and nothing less than God, who has come to us of his own will, out of his own love for us, indwelling us. This is an extraordinary mercy. St Peter speaks of the outcome of this truth as our sharing in God's 'own glory and excellence' and 'becoming partakers of the divine nature'.[7] What a thought! Can it be true of us? Surely this is a hope too far! But St John encourages us thus; 'Beloved, we are God's children now; it does not yet appear what we shall be, but we know that when he appears we shall be like him, for we shall see him as he is'. Meanwhile we must play our part in this work of grace within us that is leading us on towards our eternal salvation. So he adds, 'And everyone, who thus hopes in him, purifies himself as he is pure'.[8] But to succeed in this we also need grace, the grace that 'follows'.

So there is also the grace that 'follows', actual grace. It is called actual because it shows itself in acts, so that in the words of the Collect we become 'continually given to all good works'. But the outworking of actual grace is not only in exterior acts of love and sacrifice; it is also experienced in the way our interior lives are changed and purified. We are reminded here of the Advent Collect, in which we pray for grace to 'cast away the works of darkness and to put upon us the armour of light'. These are primarily interior activities. It is within that the battle rages, and it is within that the grace of God is for ever active. However, no matter how bitter the struggle is, we must believe that this grace is 'sufficient' for us.[9] It is never too weak for what must be done or suffered, that we may live victoriously. If we feel weak, that says St Paul is probably a very good thing. Pride is the greatest enemy of God's grace, and only when that has been utterly subdued can

5 1 Cor 1:2 et al   6   Jn 14:23   7   2 Pet 1:3-4   8   1 Jn 3:2-3
9 2 Cor 12:9

God's grace wholly work its gracious will. Grace, therefore, must work first within us, before it can show itself outwardly in our lives.

But as we cooperate with God's grace and become obedient to God within, we are enabled by the same grace of God to live properly, 'showing forth thy praise, not only with our lips but in our lives; by giving up ourselves to thy service and by walking before thee in holiness and righteousness all our days'.[10] So we go on to pray in this Collect 'continually to be given to all good works'. But first the seed, then 'the blade, then the ear and then the full grain in the ear'.[11] There are no short cuts to the Christian life. Unless God's grace 'prevents and follows' us, we are not going 'continually to be given to all good works'. Certainly we are to 'work out our own salvation with fear and trembling'. (Or should we say work at our own salvation?) But even as we do, we only do so because through his grace 'God is at work in us, both to will and to work for his good pleasure'.[12]

As we have noticed, the Reformers added the word 'all' to the original Collect. We are not to pick and choose what good works to do. St James teaches us not 'to show partiality' in doing good, and roundly declares that any such partiality is sinful.[13] 'Whoever keeps the whole law but fails in one point has become guilty of all of it' is his ruling. And it does sound fierce! But the bad tempered man cannot hide behind a willingness to be generous, or the liar behind the fact that he is always kind. We must seek to be good in, as it were, all directions. To this end the grace of God helps us. First, in showing us our weaknesses of character and guiding us to repent of them, and, secondly, in encouraging us to do better. No doubt perfection is beyond us here, but we cannot consequently deem our Lord's instruction, 'You, therefore, must be perfect, as your heavenly Father is perfect',[14] as a saying that cannot possibly refer to us! Jesus is our example as well as our Lord. The addition, therefore, of the little word 'all' adds a tremendous challenge

10 The General Thanksgiving   11 Mk 4:28   12 Phil 2:12
13 Jas 2:9   14 Matt 5:48

to this prayer. One might say the challenge was strong enough without it, with the word 'continually' to remind us that there can be no let up in our endeavours to live good lives. But it adds to it.

In all this the Collect is simply being true to the hard side of the Gospel. The way to the life of 'glory and excellence' hereafter, to which St Peter referred, is via the life of glory and excellence here, which is the crucified life. So in the Collect for the Annunciation we pray that God may 'pour his grace into our hearts, that by his Cross we may be brought unto the glory of his Resurrection'. That is what the grace of God will do for us, whether we like it or not! It is our duty to assist it to do this for us and in us by cooperating by faith. So St Paul adds that word to his ruling 'by grace you have been saved', when he repeats it. 'By grace you have been saved through faith'.[15] As we trust God the grace that is habitual within us becomes actual too, and so enables us ' continually to be given to all goods works'. At least it is to that required and blessed end that we pray in this Collect.

15 Eph 2:8

TRINITY XVIII

Lord, we beseech thee, grant thy people grace to withstand the temptations of the world, the flesh, and the devil, and with pure hearts and minds to follow thee the only God; through Jesus Christ our Lord. Amen.

This is the Gelasian Collect, which was literally translated in 1549, but significantly changed and lengthened in 1662. In the original Collect there was no mention of the world and the flesh but only of the Devil, and for 'withstand the temptations of ' it had 'avoid the infection of '. The first change no doubt reveals a desire to bring it into line with the service of Baptism, in which we are taught that the Devil is not the only source of our temptations. The second has other implications that may best be left for discussion in the commentary. Further, the word 'hearts' was added in 1662 in the final petition.

Once again we start by asking for grace, the essential gift of God, without which we are so powerless in the face of our enemies. We pray here specifically for 'grace to withstand' what is dangerous and aggressive. 'The world, the flesh and the Devil' are not passive forces which can simply be avoided, like an obstacle in our path. They are active forces that seek our spiritual death and must be withstood. In the medieval Collect the Devil only was mentioned, and was likened to some deadly disease. In that analogy we recognise the realities of the times when so many died young from diseases now rendered harmless or completely eliminated. His constant malign presence is, certainly, well illustrated by the Collect's original wording, but nonetheless the change from 'avoid' to 'withstand', and 'infection' to 'temptations', is a real improvement. We cannot tip-toe cautiously through life. We are called to 'fight the good fight with all (our) might'.[1] So 'withstand' for 'avoid' is a more realistic word for us to use in the context of our spiritual experience.

Both the Old and the New Testaments speak a lot of battles and fighting. Indeed to many the Old Testament is oppressively bloodthirsty stuff, and they cannot see what connection there is between the battle-scarred Lord of Hosts and our Father in heaven, to whom Jesus taught us to pray. Only he seems to reappear in the Book of Revelation in a very disconcerting way, locked once more in battle, this time in heaven itself! We cannot avoid the truth that this is a spiritually, as well as a physically dangerous world. The Christian is called to spiritual warfare, and courage in the face of the enemy is in that war too a vital virtue. As we read of the wars fought in God's Name and under his leadership in the Old Testament we should spiritualise the enemies, and then they become full of help and encouragement. The response of David to the giant Goliath is sublime. 'You come to me with a sword and with a javelin; but I come to you in the name of the Lord of Hosts, the God of the armies of Israel, whom you have defied'. And so he makes good his threat to kill the giant and bring about the defeat of the Philistine armies.[2]

Sometimes the stories show that we have to take the battle to the enemy, but at other times they teach that we must simply stand our ground and let God do it all. Equally sublime is the example of Moses. 'Moses said to the people, "Fear not, stand firm, and see the salvation of the Lord, which he will work for you today; for the Egyptians whom you see today you shall never see again. The Lord will fight for you, and you have only to be still"'. And once again God destroyed the enemies of his chosen people. 'The waters returned and covered the chariots and the horsemen and all the host of Pharoah.... not so much as one of them remained'.[3] In both these stories, and others like them, we see contrasted those who have faith and courage, and those who have neither. This is the special theme of Hebrews, Chapter 11, in which the Old Testament heroes are praised for their faith

1   J. S. B. Monsell – Well-known Hymn: 1 Tim 6:12   2   1 Sam 17:45-47
3   Ex 14:10-29

and the courage that lies at the heart of faith. Through faith they 'conquered'.[4] Here, too, we are praying for the grace that inspires such victorious, courageous faith. Such faith ensures that we may 'go forth in the strength of the Lord God',[5] 'because there is none other that fighteth for us, but only thou, O God'.[6]

We have already mentioned the double-edged meaning of the word temptation (see Epiphany IV). We are tempted by the Devil and his allied forces, the world and the flesh. But in our temptations we are to recognise also God testing us, and, as we turn to him in faith, to discover his saving power. Before we set out each day, we are to put on the whole armour of God in order to 'withstand the temptations' of those ever-present forces in rebellion against God. They cannot be avoided. They are waiting for us.[7] In all this, however, God's grace will always be sufficient for us.[8] But it will equally always be required. How can we face each day without it? This should be our daily prayer, and the essence of it is contained in the Lord's Prayer, which surely we do use daily.

The obvious link that this Collect has now with our Baptism should also remind us that we have at the very beginning of our Christian lives been fully armed to 'withstand the temptations of the world, the flesh and the Devil' in that Sacrament. Sufficient grace to last a lifetime and, indeed, all eternity, was given us then. We renew this sufficient grace, as it were, whenever we receive Communion. This grace is like the oil in the widow's cruse and the meal in her tub that Elijah blessed. We are to feed upon it daily, and indeed many times a day, and it will always renew itself.[9] The Sacraments and prayer are 'means of grace'[10], and the use to which this grace is to be put is to 'withstand' the powers of evil that are a constant danger to us.

The manner of our 'withstanding' is put in the Baptismal Service in a very

4   Heb 11:33   5   Ps 71:14   6   Morning and Evening Prayer
7   Ps 56:2   8   2 Cor 12:9   9   1 Kgs 17:16
10 General Thanksgiving – also Catechism

positive way. We are to renounce these evil forces. We cannot escape ' out of the world' as Jesus knew well,[11] but we are not to be 'conformed to this world'. How hard, however, this is for us. We probably do not realise how the world moulds our attitudes, or how powerful worldly conventions and manners are in forming our opinions. Inevitably we are all people of our time. However, St. Paul stresses that instead of being conformed to the world and its opinions and standards we are to be 'transformed' in our minds, seeking only the will of God for us and all that is 'good and acceptable and perfect'.[12] For this to happen in our lives prayer, the Sacraments and the study of Scripture are essential. Through them we 'learn what is pleasing to the Lord,'[13] and receive grace to do it. Doing his will is always the answer, and to discover what that might be must be our constant desire. This truth leads us naturally to the final petition.

The prayer there that we may 'follow' God 'with pure hearts and minds' reminds us inevitably of the Collect for Purity in the Holy Communion Service. What a beautiful prayer that is, and how suitable it is for regular use in our private prayers. St. Paul speaks to the Ephesians of us being 'renewed in the spirit of our minds'.[14] This renewal is to lead to 'true righteousness and holiness', which is surely the end implied in this Collect, as we 'follow thee the only God'. In the original Collect our hearts were not mentioned, and the addition of that word is surely a helpful one. As the Collect for Purity stresses, in spiritual matters we think and understand with our hearts as much as with our minds. It is there, too, that we make our resolutions. It is from the depths of our hearts that we love and trust and hope. Our reaching out to God and our 'following' in a spirit of discipleship is initially and essentially, therefore, an internal journey.

If we are to 'follow God' in the purity of our 'hearts and minds', we are to be totally committed to the enterprise. 'The pure in heart' that are so blessed

11 Jn 17:15   12 Rom 12:2   13 Eph 5:10   14   Eph 4:23

by God are those who, because they are totally committed to God, have no false love for any false god lurking in the hearts. It is our devotion to God that must be pure, not just our actions and attitudes towards our fellow men and women, but then the latter is not possible without the former. To know how we must behave towards others we must know how we are to behave towards God. So it is that the blessing given to 'the pure in heart' is that 'they shall see God'.[15] Like Moses, even in this world of many temptations and much evil, if we are faithful and true in our discipleship of Jesus we shall see 'him who is invisible',[16] for 'he who has seen me', said Jesus, 'has seen the Father'.[17] So the strange phrase 'follow thee the only God' must be taken directly with the phrase 'through Jesus Christ our Lord' that follows it. It is as we become a disciple of Jesus that we become a 'follower of God'. This prayer, then, is one to inspire us in our efforts to be such a disciple, or 'follower'. In spite of the difficulties that we are sure to encounter, and that are underlined in this Collect, we may yet hope to be one, for God's grace, for which we pray here, will make it possible. How splendid if it can be said of us, even as it was of Andrew and John, 'Jesus saw them following'.[18]

---

15 Matt 5:8   16 Heb 11:27   17 Jn 14:9   18 Jn 1:38 (A.V.)

TRINITY XIX

O God, forasmuch as without thee we are not able to please thee; mercifully grant, that thy Holy Spirit may in all things direct and rule our hearts; through Jesus Christ our Lord. Amen.

This is the Gelasian Collect significantly changed in 1662 to mention the Holy Spirit. The petition originally had prayed that God's 'mercy' might direct our hearts, and this is how the Collect read in the 1549 Book. There was also in the original no desire expressed that this might happen 'in all things'.

This is a particularly beautiful and easily remembered prayer, and is used frequently, perhaps with some suitable amendment, at many Church gatherings and prayer meetings. It says so much in so few words. It reminds one of the Collect for Purity at the start of the Holy Communion Service, which is perhaps even better known and seems to encapsulate the Gospel. In its opening with its double negative and in its special request for the help of the Holy Spirit it is like the Collect for Quinquagesima. In other aspects it recalls the Collects for Trinity XV and XVI, and also Whitsunday. It may at first sight seem surprising that so few Collects call specifically upon the Holy Spirit, but then so many ask for the grace of God, which, it may be argued, amounts to the same thing. In this Collect, at any rate, the Reformers have preferred to mention the Holy Spirit by name rather than as an attribute of God, and the Collect is greatly strengthened in consequence. It is God himself that we want to guide us, not some intermediary, however akin to God or close to God it or he or she may be. This is the point that the author of Hebrews makes as he begins his Epistle. 'God spoke of old to our fathers by the prophets, but in these last days he has spoken to us by his Son'.[1] In the Collect's opening, moreover, we make it clear that 'without God' we can do nothing worthy of our calling, let alone worthy of praise, so we pray that he himself come and help us. And that is what he does. This, therefore, is a prayer that we know very well he will answer. It is we who block the way of the Holy Spirit. It is not he who is reluctant to come to us.

Innumerable Collects stress our dependence on God, as this one does. But here the desire is expressed that we should 'please' God. This is a thought that is present in the Collects for Trinity I and X, and we considered it in the commentary on them . Without God, however, we also cannot experience any real pleasure, a different but related thought. It is 'in his presence' only that there is 'the fullness of joy', and only 'at his right hand' is there 'pleasure for evermore'.[2] How can we be happy if God is not pleased with us? We want to 'rejoice and be glad', but how can we if our lives are a disappointment to our heavenly Father? Jesus, however, said we may 'rejoice and be glad', and has taught us how. These words come at the end of the Beatitudes, with which the Sermon on the Mount starts, which is introduced by the words, 'He opened his mouth and taught them'.[3] We should remind ourselves that the Greek word 'makarios', that is traditionally translated 'blessed' and starts each of the Beatitudes, can be translated 'happy', and is so translated in some modern versions. But we are referring, of course, to a heavenly rather than an earthly happiness, a happiness that is eternal rather than transitory. This is a happiness that is one with 'the joy that no man can take from us', that is a fruit of the Spirit and mentioned by Jesus as one of his special gifts to his disciples.[4] Only as the Holy Spirit 'directs and rules' our lives can we know this special happiness.

There is no way, however, that we can live in the manner envisaged in the Beatitudes 'without God'. The life envisaged there is not only very hard, but

1   Heb 1:1   2   Ps 16:12   3   Matt 5:1-12   4   Jn 16:22. Gal 5:22

also most unnatural. Yet such a life would not only be very pleasing to God, but also, mysteriously, a truly happy one for us too. Since it would be a life full of love, peace and joy, it would be worthy of the description blessed. But it would also be a life that would have to look beyond this one for its full reward. 'Rejoice and be glad, for great is your reward in heaven' said Jesus, even though here we may experience much suffering. There is the place where the inhabitants fully please God, and where they fully 'enter into the joy of their Lord'.[5] As it was with our Lord, this fullness of joy is a 'joy that is set before us'[6] in heaven, where he has gone 'to prepare a place for us'.[7] And the word 'direct' in this Collect underlines the encouraging truth that it is God's Spirit that is for ever guiding us to fill that place our Lord has prepared for us.

Then we pray for the Holy Spirit to take full charge of us, 'in all things to direct and rule our hearts'. The ordinary man, the Gentile of St. Paul's Epistles, lives after the dictates of the flesh; the Christian, however, is to live after the promptings of the indwelling Spirit. 'The mind that is set on the flesh is hostile to God', indeed 'to set the mind on the flesh is (spiritual) death', according to St. Paul.[8] This is the folly and sin of being in all things directed and ruled in our hearts by the world's wisdom and the body's appetites. Through Christ, however, men and women everywhere may receive a better ruler and guide, the Spirit of God, who comes eager to indwell us.[9] This indwelling Spirit is far superior even to the Jewish Law that had directed and ruled the people of Israel hitherto. Though of God, the Law was an uncertain and joyless light compared to the new light of the Holy Spirit. Indeed being under the Law was like being in the darkness of captivity and slavery compared with being under the guidance of the Spirit, which was like enjoying 'the glorious liberty of the children of God'.[10] By receiving the Spirit of God the Jew was 'discharged from the Law... which held him captive... so that he might serve under the new life of the Spirit'.[11]

5   Matt 25:21   6   Heb 12:2   7   Jn 14:3   8   Rom 8:6-8
9   Rom 8:9   10 Rom 8:21   11 Rom 7:6

This teaching of St. Paul is no less true for modern man. The Spirit of God, released upon mankind in a new way through Jesus Christ, may now 'in all things direct and rule our hearts'. It is to be a controlling force in our lives, taking possession of all our faculties and characteristics, be they physical, mental or spiritual. We pray specifically here only that he may 'direct and rule our hearts'. But although the heart may stand for the mainspring of our lives, after the teaching of Jesus, (what comes out of a man... out of the heart of man, defiles a man',[12]) the operation of the Holy Spirit cannot be confined to what we might call spiritual things. Our prayer here concerns 'all things', which include the actions of our bodies and the working of our minds. The Holy Spirit works for our holiness, and that includes our wholeness. Body, mind and spirit are included in the 'all things' of our prayer. 'The body... is for the Lord... Do you not know that your bodies are members of Christ'.[13] Also, through the Spirit's indwelling, we are to experience 'renewal of our mind'[14] even to 'have the mind of Christ'.[15] We are to present all of ourselves to God, 'which is our spiritual worship', and he will make us his own, treating us even as his children. 'For all who are led by the Spirit of God are sons of God'.[16] Holiness and sonship are indeed the supreme gifts of the Spirit, and if he indwells us there will be fruits to enjoy also.

These fruits of the Spirit are the characteristics of the Saints. They are 'love, joy, peace, patience, kindness, goodness, faithfulness, gentleness and self-control' according to St. Paul.[17] How are we to know if we are being 'directed and ruled' by the Holy Spirit? We can examine our lives for these fruits. To pray this prayer, therefore, is a serious challenge to us. The consequences are potentially marvellous, but we are nonetheless sometimes wont to ask for more than we realise when we use the Collects! We must remember that we are called to holiness, no less.[18] We are through 'the Spirit of his Son in our hearts' God's children.[19] 'The love of God has been poured into our hearts through the Holy Spirit which he has given to us'.[20]

12 Mk 7:20   13 1 Cor 6:13-15   14 Rom 12:2   15 1 Cor 2:16
16 Rom 8:14   17 Gal 5:22   18 1 Thess 4:7   19 Gal 4:6
20 Rom 5:5

'If we live (therefore) by the Spirit, let us also walk by the Spirit'.[21] That is the burden of this challenging prayer. It slips very easily off the tongue. Its implications, however, are tremendous. It is not a prayer to say lightly, but if said with all sincerity, it is one to comfort as well as challenge us. We are in fact never 'without' God, and in the power of the Holy Spirit 'all (good) things' are possible,[22] even that we too may be 'numbered with thy Saints in glory everlasting.'[23]

21 Gal 5:25   22 Phil 4:13   23 Te Deum

TRINITY XX

O Almighty and most merciful God, of thy bountiful goodness keep us, we beseech thee, from all things that may hurt us; that we, being ready both in body and soul, may cheerfully accomplish those things that thou wouldest have done; through Jesus Christ our Lord. Amen.

This is the Gelasian Collect, and in translation Cranmer made a protestant-minded change, changing 'being propitiated' (propitiatus) to 'of thy bountiful goodness'. Since the original was probably a reference to the sacrificial nature of the Mass, it was not acceptable to the Reformers.

Another change was made by Bishop Cosin in 1662. The original (liberis mentibus), correctly translated by Cranmer in 1549 'with free hearts', was changed to 'cheerfully'.

––––––––––––––––

Once again we start by asking for God's protection. And we do so once again with confidence, for we pray to an 'Almighty and merciful God' who is full of 'bountiful goodness'. Bountiful means full of bounty, which are gifts given with regal generosity. So we have Queen Anne's Bounty and the Maundy Bounty. In spite of being somewhat archaic, it is a particularly appropriate word to use when we are considering the goodness and generosity of God, and this attractive phrase comes again in the Collect for Trinity XXIV (cf also Advent IV). In the Collects we are constantly recalling these qualities of God. (Trinity VI, VII, XII et al). He is a loving Father, who knows how to 'give good gifts to his children',[1] and we are never to doubt this.

Nevertheless we live in a world in which many things 'may hurt us'. We pray here that we may be kept from them. And what could be more natural

1 Lk 11:13

for the children of such a Father than to hope for such a thing? But as we have considered earlier (Trinity XV) there is no way in which we can escape some hurtful experiences. Indeed Scripture and common sense teach us that some such experiences are beneficial for us, for we are sinners. Moreover both hardship and difficulty are all part of our vocation as Christians, for Jesus calls us to enter the battle that rages in a world so estranged from God, so unloving and so cruel, and in the power of his Spirit to help forward its redemption.[2] As with temptation, so with hurtful things, what we know is both that we shall experience them, and also that through his grace we will not be overwhelmed by them. His grace is going to be sufficient for us[3] - some key texts are bound to be repeated again and again, as we consider the basic truths of the Christian faith and the spiritual life. So this prayer to 'be kept from' should include the idea of being 'seen through' the many 'things that may hurt us'.

In the second petition in this Collect we mention both 'body and soul'. In the first petition, similarly, we can add for ourselves the words "both physical and spiritual", as being included in the 'all things that may hurt us', knowing that the latter are by far the more dangerous.[4] The main means of grace, through which we receive the 'bountiful goodness' of God, are Word and Sacrament and prayer. But we should not forget that there are other sources of help, in particular such as come to us from those in heaven. At this time in the Christian year we will have recently celebrated the Feast of St. Michael and All Angels, and in the Collect for that day we pray that 'by God's appointment they may succour and defend us on earth'. We learn from Jesus that each of us has a guardian Angel[5], who is near God 'ready to accomplish' on our behalf whatever God 'wouldest have done'. It is a beautiful and comforting thought. There are, also, the prayers of our friends and of the whole Church, on earth and in heaven, to assist us. St. Paul often spoke of his reliance on the prayers of others. 'You also must help

2   2 Cor 5:19, Col 1:24   3   2 Cor 12:9   4   Lk 12:4   5   Matt 18:10, Acts 12:11

us by prayer', he says to his friends in Corinth.[6] Of such truths we should
be spiritually aware as being all part of the 'bountiful goodness' of God,
whereby we are 'kept from' and seen through 'all things that may hurt us'.
Indeed we should consciously develop both our reliance on such heavenly
aid and on the prayers of our earthly friends. (See also commentary on
Trinity II.)

God is ready to keep us, so we must be ready to obey him. He will protect
us in his service, so we must be eager to serve him and our fellow men. As
we noted the original Collect had 'with free hearts', which was changed to
'cheerfully'. Both, however, are equally helpful, and can surely be taken
together as two sides of one coin. Freely and cheerfully we are to be ready
to accomplish God's will, for this behoves us who have received so much 'of
his bountiful goodness'. We are always dependent creatures but, as an
essential part of our creation, we are also made free so that we may give
ourselves in God's service gladly and willingly. Sin prevents us enjoying
this 'glorious liberty'[7] (another often repeated text). But we can now obey
God, not as a slave obeys his master, but eagerly out of love as one would
a friend.[8] God loves, as we all do, 'a cheerful giver'.[9] It has been suggested
that the change from 'with free hearts' to 'cheerfully' was made in order to
link the Collect better to the theme of the Epistle, where St. Paul speaks
of us as being 'filled with the Spirit, speaking to (each other) in psalms and
hymns and spiritual songs, singing and making melody in our hearts to the
Lord', and in this cheerful and eager manner serving each other.[10] Whatever the reason it gives a refreshing and optimistic note to the Collect, and
reminds one of the assurance of Jesus to his dispirited and fearful disciples,
'in the world you have tribulation, but be of good cheer, I have overcome the
world'.[11]

---

6 2 Cor 1:11   7 Rom 8:21   8 Jn 15:15   9 2 Cor 9:7
10 Eph 5:18-20   11 Jn 16:33

The key word in the final petition is 'accomplish'. Francis Drake wrote a famous prayer as he set out on his voyage around the world, in which he prayed that God might enable him never to forget that it is not the beginning but the continuing of an enterprise, until it be thoroughly finished, that yields the true glory. That is exactly the meaning behind the word 'tetelestai' that Jesus spoke from the Cross; it means 'it is (thoroughly) finished'.[12] He is referring to the redemption of the world, and saying that, that which was begun, has been continued, and has now been fully accomplished. This is an aspect of the Crucifixion which does not apply to Jesus only. We know that we are all called to 'take up our cross daily' and follow him.[13] We are all to be 'crucified with Christ'.[14] So we too must seek in life to accomplish whatever we begin by continuing at the task until it be thoroughly finished, and this, of course, must apply particularly to the major task of our lives, which is the doing of God's will within the context of our own particular vocation, regardless of the cost.

We read in the Gospels of a rich young man, who wanted to follow Jesus, but could not do what Jesus 'wouldest have done'.[15] We hear also of others, who wanted to follow Jesus, but who first wanted to take leave of their families and not start to do straightaway what Jesus 'wouldest have done'.[16] They are to be contrasted with Peter and Andrew and James and John who left their jobs, and in the case of the latter brothers 'their father Zebedee in the boat' as well,[17] in order 'to cheerfully accomplish' whatever Jesus wanted them to do. We simply cannot get round the apparent harshness of the Gospel's demand that we put God's will first absolutely and irrevocably. In our hearts there are not to be any ifs and buts about it. God's will must come first all through our lives. 'No one who puts his hand to the plough and looks back is fit for the kingdom of God'.[18]

The harshness of this overriding demand is, however, only apparent. To obey is to be blessed, and to obey absolutely is to be blessed eternally. 'Do whatever he tells you', said Mary to the servants. And when they received

12 Jn 19:30   13 Lk 9:23   14 Gal 2:20   15 Matt 19: 21,22
16 Lk 9:57-62   17 Mk 1:20   18 Lk 9:62

their inexplicable instructions to fill the water pots with water we are told that 'they filled them up to the brim'.[19] This cheerful obedience was the prelude to our Lord's first miracle. So, too, the fearful demand that Jesus should drink the cup of sacrifice was not only for our redemption, but also for his glorification. 'Yet cheerful he to suffering goes, that he his foes from thence might free'.[20] We can only 'cheerfully accomplish those things that (the Father) wouldest have done', if we are sure that such obedience is for the best, both for ourselves and for others. This we can only know by faith, but such knowledge is an essential part of faith. 'It is the assurance of things hoped for, the conviction of things unseen'.[21] 'For the joy that was set before him Jesus endured the Cross'.[22] A similar faith and hope can make us 'ready both in body and soul' to obey God regardless of any sacrifice involved. We know that the obedience that took Jesus to Calvary led on to his Resurrection and glorious Ascension. So by faith and hope we may know (if we may compare little with great) that a similar obedience to God's will will lead on for us to our own eternal salvation. Therefore his 'bountiful goodness' will surely bring blessings more than we can conceive of upon those who freely and cheerfully seek to do his will.[23] This then is a prayer full of Christian assurance, as well as challenge.

19 Jn 2:5-7   20 S. Crossman – Passiontide hymn, 'My Song is Love Unknown'
21 Heb 11:1   22 Heb 12:2   23 1 Cor 2:9

TRINITY XXI

Grant, we beseech thee, merciful Lord, to thy faithful people pardon and peace, that they may be cleansed from all their sins, and serve thee with a quiet mind; through Jesus Christ our Lord. Amen.

This is the Gelasian Collect, and surely one of the simplest and most beautiful in the Prayer Book.

Other Collects refer to 'thy faithful people' (notably Whitsunday). We pray here first for those precious gifts of God, pardon and peace, but, as we do so, perhaps we should note that we pray only that they be granted to 'thy faithful people'. We recognise here by implication the truth that there is no pardon for the unrepentant and the unforgiving,[1] and that there is no peace for the wicked and the worldly.[2] Faith is linked inextricably with repentance, for faith without repentance is a counterfeit faith. Faith is also linked with a rejection of the world and a serious effort 'to do justice, and love kindness, and to walk humbly with (our) God'.[3] Although God's gifts are free, there is yet, as it were, a price to be paid. The price is that they must be received. And for us to step forward and receive them we must have faith. They are not placed into our laps, but only into our willing hands. But if we are willing to receive them, we shall surely be given them. 'Thy faithful people' have their reward, pardon and peace, yet they must always acknowledge that their reward is a gift.

Faith in our Lord's parables is shown to be an active and not just a passive virtue, just as pardon and peace are positive and not just negative gifts. There is certainly a passive element in faith. The farmer having sowed his seed in faith must then wait in faith for a long time before he can 'put in the

---

1 Matt 6:15   2 Ezel 7:25, Jn 14:27   3 Mic 6:8

sickle, because the harvest has come'.[4] There is also a negative side to both pardon and peace. Pardon is to do with 'taking away', and peace involves 'being rescued from'. But all three are mainly active and positive words. Faith is moving towards God, actively embracing his will and positively obeying his commandments. Pardon involves a positive acquiring of the strength to live a better life. Peace is to do with experiencing the fruits of victory over our great Enemy.

This truth is emphasised by the second half of the Collect's petition. There we pray that we may enjoy both the negative and the positive aspects of these gifts from God, 'the cleansing' of our lives from sin and the power to 'serve' God positively.

These gifts of 'pardon and peace' are, moreover, gifts that we must receive repeatedly. All the time we are being reinfected by sin. All the time our peace is being shattered. But if we remain faithful and repentant these gifts will be constantly renewed in us. There is a sense, of course, in which we have been washed once for all 'by the precious blood of Jesus'. This is sacramentally established in Holy Baptism. 'He that has bathed does not need to wash, but is clean all over'.[5] But in the sacrament of Holy Communion we recognise that this cleansing of 'our sinful bodies' and 'our souls' must yet be renewed regularly, so that 'we may evermore dwell in him and he in us'.

Perhaps it is important, too, to recognise our sense of spiritual fellowship in this matter of 'pardon and peace', as well as in the matter of faith. We share all three, and in all three we are linked with others within the fellowship of the Church. So we have a common faith, expressed in a corporate Creed. So, too, we experience a shared forgiveness of our sins, and we are to be 'eager to maintain the unity of the Spirit in the bond of peace'.[6] We cannot have these gifts and keep them to ourselves. As with the

4   Mk 4:29   5   Jn 13:10   6   Eph 4:3

man who received the one talent and did nothing with it, they may be taken from us.[7] We can prove ourselves unfaithful, and therefore unworthy.

We should, however, in these matters draw upon each other for strength. We are to be faithful in the sense of keeping faith with each other, as well as in the sense of putting our trust in God. We are to forgive each other, as well as to seek forgiveness of God, and the blessedness of God's gift of pardon depends as much on our readiness to do the former as the latter. So too with peace; we cannot experience peace with God if we are at war with our neighbours.[8] All this is involved in this prayer, which is not a private prayer but a prayer of the Church.

Finally we pray that we may experience the joy of a quiet mind. The Latin (secura mente) is helpful and suggestive. There is a strength in the word 'quiet' that may be lost on us, and so to speak of a 'secure mind', although hardly a correct use of English, has much to recommend it. 'Quiet' is like the words 'meek' and 'poor'. They can be badly misunderstood. They all refer to qualities that are strong. Those who possess them are people who have their security in God; they have built their lives upon the rock and are safe amid life's storms.[9] They are very blessed.[10] They are not immune from the troubles of the world, indeed quite often they are the special object of aggression simply because they do not stimulate fear in evil people. Such, said the Psalmist, 'imagine deceitful words against the quiet in the land'.[11] But they are nonetheless the great survivors; 'the meek shall inherit the earth'.[12] They have extraordinary power for 'in quietness and in trust shall be their strength'.[13] No-one in our wicked and dangerous world is more secure than the man that 'serves God with a quiet mind', for his security is within his soul, that place 'where thieves cannot break in and steal'.[14]

The word 'quiet', however, speaks especially to us of the call to serve God not only in the hurly burly of life, but in the secret place of our heart, in that

7   Matt 25:25   8   Jas 3:18   9   Matt 7:24-25   10 Matt 5:3-5
11 Ps 35:20   12 Matt 5:5   13 Is 30:15   14 Matt 6:21

inner place to which we can withdraw, and 'shut the door, and pray to our Father who is in secret'.[15] It is strangely hard to do this, for one might imagine this is the easiest of all forms of prayer. After all no apparatus is needed. All is always ready. What prevent us from enjoying this quiet form of prayer are our restless minds and unsettled wills. In the prayer of quiet we have to use our memory, our mind and our will, and these may all be confused and agitated. They so often are.

The purpose of this form of prayer is that we may grow in our appreciation of God's love of us, and so in our love of God, who loves us so much. Through it we are seeking to respond to God's love of us, for it is as St. John says, 'In this is love, not that we loved God but that he loved us'.[16] Such prayer, traditionally called 'affective prayer', because it is to do with the affections, consists mainly of spiritual acts of love toward God. In this the will is the most involved faculty. Fr. Baker speaks of this quiet prayer as 'the affective prayer of the will'. 'I will love thee, O Lord my strength', said the Psalmist.[17] The accent should be placed equally on the second and third words.

To practise this prayer of quiet we need to draw aside from time to time, and ideally regularly and frequently. Jesus went away alone quite often to find the quiet he needed to pray in this manner. 'In the morning, a great while before day he rose and went out to a lonely place, and there he prayed'.[18] Sometimes he went apart with companions, and in this Peter, James and John were specially favoured.[19] 'Come away by yourselves to a lonely place, and rest a while', he said to all his Apostles after they had returned from an evangelistic exercise.[20] This has always been seen as a call to us to go into Retreat from time to time, either alone or in groups, and so give ourselves a chance to develop the prayer of quiet and to learn to be at ease in silence with God.

'Be still then and know that I am God', said the Psalmist.[21] Dorothy Kerin of Burrswood said, 'He giveth himself to his beloved in quietness'.[22] Our knowledge of God is so much dependent upon our ability to be quiet with

15 Matt 6:6   16 1 Jn 4:10   17 Ps 18:1   18 Mk 1:35
19 Mk 9:2, 14:33   20 Mk 6:31   21 Ps 46:10
22 Burrswood Healing Service

him. In the quietness of our secret place we are to have loving communion with God, which is the true heart of the knowledge of God. In the Bible the words know and love are sometimes interchangeable. Especially this is true when it speaks of the intimacy of sexual love, so 'Adam knew Eve', that is made love to her.[23] We can in fact only really know the people whom we love, and who love us, because they are the ones we reveal ourselves to, and who reveal themselves to us. So love and knowledge in human relationships are two sides of one coin, and it is so with our relationship with God. It is not, therefore, the theologians who necessarily know God, though they know about him[24]; it is the Saints who know God, because they truly love him. We are all 'called to be Saints'[25], that is to know and love God. We will certainly want to serve him in the busy world and in practical ways. But we must also want to have a personal and intimate relationship with him in 'a quiet spirit', which in God's sight is 'very precious'.[26] To this end we should all learn to pray quietly, in a quiet spirit and a quiet mind. 'My soul waiteth still upon God', said the Psalmist, 'for of him cometh my salvation'.[27]

23 Gen 4:1   24 Matt 23:2-3   25 1 Cor 1:2   26 1 Pet 3:4
27 Ps 62:1

TRINITY XXII

Lord, we beseech thee to keep thy household the Church in continual godliness; that through thy protection it may be free from all adversities, and devoutly given to serve thee in good works, to the glory of thy Name; through Jesus Christ our Lord. Amen.

This is the Gregorian Collect. It is similar to the Collect for Epiphany V, and even more so in the Latin where their openings are identical.

We meet again here the word household to describe the Church, and we discussed its biblical meaning in the commentary for Epiphany V. Once again the Latin is familia, which is translated here, and in the Collect for Epiphany V, 'household', but in the Collect for Good Friday more literally 'family'. To our ears the word 'household' is wholly uninspiring and smacks of government forms and community charges. The word 'family', in contrast, is one that speaks traditionally of love and security. If the prayer read 'Lord, we beseech thee to keep thy family the Church in continual godliness' surely no one would complain.

Nevertheless to-day our understanding of the word family is under threat, and we can no longer take it for granted that it means to all what it has traditionally meant. The family life of the nation is disintegrating in an astonishing manner. Divorce is commonplace, and the 'one parent family' part of the new social jargon. A large number of people are growing up in our country ignorant of what was universally understood by the term 'family life'. Perhaps today the word household has, therefore, more meaning in some places than the word family, being a more truthful description of the place where many live. And how truly tragic this situation is, even though it is beginning to be accepted as normal, or, rather, because it is beginning to be accepted as normal.

When, however, we think of the Church's fellowship in a Parish, the word family is, of course, so much to be preferred. In that context 'household' is virtually meaningless, although it is more biblical. This may seem to us very strange. Even when St. Paul speaks about men and women, whether they be Jews or Greeks, 'having access in one Spirit to the Father', he still does not go on to use the word family to describe their fellowship, but prefers formal words like 'citizens' and 'members of a household'. 'You are fellow citizens with the saints and members of the household of God'.[1] Perhaps it was because the word family (patria in Greek) is only used once in the New Testament, and then not to describe the Church but mankind as a whole, that the Reformers chose to translate the Latin 'familia' by the more biblical word 'household'. This Ephesians' text, moreover, may well have been in their minds. It makes at all events the perfect background to such a prayer as this. We are praying here that the Church may be 'kept in continual godliness', that is in that spiritual state that befits those who can be described as 'fellow citizens with the saints and members of the household of God'.

The word 'continual' deserves to be pondered. The connection between the word household and the Holy Communion was particularly considered in the commentary for Epiphany V. It is through our meeting regularly together at Holy Communion, more than in any other way, that we are 'kept in continual godliness'. In so doing each of us keeps his or her place in the fellowship of the spiritual family of the Church, and therefore we must continually take our place at the table if that fellowship is to be kept strong. We must also continually use the family prayer; to do so reminds us of our family obligations and helps maintain the life of the family. We must also regularly read the Bible, the family book. As we do so, we should remember how it is read by all other members of the family in all their hundreds of different languages. These three, then, the Eucharist, the Lord's Prayer and the Bible unite us all, and 'keep us in continual godliness' if continually used.

1   Eph 2:19

We go on to pray in a more familiar manner for protection from the power of evil and freedom 'from all adversities'. Again and again in the Collects this has been the burden of our prayer, and there is no need to repeat what has been said in several previous commentaries. In the special context of this prayer, however, we should, perhaps, stress the importance of acknowledging our weakness in the face of the power of the Evil One. To do so is part of the truth, and it is only the truth that can set us free.[2] To confess this truth, as we do here, is a first step towards our obtaining the freedom from 'all adversities', for which we pray.

There is, however, something worthy of special notice in this Collect. Though we pray for protection 'from' and freedom 'from all adversities', we do so 'for' a very positive purpose, that we may be 'devoutly given to serve thee in good works'. Our prayer is made a truly Christian prayer thereby. We are not, as it were, merely looking around us fearfully, but also looking forward in an eager spirit. We are looking to serve, even though we are not unmindful of the context and the likely cost. We know that we are called 'to launch out into the deep', where there can be many dangers.[3] Here Canon Masterman makes the penetrating observation that in reality we are probably safer if we go out bravely to face adversity, than if we shrink back and do nothing. Christ's call is for us to take up our cross, whereas it is 'our adversary the Devil'[4] who is ever on the watch to tempt us to evade that duty. We are called to 'glory in tribulations'[5] and to 'rejoice that we are counted worthy to suffer'[6]. If we only paddle about in the shallows of Christian service, we are not as likely to experience freedom 'from all adversities' as we might expect. We have to put on the whole armour of God, and if we do, God will not only use us, but also protect us. We shall become 'more than conquerors through him who loved us'[7] according to the promise contained in God's Word. How paradoxical the Gospel sometimes seems! The way of danger can be the way of salvation, and the way of safety the way of greatest danger.

2 Jn 8:32   3 Lk 5:4, 8:23   4 1 Pet 5:8   5 Rom 5:3
6 Acts 5:41   7 Rom 8:37

Finally we are reminded in this Collect of the true purpose of his protection and of our service. It is to glorify his Name. Jesus said, 'I glorified thee on earth'.[8] The Church, his new earthly Body, is to continue to glorify God. 'Hallowed be thy Name' is the first element in the Lord's Prayer, and it means, 'May God be glorified'. The whole of creation is to glorify God and we are, as it were, creation's chief worshippers. Through Christ we are to bring all things into subjection to this one glorious purpose. When this is done it will be perceived to be freedom indeed. Nowhere is this tremendous truth better put than in Romans 8. St. Paul declares that our sufferings in the service of God are as nothing 'compared with the glory' to which these sufferings in Christ are taking the whole world. They are helping the universe, no less, to find its freedom from 'its bondage to decay' and to share in the 'glorious liberty of the children of God'. 'We know', he says 'that the whole creation has been groaning in travail together until now'.[9] But 'now' things are beginning to change. Christ has come. God has acted. The Spirit is here. The redemption of all things is 'at hand'.[10] Now we, who are members of the Church, are being called to serve this end, the glorification of God. The time will come when 'all things are put in subjection under him'. 'Then the Son himself will also be subjected to him who put all things under him that God may be all in all'.[11] This is the ultimate vision of divine glory that we may have before us as we seek 'devoutly to serve God in good works to the glory of his Name'. It is one in which we are all to share.

There is, however, always a temptation for us to see everything only as it affects us, and therefore to believe all is done for our sakes rather than for God's. Even when we know this cannot be so, we are tempted to believe it. Just as it is easy to believe the sun goes round the earth, because that is what it appears to do, so it is easy to believe that God is concerned only for us, as if man was the centre of all things. From where we stand it can so easily seem like that. But it falsifies everything if we make this elementary error. Even our redemption was not won by Christ solely for our sake. He came to redeem us primarily for the Father's sake, that the Father might

8 Jn 17:4   9 Rom 8:18-22   10 1 Pet 4:7   11 1 Cor 15:28 (A.V.)

be glorified by us as was his due. We, who were made in God's image, had lost that image, and this loss dishonoured God. And God's honour and glory is alone what supremely matters. So the reason why our redemption in Christ, who gives back God's image to men, is such a glorious thing is that it redounds to God's glory. This is the supremely important truth Christ speaks of in his famous prayer to the Father in John 17. This is a central but often forgotten aspect of the Gospel.

For us, however, glory will always be linked with the Cross. This truth cannot be evaded, indeed it must be emphasised. 'It had been granted to us, not only to believe, but also suffer for his sake', said St. Paul to the Philippians.[12] The ear of faith picks out the 'us' and recognises the ever present tense in which the Word of God speaks to us in the Scriptures. 'It' (this faith that will suffer if required to do so) 'has been granted to us' as a privilege; it can make even our lives glorious. But we will be tested by God to see whether or not we have really received it! In the event such testing may indeed include much suffering, indeed so much that it may cause some to reject this privilege.[13] But if we prove our faithfulness, our faith, tested and tried, will bring such great blessings.

First, we ourselves shall be saved to share in 'an inheritance' and 'a salvation' prepared for us by God.[14] And, secondly, and still more importantly, 'our faithfulness' will also 'redound' to God's glory.[15] It is through such faith that the ways of God make real progress on earth and the general good is truly served. They are the 'good works' that men see and then glorify God.[16] They alone do lasting good, for they are 'devoutly given', done out of faith for Christ's sake. Such 'good works' contribute to the redemption of the world and the glory of God. What a thought! But is not this what St. Paul meant when he said, 'I rejoice in my sufferings for your sake, and in my flesh I complete what is lacking in Christ's afflictions'?[17] And are not these the 'greater works' that Christ prophesied that his future disciples would do, because they believe in him and because he has gone to the Father?[18]

12 Phil 1:29   13 Matt 13:20-21   14 Rev 7:13-17   15 1 Pet 1:6-7
16 Matt 5:16   17 Col 1:24   18 Jn 14:12

TRINITY XXIII

O God, our refuge and strength, who art the author of all godliness; be ready, we beseech thee, to hear the devout prayers of thy Church; and grant that those things which we ask faithfully we may obtain effectually; through Jesus Christ our Lord. Amen.

This is the Gregorian Collect.

The opening has an Old Testament ring about it, especially reminiscent of the Psalms. 'Lord, thou hast been our refuge'.[1] 'God is our hope and strength'.[2] It is not likely that today Christians would naturally start, 'O God, our refuge and strength'. Perhaps this is not only because it sounds archaic, but also because it may appear that we are living in securer times and with so much more ability to help ourselves than used to be the case. Yet surely we live in times of even greater underlying uncertainty than did the people of medieval Europe, let alone the Israelites 2000 years earlier. If the threat of nuclear war has receded, it remains. If man has the power to invent more and more means to make human life easier and to last longer, these same inventions have within them, so we now discover, hidden dangers, some of which are so great as to have the powers to destroy even that vital protection to our lives, the ozone layer around the planet. Man, we know, does not have all the answers. The world is still a very dangerous place. This sense of danger is still a powerful cause for prayer. 'O God, our refuge and strength' is not, therefore, an opening to prayer that has become outdated, however untypical it may sound.

The invocation continues on a more straight-forward devotional level. Godliness, however, is also not a word that we find easy to use these days. It translates the word 'pietas', but piety is certainly no better. There is,

---

1   Ps 90:1   2   Ps 46:1

moreover, a play on words here that is lost in the English, for devout is 'pius' in Latin. We are praying, therefore, that he who is the author of 'piety' may hear our 'pious' prayers! The words devout and devotion, however, are probably quite acceptable to us all; we understand them, admire those who personify them and desire the qualities they represent. So when we pray that the Church may be heard for its 'devout prayers', we recognise we are talking about the spiritual quality of the Church's life. This, we know, is what really matters.

That play on words reminds us that this quality is not of our creation, but of God's gift. He is the author of this quality of godliness or true devotion. So if the Church is to pray truly 'devout prayers' they are going to be prayers inspired by God. 'We do not know how to pray as we ought', but God in the power of his Holy Spirit inspires us to pray 'according to the will of God'.[3] These are the only prayers that matter. Prayers emanating from our shallow insight into things or from our prejudiced points of view are not really 'devout prayers', however sincere we may be in praying them. All 'devout prayers' are variations on the one theme, 'thy will be done'. It is no good us beseeching God for what is contrary to his will; mercifully he will not give it us. 'Devout prayers', therefore, are such as in every sense and every circumstance seek to cooperate with God's will.

This truth is one of the main reasons why liturgical prayer is so vital and fruitful. There is no doubt a time and place for spontaneous prayers within the general prayers of Christians, but so often they simply represent our will rather than God's. As such they cannot be described as 'the devout prayers of thy Church', but only as the sincere requests of some Christians. The liturgical prayers of the Church, however, have a breadth and depth about them that make them more of him than of us. They bear constant repetition, therefore, and never fail to be meaningful. They are improved certainly by being led in a devout manner, but it is not the way they are said that makes them 'the devout prayers of thy Church'. They are that in

3   Rom 8:26-27

themselves, and foremost among these 'devout prayers' are our Prayer Book Collects. It is this truth about them that makes them so exceedingly precious, and merits this phrase as the title for this book.

The second part of the petition speaks about faithful prayer and effectual prayer. They are surely the same kind of prayer. One of the strangest stories in the Gospels, that of the withering of a fig tree on the Monday in Holy Week, teaches us this. St. Mark ends our Lord's comments on the episode like this. 'Therefore I tell you, whatever you ask in prayer, believe that you have received it, (or are receiving it) and it will be yours'.[4] This is changed slightly by St. Matthew, 'Whatever you ask in prayer, you will receive if you have faith'.[5] St. Luke omits this story, but has another rather like it to do with a sycomore tree.[6] It also stresses the effectiveness of prayer that is full of faith. In St. John, Jesus also talks about the effectiveness of prayer 'in his Name'.[7] And the same emphasis is found in the Epistles too.[8] That true faith opens the door to the miraculous is a truth that we come across repeatedly in the New Testament,[9] and we must believe that it will be the same for us who pray in Christ's name, for 'Christ is the same yesterday, today and for ever'.[10] Faithful prayer, therefore, is effectual prayer.

But what we are saying here must be governed by the truth of what we have just been emphasising. True prayer can only be such as cooperates with the will of God, and true faith must similarly be directed to the same all essential end. True faith is never selfish any more than true love is; 'it does not insist on its own way'.[11] Always our prayers must be governed by the spirit of faith that says, 'Nevertheless not my will, but thine, be done'.[12] But true faith and true prayer unblock the way for God's will to be done, just as surely as sin and disobedience block that way. That is their power. So the Church, and all members of the Church, must strive to possess this

4   Mk 11:24   5   Matt 21:22   6   Lk 17:6   7   Jn 16:23-24
8   Jas 5:13-18   9   Matt 9:22 et al   10 Heb 13:8   11 1 Cor 13:5
12 Lk 22:42

faith that puts God's will first, and to pray only in the power of that faith. Then what 'we ask faithfully' we will most assuredly 'obtain effectually'.

Perhaps there is one other side to this matter that may be emphasised here. St. Benedict had as his motto 'orare est laborare' (to pray is to work). His monks were to be a very active order, but first they were to see prayer as the most effectual and creative of all their activities. They were not to view prayer as simply that which fuels other activity. In itself it was to be seen as the most active of occupations. This is hardly a view shared by all in the Church, and it is certainly not one understood by those outside it. Consequently many, who would pride themselves on being active Christians, being involved in all manner of good works, do not attend worship regularly or pray in private in any but the most perfunctory manner. Is this not the real hindrance to the Church being the instrument of God's will in the world? Where the active nature of prayer is fully understood, as it is, to take an obvious example, among the Missionaries of Charity founded so recently by Mother Teresa, the results are 'effectual', even miraculous. Such then are 'the devout prayers of thy Church', prayers that are faithful and therefore effectual, and that they should always be so is the main concern of this Collect.

TRINITY XXIV

O Lord, we beseech thee, absolve thy people from their offences; that through thy bountiful goodness we may all be delivered from the bands of those sins, which by our frailty we have committed: Grant this, O heavenly Father, for Jesus Christ's sake, our blessed Lord and Saviour. Amen.

This is the Gregorian Collect, with small but significant changes. (See commentary)

———————————

There are two parts to the petition in this Collect. The first is for the absolution of our sins, and the second is for deliverance from their power to hold us, even after we have repented of them. These are united requests, but not precisely the same. We get a perfect example of their unity, yet difference, in the story of Jesus' healing of the paralytic that was brought to him by four friends. There he first forgave the man his sins, and then he healed him of his paralysis. In the way the story unfolds it is clear that the two were connected and the deliverance followed on from the absolution. It is a story[1] that will help us in various other ways as we consider the meaning and implications of this Collect.

First, however, let us notice that we pray for absolution of our sins. Absolution is the prerogative of God, and in this the Pharisees were right. 'Who can forgive sins but God alone ? '[2] But God 'hath given power and commandment to his Ministers to declare and pronounce to his people, being penitent, the Absolution and Remission of their sins'.[3] This is emphasised on three occasions in the Gospels as being central to the ministry of the Church as a whole, and so of the ordained clergy, who minister in the Church's name.

1   Mk 2:1-12   2   Mk 2:7
3   Prayer of Absolution in Morning and Evening Prayer

Two of these passages come in St. Matthew's Gospel, and are part of those few stories and sayings in that Gospel that are not found in either St. Mark or St. Luke. Their context is some general discussion between Jesus and his disciples about the ministry of the Church that Jesus was so soon to found. In the first of these St. Peter is specially mentioned; 'I will give you the keys of the kingdom of heaven, and whatever you bind on earth shall be bound in heaven and whatever you loose on earth shall be loosed in heaven'.[4] Then later he said to all, 'Truly I say to you, whatever you bind on earth shall be bound in heaven and whatever you loose on earth shall be loosed in heaven'.[5] The wording, except for the opening, is identical. The text, relating to St. Peter and the keys, is one that is much discussed, pointing, as it does, to the primacy of St. Peter, and then to what has been claimed to follow from that position of primacy. But the combined sense of these two Matthean texts, especially when taken with John 20 v 23, the other occasion on which this matter is specially mentioned, seems to confirm the claim held by Anglicans and others who are not Roman Catholics, that the power to absolve was left as a basic aspect of the ministry of the whole Church, rather than that of the ministry of one man and those with whom he may share it.

When we look at the Johannine text[6] we notice that the scene is Easter evening in the Upper Room and 'the disciples of Jesus are gathered there'. We are not told who they were. St. John, however, never speaks of the Apostles, only of the disciples and the Twelve, so the implication is that more than the Apostles were present. (See also Luke 24:33). To them he says almost identical words to those found in St. Matthew. 'If you forgive the sins of any, they are forgiven; if you retain the sins of any they are retained.' But it is important that we should note that immediately before these words comes the solemn declaration, 'Receive the Holy Spirit'. This authority, then, to absolve, and to refuse absolution, is clearly linked in St. John with the supreme gift of the Holy Spirit. It is the Holy Spirit that

---

4   Matt 16:19   5   Matt 18:18   6   Jn 20:23

constitutes the Church as the mystical Body of Christ, and who ordains its ministers to communicate his sacramental grace. This grace is mediated through the indwelling Spirit, but the authority remains Christ's, who 'has power on earth to forgive sins'.[7] This is put succinctly in our Prayer Book in the prayer of Absolution said by the Priest to private penitents as set out in the Visitation of the Sick. 'Our Lord Jesus Christ... hath left power to his Church to absolve all sinners who truly repent and believe in him'. Man in himself has not this power ever, but man may be God's instrument. Through the Church we may hear his words, (and how blessed they are), 'My son your sins are forgiven you', but can we, like the paralytic in the story, 'go home' a new man?

———————

The second half of the petition is for deliverance from 'the bands' of our sins. Forgiveness is one thing and deliverance is slightly different. We may note that in the Lord's Prayer the prayer for forgiveness and deliverance follow each other as two separate petitions. The consequences of our sins, on others and on ourselves , can be so deepseated. We may be forgiven a bad tempered word or action, but how can we be delivered from an evil temper that demands revenge and delights in violence? We may be forgiven a lie, but how can we be delivered from a boastful spirit that loves to exaggerate or a prejudiced outlook that refuses to accept the truth? Jesus not only healed the ordinarily sick, who had some temporary affliction, like a fever, that could be put right and then all was well, and our doctors can do the same; but he also drove out evil spirits that were driving people mad and to suicide. These are cures that his disciples found impossible to perform[8], and even though he has given to the Church the power to perform them[9] we find it no easier today. In the Absolution in the Holy Communion Service the Priest is empowered to say that God both 'pardons and delivers us from all our sins'. It is not always, however, that we experience this deliverance, even though we may know by faith our forgiveness, and experience much

7   Mk 2:10   8   Lk 9:38-40   9   Mk 16:17

comfort from that knowledge.

In this matter we are brought back to the biblical concept of sin as a form of inner slavery, from which we need to be set free. The Collect speaks of 'the bands' with which sin binds us. Another prayer in the B.C.P., found in its section of special prayers recommended for general use, speaks of us being 'tied and bound with the chain of our sins'. This 'slave theology' is specially emphasised by St. Paul, as we have already had occasion to notice. (Christmas, Trinity XIII). It lies at the heart of our troubles in the spiritual life. Would that it was an easier matter than it is. 'Wretched man that I am!' said St. Paul. 'Who will deliver me from this body of death?'[10] Is it not the same for us?

'Thanks be to God', however, there is an answer. God in 'his bountiful goodness' longs to deliver us as much as we long to be delivered. But 'our frailty' is not easily ended. The process of penitence and trust and obedience is one that must always continue while we are here, and such prayers as these will always be applicable to our situation. 'If we say that we have no sin, we deceive ourselves, and the truth is not in us, but if we confess our sins, God is faithful and just to forgive us our sins and to cleanse us from all unrighteousness'.[11] Deliverance implies a positive cleansing, being able 'hereafter to live a godly, righteous and sober life to the glory of (God's) holy Name'.[12] It is only the Holy Spirit indwelling us, however, that can enable this to happen, 'so that at the last we may come to his, (and our), eternal joy'.

In the Burrswood Healing Service devised by Dorothy Kerin it says, 'Anything falling short of the glory of God is sin. In particular, resentments, anger, unresolved frustrations and lack of forgiveness to any who have wronged us, provide powerful blocks to healing. Repentance is the willingness to change one's whole attitude, relationships and way of life'. Deliverance may demand hard choices. The drug addict and the alcoholic have to give up and never ever touch again that which had enslaved them. The rich

10 Rom 7:24   11 1 Jn 1:8-9
12 General Confession in Morning and Evening Prayer

young man who wanted to be a disciple had to sell all his possessions. He could not pay the price, and 'went away sorrowful', still the slave of his wealth. 'How hard it is to enter the kingdom of God!....But all things are possible with God'.[13] Two small changes were made by the Reformers in the translation of this Collect, which seem arbitrary, but are nonetheless suggestive and interesting. In the Latin the adjective 'all' does not appear. In the 1549 translation, however, it appears before 'sins', (all those sins), and then in the 1662 version it is moved to qualify 'us', (we may all). It could surely very well be used in both places. We all want this deliverance, and we want it for all our sins.

So absolution is not the end of our struggle with the evil within. Deliverance is the end. And even though that is something we usually have to wait for, we would give up in despair if we were not sustained by our trust in the 'bountiful goodness' of God, who in Jesus has come to die for us, that we 'should not perish, but have everlasting life'.[14] It is a comfortable word. Full deliverance is the hope that is set before us, which for most of us certainly cannot be expected in this life. The paralytic, absolved and delivered, went 'home' a new man. We too seek that 'home' where deliverance from the power of the Evil One is complete and where we may experience fully the newness of life, free from 'the bands of our sins', that is our ultimate inheritance in Christ. We will probably not find it in this life, but it is there to be found, as a hope that is set before us.[15] (See also the commentary on the Collect for Ash Wednesday.)

13 Mk 10:24-27   14 Jn 3:16   15 Rev 21:1-7

TRINITY XXV

Stir up, we beseech thee, O Lord, the wills of thy faithful people; that they, plenteously bringing forth the fruit of good works may of thee be plenteously rewarded; through Jesus Christ our Lord. Amen.

This is the Gregorian Collect, with one surprising change that seems to reinterpret its meaning. (See commentary)

In the Sarum Missal this Sunday had another title, the Sunday next before Advent, and is still often so called. It is the last Sunday of the Christian year. Unofficially it is called Stir-up Sunday from the Collect, and in this the Collect is unique in giving the Sunday its popular title. (Although Mid-Lent Sunday may perhaps owe something to the Collect for its popular title Refreshment Sunday, it owes much more to its Gospel; and in any case it is more often called Mothering Sunday, a title taken from the Epistle). In earlier times, when Christmas cakes and puddings were always made at home, it was traditional for the family to stir the sticky mixture together, making appropriate wishes and resolutions, thereby reminding themselves that Christmas was now only a few weeks off.

———————————

The will is our spiritual heart. In the Bible it is often called the heart, as when the Psalmist declares 'My heart is fixed', 'His heart is established', and 'I will give thanks unto thee with my whole heart'[1] Many other texts using similar phrases describe the settled will of the true believer. Our will is the faculty with which we desire God's will to be done, and that is to be our true desire. Without doubt this was true of Jesus, and so it must be true of his disciples, who are his mystical Body. Unless we desire God's will we are not his 'faithful people'.

1 Pss 57:7, 112:8, 9:1

This may be true of us without, however, being sufficiently true of us! We may desire God's will, but in a lazy half-hearted way, not at all 'with our whole heart'. So the prayer is thoroughly relevant. 'Stir up, we pray thee, O Lord, the wills of thy faithful people'. Indeed, how lacking in energy we are! How unenthusiastic in our prayers and in our service! How timid and ineffective in our witness! We need bestirring, and we pray here that God will do this within us. The Old Testament text that is more frequently quoted in the New Testament than any other is Isaiah 6:9-10, which declares, among other things, that 'this people's heart has grown dull'. It was a text that prophesied the rejection of the Messiah and so seemed to explain the inexplicable, that when the Messiah came he was not only not recognised, but also rejected by his people. But do not those particular words apply still? Christian hearts can grow so dull, and badly need bestirring. Perhaps this is an especially appropriate prayer as we come to the end of the Christian year and stand on the threshold of a new one.

Advent is a penitential season, and, although not as widely recognised and kept as such as Lent, it is always a time of special Church activity. We are preparing for Christmas, and that in itself is a stirring consideration. Nativity plays and rehearsals for the Christmas Carol Service are sure to play their part in stirring up large sections of the faithful. It is a traditional time for Confirmation classes to start, if candidates are to be ready in the Easter-Whitsun season when so many Confirmations take place. The traditional subjects for Advent preaching, judgement and its consequences, will also no doubt be the means of stirring up 'the wills of thy faithful people', who should augment this traditional liturgical fare by their own Advent resolutions. Advent, then, is to be a time of spiritual activity and of new year resolutions, and to encourage this would seem to be the special purpose of this Collect for the Sunday next before Advent.

Wittingly or unwittingly Cranmer changed the sense of the second half of this Collect. Now the 'good works' mentioned seem to apply wholly to us and to our choosing, and, as a result of our doing them well, we can hope to be well rewarded. The original, however, gives a different sense and one that, one would imagine, would have been more agreeable to the Reformers; hence one's surprise at the change made in translation. There the 'good works' were rather good deeds of God's choosing or godly works (divini operis), and we are to busy ourselves in them. Jesus said to Peter and Andrew, 'Follow me and I will make you fishers of men'[2] We are men and women under authority, who do not choose what we do. 'If you love me', said Jesus, 'you will keep my commandments'. 'And apart from me you can do nothing'.[3] The Collect certainly urges us on to energetic activity as befits God's 'faithful people', but it is perhaps just as bad for us to be self-centred and self-regarding in our activity as it is for us to be lazy - and just as likely! Jeremiah said that we are not to glory in our own wisdom or our own power or our own resources, but only in our understanding of God's will and our knowledge of his ways.[4] Isaiah also warned that God's ways are so different to ours.[5] And Zechariah declares that in all our doings our motto must be, 'Not by (my) might, nor by (my) power, but by God's Spirit'.[6] Only then will our activities be truly fruitful, and therefore worthy of reward. (cf. Trinity XIV)

The idea of lives being fruitful and worthy of reward is found in several parables, and especially in St. John 15 in the parable of the vine, the branches and the grapes. Christ is the vine, we are the branches. The grapes are the good works that are therefore both of him and of us. Only as we 'abide in him' can we 'bear much fruit'. This parable of Jesus is similar to Isaiah's parable of Israel being the vineyard specially planted by God. In that parable the prophet says that God, the husbandman, looked for good sweet grapes, but found only bitter wild ones.[7] So with us: we can be very busy and in some respects fruitful, but what is the quality of the

2 Mk 1:17   3 Jn 14:23, 15:5   4 Jer 9:23   5 Is 55:8
6 Zech 4:6   7 Is 5:4

fruit? 'The fruit of the Spirit', says St. Paul, 'is love, joy, peace, patience, kindness, goodness, faithfulness, gentleness, self control'.[8] We have to examine our lives and our work by that list, and so enquire if the life of Christ flows through our lives and our fellowship. In the spiritual life the true fruit is itself an essential part of the reward.

When Jesus was teaching this in his parable he was on his way to the garden of Gethsemane. There he was to meet Judas for the last time. Perhaps, says Bishop Loyd, he was thinking of Judas especially when he said, 'Every branch of mine that bears no fruit shall be taken away' and 'if a man does not abide in me he is cast forth as a branch and withers'.[9] It is possible, according to Judas's example, for us too to be completely wrong about everything, and end up opposing what we really want to support. Like the Galatians we can 'turn to a different gospel'. 'Having begun with the Spirit' we can end up with 'the flesh'.[10] The Church and Christians have from time to time done some very evil things and been motivated by some very evil ideas, all with the desire to serve God. That is why we surely must interpret the 'good works' of the present Collect in terms of the original Collect; they must be works of God's choosing. Is not this truth behind so much of the fierce debate now agitating the Church? And therefore its importance? There is no virtue in the Church and Christians being busy about the wrong things.

Finally the Collect ends with the hope of reward by God for good works done. To Christians the whole idea of divine rewards and punishments is complex and difficult. Nevertheless in the Old Testament it is set out as something manifestly simple and straightforward. God is sovereign and God is just. So the good are rewarded and the evil punished. What could be easier to comprehend than that? And if one asked what constituted good and evil the answer was equally simple, keeping or disobeying the Law. 'By

8   Gal 5:22-23   9   Jn 15:1-6   10   Gal 1:6, 3:3

them (the commandments of God comprising the Law) is thy servant taught and in keeping of them there is great reward'.[11]

However, in spite of this basic simplicity, experience showed that this was not always what happened. So it was postulated that God's final judgement is delayed, even to the end of all things, to a Day of Judgement. This final Day is called by Isaiah 'the Day of vengeance of our God'.[12] In the New Testament this idea is certainly preserved, and we hear St. Paul declaring that we are simply to do good, regardless of the immediate consequences, and leave the outcome to God.[13] In Revelation, too, we see this Old Testament faith confirmed. 'The books were opened... and the dead were judged by what was written in the books, by what they had done'.[14] In 2 Timothy we see the fate of St. Paul and Alexander the coppersmith, who greatly harmed his ministry, contrasted. For St. Paul there is a crown of righteousness awaiting him, for Alexander something different, for 'the Lord will requite him for his deeds'.[15]

However, we cannot but notice a certain confusion of teaching on this issue in the New Testament. This is because it is central to the New Testament understanding of religion that it is not really the keeping of the letter of the Law that matters; rather it is having the virtues of faith, hope and love towards God indwelling the soul and living by the Spirit that is all important. To live righteously is good, but this is seen as of secondary importance, being like the good fruit that grows on a good tree. It is the tree that matters most. This good tree, as we have already emphasised, is Christ himself, and we are to see ourselves as living in and through him. 'I know', says St. Paul, 'nothing good dwells within me, that is within my flesh'.[16] But through the indwelling of the Holy Spirit things can be so different, and he is, as he says, now living a new life altogether. 'It is no longer I who live, but Christ who lives in me'.[17] So we can look to share in Christ's reward because we live in him. That is the point. That for us is the 'plenteous reward'. 'But as for me, I will behold thy presence in righteous-

11 Ps 19:11   12 Is 61:2   13 Rom 12:19   14 Rev 20:12
15 2 Tim 4:8, 14   16 Rom 7:18   17 Gal 2:20

ness, and when I awake up after thy likeness, I shall be satisfied with it'.[18] So we may look for a heavenly reward, because we are 'in Christ'. 'It was for the joy that was set before him that he endured the Cross'.[19] We are to follow in the same spirit. While we are here we must simply and quietly do God's will and, having done it, expect no special reward, for we are servants who have done no more than is required of us.[20] Our only reward here is 'knowing that we do thy will'.[21] Hereafter, however, our reward is to be with Christ and share in his reward. So St. Paul again, 'I do all for the sake of the Gospel, that I may share in its blessing'. 'For (Christ's) sake I have suffered the loss of all things and count them as refuse in order than I may gain Christ and be found in him... and if possible I may attain the resurrection from the dead'.[22] Where he is we shall be also,[23] and for his 'faithful people' there can be no more 'plenteous reward' than that.

---

18 Ps 17:16   19 Heb 12:2, Jn 17:5   20 Lk 17:9-10
21 The Prayer of St. Ignatius   22 1 Cor 9:23, Phil 3:8-11   23 Jn 14:3